T0214273

Lecture Notes in Artificial Intelligence   11979

Subseries of Lecture Notes in Computer Science

More information about this series at http://www.springer.com/series/1244

Mar Marcos · Jose M. Juarez · Richard Lenz ·
Grzegorz J. Nalepa · Slawomir Nowaczyk ·
Mor Peleg · Jerzy Stefanowski · Gregor Stiglic (Eds.)

Artificial Intelligence in Medicine

Knowledge Representation and Transparent and Explainable Systems

AIME 2019 International Workshops, KR4HC/ProHealth and TEAAM
Poznan, Poland, June 26–29, 2019
Revised Selected Papers

Springer

Editors
Mar Marcos 🆔
Universitat Jaume I
Castellón, Spain

Richard Lenz 🆔
Friedrich-Alexander-University
of Erlangen-Nuremberg
Erlangen, Germany

Slawomir Nowaczyk 🆔
Halmstad University
Halmstad, Sweden

Jerzy Stefanowski
Poznań University of Technology
Poznan, Poland

Jose M. Juarez 🆔
University of Murcia
Murcia, Spain

Grzegorz J. Nalepa 🆔
Jagiellonian University and AGH University
of Science and Technology
Kraków, Poland

Mor Peleg 🆔
University of Haifa
Haifa, Israel

Gregor Stiglic 🆔
University of Maribor
Maribor, Slovenia

ISSN 0302-9743   ISSN 1611-3349   (electronic)
Lecture Notes in Artificial Intelligence
ISBN 978-3-030-37445-7   ISBN 978-3-030-37446-4   (eBook)
https://doi.org/10.1007/978-3-030-37446-4

LNCS Sublibrary: SL7 – Artificial Intelligence

This Springer imprint is published by the registered company Springer Nature Switzerland AG
The registered company address is: Gewerbestrasse 11, 6330 Cham, Switzerland

Preface

The Artificial Intelligence in Medicine (AIME) society was established in 1986 with the main goals of fostering fundamental and applied research in the application of Artificial Intelligence (AI) techniques to medical care and medical research, and providing a forum for discussing any progress made. For this purpose, a series of AIME conferences have been organized on a biennial basis since 1987. The last edition of the AIME conference was held in Poznan, Poland, in June 2019. Two workshops were organized in conjunction with the AIME 2019 main conference. The first one was the 7th Joint Workshop on Knowledge Representation for Health Care and Process-Oriented Information Systems in Health Care (KR4HC/ProHealth 2019). The second AIME workshop was the First Workshop on Transparent, Explainable and Affective AI in Medical Systems (TEAAM 2019). This volume contains a selection of the best papers presented in the KR4HC/ProHealth 2019 and TEAAM 2019 workshops.

The KR4HC/ProHealth 2019 workshop was the seventh time that two separate research communities merged to address common medical issues, to discuss new trends, and to propose solutions to healthcare issues by means of the integration of knowledge representation and process management technologies. As part of medical informatics, the knowledge-representation for health care (KR4HC) view focuses on representing and reasoning with medical knowledge in computers to support knowledge management, clinical decision-making, healthcare modeling, and simulation. As part of business process management, the process-oriented information systems in healthcare (ProHealth) view focuses on using business process management technology to provide effective solutions for the management of healthcare processes.

In total 13 papers were submitted to the KR4HC/ProHealth 2019 workshop, among which 7 papers were full research papers and 6 were short papers describing preliminary research, position papers, or demonstrations of implemented systems. All submitted papers underwent a single-blind peer-review process, in which each submission was reviewed by at least three Program Committee members. Based on the review reports, the Program Committee chairs accepted a total of 11 papers for oral presentation during the workshop, 5 papers for full presentation (20 minutes), and 6 for short presentation. In addition to oral presentations of accepted papers, the workshop had a keynote speech delivered by Prof. Wojtek Michalowski, from the University of Ottawa (Canada), as well as a final panel discussion with the participation of all attendees. In his keynote speech, Prof. Michalowski covered different aspects related to the use of logic-based approaches for the management of multi-morbid patients. The KR4HC/ProHealth 2019 papers presented in this volume correspond to the works selected for full presentation, which largely coincide with the best-rated papers after the review process.

The TEAAM 2019 workshop aimed to provide a forum for discussing AI approaches that are comprehensive, credible, and trusted in healthcare. Today, the positive impact of AI techniques in medical care is put under the spotlight regarding clinical responsibilities, the emerging interest in regulations of algorithms, and the need of explanations. Particular attention was also paid to topics such as comprehensive and interpretable knowledge representations, identifications of the most important features in the complex machine learning (ML) models, new visualization approaches, and interactions with humans. This was the main motivation of the first edition of the TEAAM workshop.

The TEAAM 2019 workshop received 10 full paper submissions. All papers were carefully peer reviewed (single-blind review) by at least two experts from the Program Committee. The reviewers judged the overall quality, its novelty, and the relevance to the TEAAM workshop. As a result, 8 papers were finally accepted. Each paper was presented in 20-minute oral presentations. The workshop also had the privilege of hosting the keynote speaker Prof. Marcin Grzegorzek from the University of Lubeck, Germany. Prof. Grzegorzek discussed and shared his experience about human-centred pattern recognition for assistive health technologies. The workshop was concluded by an interesting discussion of participants on the current status and the role of explainable AI/ML in medical systems. The papers presented during the workshop were invited to be extended and improved to form part of this volume.

To conclude, we would like to express our gratitude to the AIME 2019 organization, to the invited keynote speakers for their participation, and to all the members of the Program Committees for their invaluable support in making the KR4HC/ProHealth 2019 and TEAAM 2019 workshops a success. We would also like to extend our gratitude to the EasyChair conference management system for the support provided, and to Springer publisher for the trust placed in this endeavor.

We hope that you will find our selection of papers of the KR4HC/ProHealth 2019 and TEAAM 2019 workshops included in this proceedings volume interesting and stimulating.

November 2019   Mar Marcos
                                                          Jose M. Juarez

Organization KR4HC/ProHealth Workshop

Program Committee Chairs

Mor Peleg   University of Haifa, Israel
Mar Marcos   Universitat Jaume I, Spain
Richard Lenz   Friedrich-Alexander-University
                       of Erlangen-Nuremberg, Germany

Program Committee

Luca Anselma   Università di Torino, Italy
Gregor Endler   Friedrich-Alexander-University
                             of Erlangen-Nuremberg, Germany
Jesualdo T. Fernández-Breis Universidad de Murcia, Spain
David Isern   Universitat Rovira i Virgili, Spain
Vassilis Koutkias   Institute of Applied Biosciences, Greece
Nekane Larburu   Vicomtech, Spain
Giorgio Leonardi   Università del Piemonte Orientale, Italy
Wendy MacCaull   St. Francis Xavier University, Canada
Begoña Martínez-Salvador   Universitat Jaume I, Spain
Martin Michalowski   University of Minnesota, USA
Silvia Miksch   Vienna University of Technology, Austria
Stefania Montani   Università del Piemonte Orientale, Italy
Øystein Nytrø   Norwegian University of Science and Technology,
                             Norway
Leon Osterweil   University of Massachusetts Amherst, USA
Manfred Reichert   University of Ulm, Germany
David Riaño   Universitat Rovira i Virgili, Spain
Brigitte Seroussi   Sorbonne Université, France
Martin Sedlmayr   Dresden University of Technology, Germany
Erez Shalom   Playwork Intelligent Physiotherapy Technology, Israel
Annette Ten Teije   Vrije Universiteit Amsterdam, The Netherlands
Paolo Terenziani   Università del Piemonte Orientale, Italy
Lucinéia Heloisa Thom   Federal University of Rio Grande do Sul, Brazil
Maria Taboada   University of Santiago de Compostela, Spain
Frank van Harmelen   Vrije Universiteit Amsterdam, The Netherlands
Dongwen Wang   Arizona State University, USA

Organization TEAAM Workshop

Program Committee Chairs

Grzegorz J. Nalepa	AGH University of Science and Technology and Jagiellonian University, Poland
Gregor Stiglic	University of Maribor, Slovenia
Sławomir Nowaczyk	Halmstad University, Sweden
Jose M. Juarez	University of Murcia, Spain
Jerzy Stefanowski	Poznan University of Technology, Poland

Program Committee

Martin Atzmueller	University of Tilburg, The Netherlands
Piotr Augustyniak	AGH University of Science and Technology and Jagiellonian University, Poland
Jerzy Błaszczyński	Poznań University of Technology, Poland
David Camacho	Universidad Autonoma de Madrid, Spain
Manuel Campos	University of Murcia, Spain
Alex Freitas	University of Kent, UK
Alejandro Rodríguez González	Universidad Politecnica de Madrid, Spain
Giorgio Leonardi	University Piemonte Orientale, Italy
Peter Lucas	Leiden University, The Netherlands
Agnieszka Ławrynowicz	Poznań University of Technology, Poland
Juan Carlos Nieves	Umeå University, Sweden
Jose Palma	University of Murcia, Spain
Niels Peek	The University of Manchester, UK
Stephen Swift	Brunel University, UK
Allan Tucker	Brunel University, UK

Contents

xii   Contents

KR4HC/ProHealth - Joint Workshop on Knowledge Representation for Health Care and Process-Oriented Information Systems in Health Care

A Practical Exercise on Re-engineering Clinical Guideline Models Using Different Representation Languages

Mar Marcos[1(✉)] , Cristina Campos[2] , and Begoña Martínez-Salvador[1]

[1] Department of Computer Engineering and Science, Universitat Jaume I,
Av. de Vicent Sos Baynat s/n, 12071 Castellón, Spain
{mar.marcos,begona.martinez}@uji.es
[2] Department of Computer Languages and Systems, Universitat Jaume I,
Av. de Vicent Sos Baynat s/n, 12071 Castellón, Spain
camposc@uji.es

Abstract. The formalization of clinical guideline knowledge is a prerequisite for the development of guideline-based decision support tools that can be used in clinical practice. Several guideline representation languages have been developed to formalize clinical guidelines and execute them over individual patient data. However, no standard has emerged from these efforts, and the core guideline elements to be represented have not been agreed upon in practice. One result is that there is little support when it comes to re-engineer a guideline modelled in a specific language into another language with different features. In this paper we describe a practical exercise consisting in modelling a guideline fragment in a target representation language starting from the same fragment modelled in a source language, having the source and target languages very different features. Concretely, we used PROforma as the source language and GDL as the target one. We also describe a methodological approach to facilitate this task. The lessons learnt from this work can be of interest not only to modellers tackling a similar task but also to developers of guideline transformation methods.

Keywords: Clinical guidelines · Guideline representation languages · PROforma · GDL · openEHR archetypes

1 Introduction

The interest of modelling clinical guidelines in terms of some guideline representation language has been extensively discussed. First and foremost, the formalization of clinical guideline knowledge is a prerequisite for the development of guideline-based decision support tools that can be used in clinical practice. Several guideline languages have been developed to formalize clinical guidelines and execute them over individual patient data. These languages follow different approaches, including document-centric models, task-network models, as well as

© Springer Nature Switzerland AG 2019
M. Marcos et al. (Eds.): KR4HC-ProHealth 2019/TEAAM 2019, LNAI 11979, pp. 3–16, 2019.
https://doi.org/10.1007/978-3-030-37446-4_1

rule-based models [14]. Besides that, some of the languages are formal, which means that they are computer-executable, while others are semi-formal, which implies that they cannot be interpreted without the intervention of the user.

However, despite more than two decades of research on guideline representation languages, no single standard has emerged from these efforts. And although there exist works seeking to identify the common basis of a number of representative languages [13, 18], in practice the core guideline elements to be represented have not been agreed upon. As result, the sharing possibilities of guideline models represented in a specific language are limited. Another consequence is that there is little support when it comes to re-engineer a guideline modelled in one language into another language with different features. This is critical since, from a knowledge engineering viewpoint, it is important to capitalize on existing modelling efforts, rather than start from scratch every time.

The research question that we investigate in this paper is whether such re-engineering of guideline models from one language into another can benefit from a methodological approach guiding the process. Our work is based on a practical exercise consisting in modelling a guideline fragment in a target representation language starting from the same fragment modelled in a source language, having the source and target languages very different features. Concretely, we have used PROforma as the source language and GDL as the target one. PROforma is a process description language grounded in a logical model of decision making and plan enactment [15]. PROforma falls in the category of task-network models. In contrast, GDL [4] is a rule-based language in which clinical logic is expressed in terms of production rules. Its most distinctive feature is that it enforces the use of openEHR archetypes [12] for the description of guideline data.

The choice of the above languages is motivated by the notable differences between them, which makes re-engineering a non-trivial task. In the case of GDL, the smooth integration with archetypes has been a key factor in the choice. Taking into account the features of the two languages, we have carried out a prior analysis to devise a methodological approach to facilitate the transformation task. The lessons learnt from this work can be of interest not only to modellers tackling a similar task, but also to developers of (automated) guideline transformation methods.

The rest of the paper is organized as follows. First, Sects. 2 and 3 describe the PROforma and GDL languages, respectively. Next, Sect. 4 describes the methodological approach we propose to guide the transformation of PROforma models into GDL ones. Afterwards, Sect. 5 presents a re-engineering exercise where we have put into practice this approach, based on a PROforma model for a fragment of the European Society of Cardiology (ESC) guideline for acute and chronic heart failure [16]. Finally, Sect. 6 concludes the paper highlighting our main contribution and discussing its limitations.

2   The PROforma Language

PROforma is a formal knowledge representation language tailored to capture clinical knowledge which has been successfully used for the deployment and execution of clinical guidelines models [15]. In PROforma, a guideline is modelled as a plan made up of one or more *tasks*. There are four types of tasks, namely: *actions*, *enquiries*, *decisions*, and *plans*. An action corresponds to an activity (e.g. a clinical procedure) to be performed by an external agent. An enquiry is a task that acquires information, i.e. the value of one ore more data items or *sources*, from the external environment (e.g. clinician, databases). A decision is a task that represents a choice among different options or *candidates*. Finally, a plan can be used to group together a set of other tasks. Since a plan can contain in turn other nested plans, PROforma allows the definition of hierarchical task networks. The tasks within a plan are usually ordered via *scheduling constraints* and/or different kinds of *task conditions*. If none are given, a parallel execution of tasks is assumed.

The specification of PROforma decisions requires additional attributes, apart from the associated candidates. Notably, each candidate can have one or more *arguments*, which are truth-valued expressions that determine the choice of that candidate. These expressions usually describe the arguments for (in favour) or against the candidate. Additionally, each candidate has a *recommendation rule*, which is an expression that is used to calculate the support for the candidate considering all its arguments. Finally the choice mode, single or multiple, determines how many candidates can be recommended by the decision.

In the PROforma graphical notation guidelines are depicted as directed graphs in which nodes represent tasks and arcs represent scheduling constraints. In this notation the shape of the nodes indicates the task type: squares are used for actions, circles for decisions, diamonds for enquiries, and round-edged rectangles for plans. In the case of scheduling constraints, the arc indicates that the task at the head of the arc cannot start until the task at the tail of the arc (antecedent task) has completed. An example of PROforma graph can be found in Sect. 5.

Regarding the execution, a task can only be considered for activation when all its scheduling constraints have been met, i.e. when all its antecedent tasks have been either completed or discarded. In that case, the task will be activated if at least one of the antecedent tasks has completed, otherwise it will be discarded. Tasks may also have different types of conditions imposing additional constraints to be met before activation, including *preconditions* and *wait conditions*. Both are truth-valued expressions that are checked when the scheduling constraints are met. In the case of preconditions, the task will be activated if the precondition holds, otherwise it will be discarded (and not considered again). In the case of wait conditions, the task will remain dormant until the condition is met. For more details on PROforma, see the OpenClinical.net resources [9].

3   The GDL Language

The Guideline Definition Language (GDL) is a formal language for expressing decision support logic [4]. It is a rule-based language that is part of the openEHR specifications [10]. GDL uses production rules in combination with openEHR archetypes, and allows linking to clinical terminologies as well as adding support for different natural languages. The specification of a guideline model in GDL comprises mainly a set of rules plus a set of archetype bindings. On one hand rules can be combined together to support single decision steps as well as more complex decision making processes. On the other hand openEHR archetypes are used both as input and output to the GDL guideline model, as a means to achieve interoperability with the Electronic Health Record (EHR).

A GDL rule is the basic building block to describe the guideline logic by means of when-then (if-then) statements. The *when part* contains a list of expressions that must hold true in conjunction before the rule can be fired, while the *then part* contains the expressions (typically assignments) that are executed as a result of rule firing. A variety of operators (arithmetic, comparison, logical) and functions (element existence, rule firing) can be used in the *when part* of GDL rules.

Formally, an openEHR archetype is a computable specification of a domain/clinical concept, in the form of structured constraints and based on the openEHR reference model [12]. An archetype describes in detail the structure and content of clinical concepts such as "diagnosis", which includes details such as name, clinical description, date/time of onset, or diagnostic certainty. In principle archetypes are defined for wide reuse and therefore they include all the relevant attributes about a specific clinical concept. However, they can be specialised to accommodate local singularities. Archetypes are a key component of the so-called dual-model EHR architectures aimed at achieving semantic interoperability of the EHR.

Typically, a GDL model [4] starts with a header section containing the guideline name, the authorship and version information, keywords, etc. Then there is a definition section listing the archetypes used in the GDL model and, for each one, the bindings linking the data elements in the archetype to the (local) variables used in the GDL rules. Within the same section it is possible to define a set of preconditions, which must hold true before the GDL rules can be executed. Next the rule section describes the guideline logic in terms of the when-then statements mentioned above and making use of the local variables defined through the archetype bindings. Finally there is an ontology section listing all the used terms as well as the descriptions of these terms in the supported natural languages.

4   A Methodological Approach to Re-engineer PROforma Models in GDL

In this section we describe a methodological approach to support the re-engineering of existing PROforma models in GDL. The only language constructs in GDL are production rules, consequently all the aspects of PROforma tasks (logic, effects and sequencing) must be expressed in terms of rules. Additionally, as mentioned before, openEHR archetypes play a fundamental role in GDL. Not only they are used for input and output to the GDL model, but also all the local variables in the GDL rules must come from some archetype. According to this, we propose to begin with the identification of the openEHR archetypes providing elements compatible with the EHR data used as input and/or output in the PROforma model. The next step is designing a set of GDL rules to capture all the details of the different types of tasks in the PROforma model (see below). While doing this, it is crucial to draft a list of all variables used in these GDL rules, other than EHR data. This will include not only the explicit data items in the PROforma tasks (such as data sources in enquiries) but also other data required for expressing the logic of tasks. Next, it is necessary to develop an openEHR archetype to hold these local variables (henceforth, *model-specific archetype*). The final step is the development and testing of the GDL model, once the data requirements have been settled by means of appropriate archetype models. The rest of the section describes practical hints for the main modelling tasks.

Identification of openEHR Archetypes for EHR Data Items. Clinical guidelines typically refer to some patient data which can be obtained from the EHR. For example, a guideline is usually applicable only to patients with specific clinical circumstances, such as an initial diagnosis. These conditions are modelled as preconditions to be tested before execution, both in PROforma and in GDL. Since GDL needs archetypes (and archetype bindings) to refer to input and/or output EHR data, it is necessary to identify the openEHR archetypes suitable for these data. For this purpose, the recommended option is to select one of the archetypes available in existing repositories, such as the CKM [11]. The option of designing and developing a new archetype from scratch should be considered only in case it is not possible to find a suitable archetype in repositories. Here it is important to note that the same archetype could play a role both as an input and as an output, when it is modified as result of the execution of the GDL model.

Design of GDL Rules and Identification of Additional Data Items. The design of the GDL rules and the identification of the additional data they require come naturally together. In general PROforma tasks have some effect on the execution state. For instance, enquiries modify the value of data items, and decisions have an implicit result. Consequently all PROforma tasks should be encoded as GDL rules, roughly speaking. Besides, the side effects of tasks very likely point to additional data items to be set in such rules. These data items can also be used to enforce the sequencing of two GDL rules, to mimic the sequencing imposed by a scheduling constraint connecting two tasks. For instance, if there is a scheduling constraint connecting the PROforma tasks A and B, and the GDL rule representing task A sets the value of a data item x, then the sequencing of the two GDL rules can be encoded by checking the existence of a value for the data item x in the conditions (when part) of the GDL rule representing task B. A similar approach can be used to encode preconditions and wait conditions, which impose additional constraints with an influence on the sequencing of tasks, beyond scheduling constraints.

Below we provide useful hints for the design of the GDL rules according to the main PROforma tasks, to be considered in combination with the previous indications:

- *GDL rules for PROforma actions.* An action in principle refers to a clinical procedure to be performed in the environment. However it is a common practice to use them also to highlight changes on important clinical aspects under evaluation, such as a final diagnosis. In both cases some data item must be listed as an additional one, either for the clinical procedure or for the evaluation. Then, the action can be encoded in GDL by means of a rule setting the value of the corresponding archetype element, usually in the model-specific archetype, representing this data item.
- *GDL rules for PROforma enquiries.* An enquiry requests the input of data for one or more sources. A single source enquiry can be encoded in GDL by means of a rule checking the existence of a data value for the source in the EHR archetype (when part), and setting the value of the corresponding archetype element to this value, if it exists (then part). If the data input request refers to an element which is not part of the archetypes selected in the previous step, it must be listed as an additional data item.
- *GDL rules for PROforma decisions.* A decision represents a choice among two or more candidates, usually based on arguments with conditions in favour of each candidate. For the sake of simplicity, here we focus on single choice decisions with a single argument per candidate. In GDL the resulting choice must be included as an additional data item, so that its value can be subsequently queried. This data item should have as many possible values as there are candidates in the decision. Additionally, one rule is required for each argument in favour of a candidate, checking the associated condition (when part), and setting the value of the corresponding archetype element representing the decision data item to the appropriate candidate (then part).

Development of openEHR Archetype (or Archetypes) for Additional Data Items. It is necessary to design openEHR archetypes to hold all the additional data items identified during the design of GDL rules. As opposed to the case of EHR data, it is not likely that existing repositories contain archetypes suitable for the specific requirements of clinical guidelines. For the same reason, the reuse chances of model-specific archetypes designed to fulfill these requirements would be rather low. Therefore, for the moment our recommendation is designing from scratch a single *ad-hoc* model-specific archetype, with appropriate data types (and terminology bindings) but without further pretensions. This is in line with some clinical models currently in the GDL GitHub repository [3].

5 Use Case: Re-engineering of a PROforma Model Fragment in GDL

We have used the 2016 ESC Guidelines for the diagnosis and treatment of acute and chronic heart failure (henceforth, ESC guideline) [16] as a use case to illustrate the methodological approach described in the previous section. It is a lengthy document (85 pages) containing recommendations for the diagnosis, assessment, and treatment of acute and chronic heart failure, for use in clinical practice. An evidence-based approach has been applied in the elaboration of the guideline, except for the diagnosis part, which is consensus-based. The guideline has text format but nevertheless contains many explanatory figures and tables. As the document states, heart failure (HF) is becoming a preventable and treatable disease by applying evidence-based guidelines, hence the importance of this guideline.

A small part of the ESC guideline has been used in our re-engineering exercise, consisting in modelling a guideline fragment in the GDL language starting from the same fragment modelled in the PROforma language. In particular we have focused on the algorithm for the diagnosis of HF in the non-acute setting. Figure 1 shows a diagram representing this diagnostic algorithm. The rest of the section describes some of the details of the starting PROforma model and its re-engineering in GDL, with illustrative examples. As editing tools we have used: the Composer Authoring Suite 3.0,[1] for PROforma; the GDL Editor 1.0,[2] for GDL; and the LinkEHR Studio,[3] for openEHR archetypes. The guideline models have been thoroughly examined and tested for validity using the the PROforma and GDL tools.

5.1 PROforma Model

The layout of the top-level plan of the PROforma model (see Fig. 2) resembles the diagnosis algorithm in Fig. 1. As the guideline states, a possible HF diagnosis should first be evaluated considering the details of physical examination, clinical history and electrocardiogram results of the patient. If all aspects are normal, then the HF diagnosis is discarded. Otherwise, further tests should be considered. These tasks have been grouped in plan Step_1_assessment_of_HF_probability (step 1). The guideline considers several clinical history and physical examination aspects. However, for simplicity the enquiries in step 1 only contain one source each, summarising the findings. If required, adding more sources to these enquiries would be straightforward. The implicit choice on whether further investigations are required or not is made explicit in task HF_or_other_diagnoses_decision, also in step 1. Note that although the previous subtasks (enquiries, etc.) are not visible in the right side of Fig. 2, they can be displayed by unfolding the hierarchical tree on the left side.

If further investigations are necessary, the task plasma_NPs_measured_enquiry queries if the test for measuring plasma natriuretic peptides (or NPs) is available locally. If so, the plan Step_2_natriuretic_peptides (step 2) asks for the results of the NP test and decides whether it is necessary to proceed with an echocardiography, depending on the appropriate numerical values (see conditions in Fig. 1). The echocardiography procedure together with the enquiry asking for its results

---

[1] https://deontics.com/technology/proforma.
[2] https://sourceforge.net/projects/gdl-editor/.
[3] http://www.linkehr.com/linkehr/.

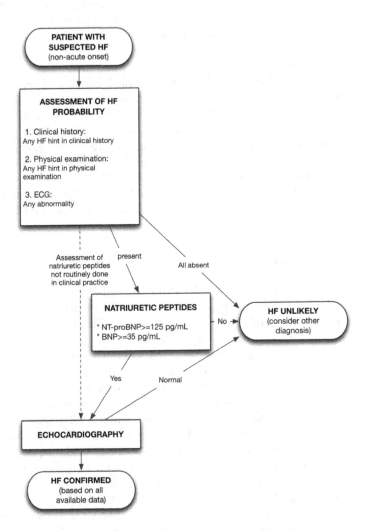

Fig. 1. Algorithm for the diagnosis of HF in the non-acute setting (adapted from ESC guideline [16]).

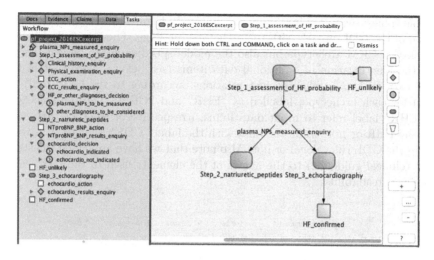

Fig. 2. PROforma model for the diagnosis of HF in the non-acute setting.

are both modelled within the plan Step_3_echocardiography (step 3). The latter can be activated either because NP tests are not locally available or because the decision in step 2 supports to proceed with an echocardio (see the two paths leading to echocardiography in Fig. 1). This has been modelled using the wait condition below:

```
plasma_NPs_measured="no"
or result_of(echocardio_decision)=echocardio_indicated
```

Notice that the use of two scheduling constraints would not be appropriate in this case, because they could make that step 3 is never considered (in case step 2 is not activated). This explains the apparent divergence between the algorithm in Fig. 1 and the PROforma graph in Fig. 2.

The two actions HF_confirmed and HF_unlikely in the top-level plan are used to reflect the changes in the diagnosis certainty. Since the action HF_unlikely can sequentially follow several other tasks, namely step 1, step 2 and step 3, a wait condition capturing these different paths has also been used in this case, concretely:

```
result_of(HF_or_other_diagnoses_decision)=other_diagnoses_to_be_considered
or result_of(echocardio_decision)=echocardio_not_indicated
or echocardio_results="Normal"
```

5.2 GDL Model

Identification of openEHR Archetypes for EHR Data Items. According-ing to the proposed methodology, we have selected the archetype openEHR-EHR-EVALUATION.problem_diagnosis.v1 from the CKM repository, which contains appropriate elements for both the diagnosis name and certainty (with possible values: suspected, probable or confirmed). Figure 3 shows the definitions section of the GDL model, with the archetype bindings. These include not only the selected CKM archetype but also the model-specific one, to be constructed after the identification of additional data items (see below). Note that in this figure two versions (archetype instantiations, according to the GDL tool) are shown for each archetype, labelled as "EHR" and "CDS". The bindings with the "EHR" label refer to input data items, irrespective of whether they come from the EHR or not, while the ones with the label "CDS" refer to data to be used in the GDL rules, local or not. Also note that we have appended the string "CG" (clinical guideline) to the names of the elements used in the GDL rules, to improve readability.

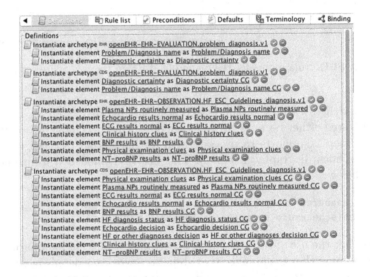

Fig. 3. Archetypes and bindings of the GDL model.

Design of GDL Rules and Identification of Additional Data Items. We have defined a set of 16 GDL rules to represent the previous PROforma model. In the case of enquiries, all the data items appearing as sources have been identified as elements for the model-specific archetype. More importantly, one rule has been added for each enquiry, checking if a data value for the element exists in the input archetype (when part), and assigning this value to the corresponding element in the (local) model-specific archetype, which is initially empty (then part). Besides, the preconditions of the task, if any, have been added to the rule as conditions.

Rules for enquiries (in general, tasks) with sequencing constraints are slightly different. To illustrate this case, the rule `Set echocardio results` is shown in Fig. 4. This rule checks if a data value for the element `Echocardio results normal` exists in the model-specific archetype, and assigns that value. The conditions of

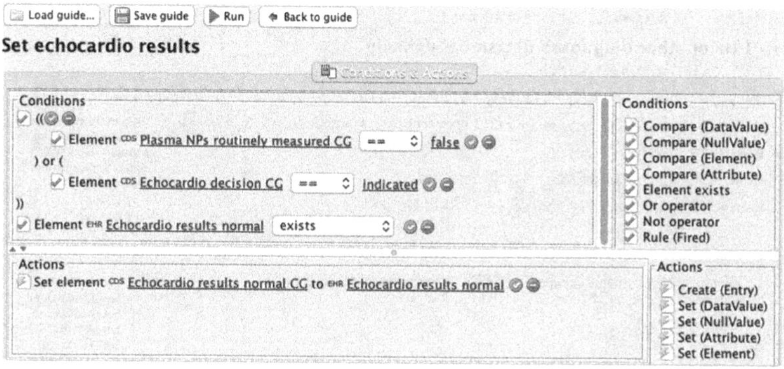

Fig. 4. GDL rule Set echocardio results.

the rule also include a disjunction to capture the sequencing constraints of the task (corresponding to the two paths leading to echocardiography, as explained in Sect. 5.1).

Regarding the decisions, additional data items to hold their result have been identified as elements for the model-specific archetype. To improve readability, these data items have been labelled with the name of the decision. Besides, one rule has been defined for each candidate, checking the conditions of the argument in favour and setting the corresponding element in the model-specific archetype to the appropriate candidate. Also for readability, rules have been labelled with the name of the decision followed by the name of the candidate. As an illustration, Fig. 5 shows the GDL rule for the PROforma candidate other_diagnoses_to_be_considered (leading to the conclusion that HF is unlikely). This candidate is part of the PROforma task HF_or_other_diagnoses_decision, in step 1 (see Sect. 5.1). The first condition of the rule checks that the decision element in the model-specific archetype has not been set yet, whereas the rest of conditions represent the actual argument to commit to this candidate.

Figure 5 refers to an additional data item which deserves further explanation, namely HF diagnosis status CG. As mentioned before, the diagnostic certainty of the openEHR-EHR-EVALUATION.problem_diagnosis.v1 archetype has as possible values suspected, probable or confirmed. These values do not correspond exactly with the ones used in the guideline, which are suspected, unlikely and confirmed. Therefore, we have chosen to use a new element in the model-specific archetype, following the terminology used in the guideline more faithfully.

Development of the Specific openEHR Archetype. A model-specific openEHR archetype, openEHR-EHR-OBSERVATION.HF_ESC_Guidelines_diagnosis.v1, has been designed to hold the additional data items identified in the development process of GDL rules. This archetype includes elements for all the data items corresponding to enquiry sources, decision results, and action effects, as well as for the data item to accommodate the guideline terminology to the one of the CKM archetype. The main elements of this archetype can be seen in Fig. 3.

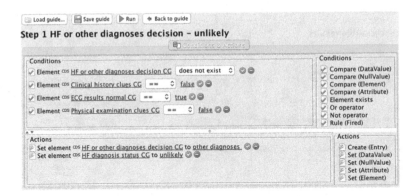

Fig. 5. GDL rule `Step 1 HF or other diagnosis decision - unlikely`.

6   Discussion and Conclusions

In this paper we describe a practical experiment in modelling a guideline fragment in the rule-based GDL language starting from the same fragment modelled in the PROforma task-network language. We also describe a methodological approach with steps to facilitate this re-engineering task, which are the ones we have followed to carry out the experiment.

Related work includes the review studies which seek to identify the common basis of a selection of guideline representation languages [13,18]. These studies draw parallels between the elements of different languages, however they do not contain practical steps and indications like the ones we propose in this work. Related work dealing with the translation of Arden MLMs into the GLIF language [17] is more similar to ours. A novel contribution of our work is the use of GDL rules and openEHR archetypes as target in the guideline transformation process. In particular, archetypes help resolve the "curly braces problem". Archetype design issues have been the focus of interest in more recent works, although unrelated to the re-engineering of guideline models we tackle in this work [1,5,6]. Our main contribution is a methodological approach to simplify the rule-based encoding of complex clinical decision making processes like the ones that can be typically modelled with task-network languages.

Our approach is generic in the sense that a similar strategy could be applied in the case of other task-network and/or rule-based languages, however the precise re-engineering indications would differ as they are largely dependent on the specific features of the languages used. Whatever the source and target language pair is considered, the re-engineering indications could be used as a starting point for the development of (semi)automated guideline transformation methods, as we have done in previous works [7,8]. This idea is in line with the transformation-based alternative for guideline model sharing described in the literature [2]. There exist inherent difficulties in the transformation-based sharing of guideline models (because of syntactic and semantic differences), however it may be the only practical way given the lack of a standard representation. Moreover, it can contribute to a better insight into the strengths and weaknesses of the different guideline representation languages.

With respect to the initial research question, our preliminary conclusion is that reliance on existing (and validated) guideline models as well as on the proposed methodology can facilitate the modelling task to a great extent, as compared to modelling a clinical guideline from scratch. This is particularly important in the case of rule-based languages like GDL due to the inherent complexity of describing decision making processes using rules, in particular in the case of processes more complex than mere single decision steps.

A limitation of our work is that it is based on a small guideline excerpt. However, it is important to note that the PROforma model used is not simple, as it includes a significant number of actions, enquiries, decisions, and tasks. It also includes a variety of task conditions that, together with the scheduling constraints, make the control flow far from trivial. Either way, our results can be regarded as a first step on which other research works can build further results.

Acknowledgements. This work has been supported by the Spanish Ministry of Economy and Competitiveness and the ERDF (European Regional Development Fund) through grant TIN2014-53749-C2-1-R, and by the Ministry of Education, Culture and Sports through grant PRX18/00350.

References

1. Anani, N.: Applying openEHR's guideline definition language to the SITS international stroke treatment registry: a European retrospective observational study. BMC Med. Inform. Decis. Mak. **17**, 7 (2017)
2. Boxwala, A.A., et al.: Toward a representation format for sharable clinical guidelines. J. Biomed. Inform. **34**(3), 157–169 (2001)
3. Cambio Healthcare Systems: common clinical models in the forms of openEHR archetypes and GDL guidelines. https://github.com/gdl-lang/common-clinical-models. Accessed 10 Apr 2019
4. Chen, R.: openEHR Guideline Definition Language (GDL). https://specifications.openehr.org/releases/CDS/latest/GDL.html. Accessed 15 Feb 2019
5. Marcos, M., Maldonado, J.A., Martínez-Salvador, B., Moner, D., Boscá, D., Robles, M.: An archetype-based solution for the interoperability of computerised guidelines and electronic health records. In: Peleg, M., Lavrač, N., Combi, C. (eds.) AIME 2011. LNCS (LNAI), vol. 6747, pp. 276–285. Springer, Heidelberg (2011). https://doi.org/10.1007/978-3-642-22218-4_35
6. Marcos, M., Maldonado, J.A., Martínez-Salvador, B., Boscá, D., Robles, M.: Interoperability of clinical decision-support systems and electronic health records using archetypes: a case study in clinical trial eligibility. J. Biomed. Inform. **46**(4), 676–689 (2013)
7. Martínez-Salvador, B., Marcos, M., Riaño, D.: An algorithm for guideline transformation: from BPMN to SDA. Procedia Comput. Sci. **63**, 244–251 (2015). 5th International Conference on Current and Future Trends of Information and Communication Technologies in Healthcare (ICTH-2015)
8. Martínez-Salvador, B., Marcos, M.: Supporting the refinement of clinical process models to computer-interpretable guideline models. Bus. Inf. Syst. Eng. **58**(5), 355–366 (2016)

9. OpenClinical CIC: OpenClinical.net (2017). https://www.openclinical.net/. Accessed 10 Apr 2019
10. openEHR Foundation: openEHR - Open industry specifications, models and software for e-health. https://www.openehr.org/. Accessed 10 Apr 2019
11. openEHR Foundation: openEHR Clinical Knowledge Manager. https://www.openehr.org/ckm/. Accessed 10 Apr 2019
12. openEHR Foundation: archetype definitions and principles (2007). https://specifications.openehr.org/releases/1.0.2/architecture/am/archetype_principles.pdf. Accessed 10 Apr 2019
13. Peleg, M., Tu, S., Bury, J., et al.: Comparing computer-interpretable guideline models: a case-study approach. J. Am. Med. Inform. Assoc. **10**(1), 52–68 (2003)
14. Peleg, M.: Computer-interpretable clinical guidelines: a methodological review. J. Biomed. Inform. **46**(4), 744–763 (2013)
15. Sutton, D.R., Fox, J.: The syntax and semantics of the PROforma guideline modeling language. J. Am. Med. Inform. Assoc. **10**(5), 433–443 (2003)
16. Ponikowski, P., et al.: The Task Force for the diagnosis and treatment of acute and chronic heart failure of the European Society of Cardiology: 2016 ESC Guidelines for the diagnosis and treatment of acute and chronic heart failure. Eur. Heart J. **37**(27), 2129–2200 (2016)
17. Wang, D.: Translating Arden MLMs into GLIF guidelines-a case study of hyperkalemia patient screening. Stud. Health Technol. Inform. **101**, 177–181 (2004)
18. Wang, D., Peleg, M., Tu, S., et al.: Representation primitives, process models and patient data in computer-interpretable clinical practice guidelines: a literature review of guideline representation models. Int. J. Med. Inform. **68**(1–3), 59–70 (2002)

A Method for Goal-Oriented Guideline Modeling in PROforma and Its Preliminary Evaluation

Mor Peleg[1](✉) ⓘ, Alexandra Kogan[1] ⓘ, and Samson W. Tu[2]

[1] Department of Information Systems, University of Haifa, 3498838 Haifa, Israel
morpeleg@is.haifa.ac.il
[2] Center for BioMedical Informatics Research, Stanford University, Stanford, CA 94305, USA

Abstract. Goal-based reasoning may be used to support clinical decision making for multimorbidity patients; medical knowledge originating in different computer-interpretable guidelines (CIGs) and from medical ontologies may be matched at the goal level. This matching may be based on CIG metaproperty specifications referring to standard medical ontologies (e.g., as the U.S. Department of Veterans Affairs National Drug File - Reference Terminology) and adhering to standard patient information models (e.g., HL7's Fast Healthcare Interoperability Resources). To support such knowledge and data integration, we developed a method for specifying metaproperty annotations within PROforma CIGs. We positioned this specification step within an existing method for CIG knowledge elicitation/specification, known as the Consensus method. Because clinicians time is costly, the research question that we evaluated in this study was whether knowledge engineers could successfully use this method to specify clinical practice guideline consensus documents in goal-annotated PROforma terms. The preliminary evaluation with nine information systems students taking an advanced knowledge representation course indicates is encouraging. We discuss the technical and conceptual modeling errors and how they could guide instruction of the goal-oriented CIG modeling.

Keywords: Computer-interpretable guidelines · Goal modeling · Multimorbidity · FHIR · NDF-RT

1 Introduction

While multimorbidity is a common condition in older patients, requiring complex treatment planning [1], clinical practice guidelines are still written with single-disease focus. Hence interactions among recommendations originating from different guidelines may occur [1]. In an earlier paper [2], we proposed a goal-based methodology for integrating computer-interpretable guidelines (CIGs) for different chronic diseases to create non-conflicting management plans for patients with multimorbidity. By annotating CIG plans and actions with terms that are taken from a medical ontology and that represent goals and physiological effects, we were able to detect unmet goals and conflicting goals and

© Springer Nature Switzerland AG 2019
M. Marcos et al. (Eds.): KR4HC-ProHealth 2019/TEAAM 2019, LNAI 11979, pp. 17–28, 2019.
https://doi.org/10.1007/978-3-030-37446-4_2

actions. We further used the CIGs' knowledge to suggest non-conflicted recommendations. We demonstrated that a Controller component that implements behavioral patterns was able to detect and mitigate such conflicts detected in the benchmark case of aspirin (recommended for secondary prevention of cardiovascular disease) causing duodenal ulcer.

This paper addresses the knowledge elicitation/specification phase of goal-based CIG specifications in the PROforma [3] CIG language. Framed in terms of the state-of-the-art elicitation methodology known as the Consensus-based method [4], our goal-based CIG modeling requires formulating the ontology-based specification according to procedural and declarative patterns for diagnosis, management, and prevention while using controlled vocabulary terms and referring to standard health data exchange standards. We therefore augmented the Consensus-based method by introducing a guide that explains the procedural patterns and the corresponding declarative patterns that could be used to create the ontology-based consensus and formal specification. The guide assists clinical experts and knowledge engineers (KE) to create collaboratively the ontology-based consensus and formal specification. We evaluated the feasibility of KEs successfully generating an ontology-based consensus via an empirical study with information systems students, who were taking an advanced knowledge representation course, performing the role of KEs.

2 Background

Several researchers have developed methods for translating clinical practice guidelines into CIGs. Shiffman described a process for translating clinical guidelines into decision support systems [5]. The steps of the process focus first on disambiguation of the text, achieving clarity, consistency, and evidence of the clinical recommendations. Then, the knowledge is encoded as executable decision rules, places for workflow integration are identified, and actions are selected from a palette of possible clinical action types. Finally, mockups for user interfaces are defined and a set of requirements for the CIG-based decision-support system are defined. However, this process has not been evaluated in practice. Further work by Shiffman focused on developing instruments [6] and tools [7] for facilitating more coherent and complete authoring of clinical guidelines and did not address formal specifications using CIG languages.

Shalom, Shahar and coauthors [4] developed an alternative process, which pays attention to the different expertise needed: clinical and technical (knowledge engineering). This methodology was also unique in introducing a coordination and communication step between these two (or more) experts, in which they together create a consensus document that removes ambiguity while sketching the guideline using the CIG language' constructs (knowledge roles). The methodology was evaluated empirically by a study that focused on the ability of the clinical experts to perform the following pipeline. Expert physicians (EPs) work together with knowledge engineers (KEs) to create the consensus, which is then marked up by clinical editors (CEs) using CIG authoring tools and is finally converted by KEs into a CIG using the CIG authoring tools [8]. Considering that clinicians' time is costly, our study examined the possibility of distributing the work that is done by EPs and KEs working together into a series of more targeted steps, each performed by either the EP or KE, for producing a goal-based consensus. An alternative approach [9] uses rules to extract the sentences and from them the process information to create the informal consensus.

3   Methods

3.1   The Extensions of the Consensus-Based CIG Modeling for Goal Annotations

Our goal-based CIG modeling in terms of the Consensus-based method [4] requires us to formulate the ontology-based specification according to procedural and declarative patterns for diagnosis, management, and prevention. The procedural patterns are formulated according to design templates that constrain the PROforma semantics; the declarative patterns include metaproperty annotations corresponding to goal, drug, and physiological effect terms and relationship taken from the National Drug File - Reference Terminology (NDF-RT) [10]. These metaproperty annotations also adhere to HL7's Fast Healthcare Interoperability Resources (FHIR) [11] data exchange standard, using a specialization of the FHIR Goal class (see Fig. 1).

We defined design patterns, in PROforma, for different stages of disease management. Figure 2 shows patterns for diagnosing secondary cause of a disease, disease treatment, and secondary prevention of a disease.

We augmented the Consensus-based method (Fig. 3), by augmenting Step 3 to include goal-based modeling supported by templates and a Guide (Fig. 4). The Guide is shown in Fig. 4 and explains the procedural patterns and the corresponding declarative patterns that could be used to create the ontology-based consensus and formal specification. Because clinical experts have very limited time, we suggest that they formulate the initial informal consensus, while the knowledge engineers (KE) create the ontology-based consensus and formal specification. These are then evaluated by the clinical expert together with the KE. This cycle is repeated until the clinical experts are satisfied with the representation and the KEs proceed to the testing phase.

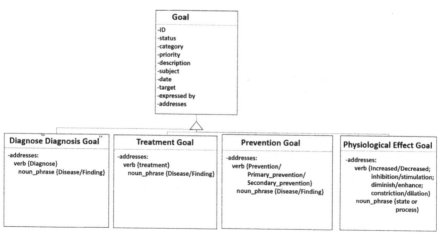

Fig. 1. Specialization of FHIR Goals based on NDF-RT properties

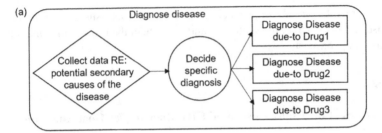

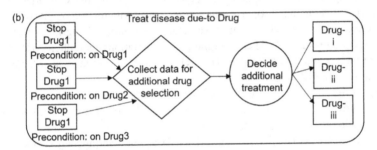

Goal: Verb: Diagnose
        NP: some [Disease/Finding]; NDF-RT.ow/#NXXX
Action: Verb: Diagnose
        NP: some [Disease/Finding]; NDF-RT.ow/#NXXX, due-to, some [Drug]; NDF-RT.owl#NYYYY

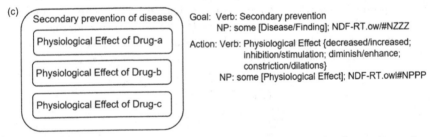

Goal: Verb: Treat
        NP: some [Disease/Finding]; NDF-RT.ow/#NXXX, due-to, some [Drug]; NDF-RT.owl#NYYYY
Action: Verb: Stop/Start
        NP: some [Drug]; NDF-RT.owl#NYYYY

(c)

Secondary prevention of disease
Physiological Effect of Drug-a
Physiological Effect of Drug-b
Physiological Effect of Drug-c

Goal: Verb: Secondary prevention
        NP: some [Disease/Finding]; NDF-RT.ow/#NZZZ

Action: Verb: Physiological Effect {decreased/increased;
                inhibition/stimulation; diminish/enhance;
                constriction/dilations}
        NP: some [Physiological Effect]; NDF-RT.owl#NPPP

Fig. 2. PROforma Design patterns. (a) diagnosing secondary cause of a disease (drug adverse effect), (b) treatment of disease due-to drug, (c) secondary prevention of disease. Plan - round-cornered rectangle, Enquiry - diamond, Decision - circle, Action - rectangle. NP-noun phrase.

3.2   Empirical Assessment of the Ability of Information Systems Students to Specify Goal Annotations

Our hypothesis was that information systems students who have taken information systems analysis and knowledge representation courses, and who have performed a tutorial

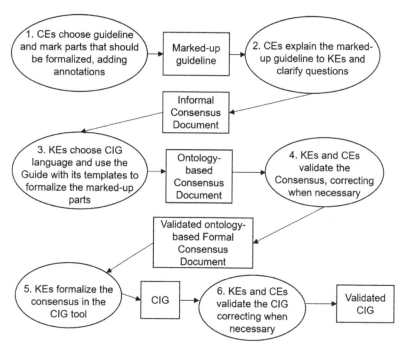

Fig. 3. Modified Consensus-building process, with Guide

on goal-based annotation, would perform well on goal-oriented PROforma modeling and annotation tasks.

In this pilot study we sought to empirically establish a proof of concept that the knowledge elicitation and specification approach is applicable. The pilot study with a small number of participants allowed us to perform qualitative analysis of the types of errors the students made and to gather insights for improving the method. In future studies we could check for statistical significance using larger samples.

Subjects Background and Training

The nine participants in the study were undergraduate information systems students in their last year of study, who were taking the Knowledge Representation and Decision Support Systems elective course. The students had prior experience in modeling organizational processes (business process management notation was taught in the Information Systems Analysis course). In the elective course, they had studied different formalisms for representing and reasoning with clinical knowledge, including rule-based and ontology-based systems. They had one lecture on computer-interpretable guidelines and took one tutorial on goal-based modeling and specification in PROforma, using the User Guide that we had developed. Versions of Figs. 1, 2 and 4 were part of the Guide. The CIGs' task networks were already drawn for the students in the tutorial. The tutorial [12] considered the specification of goal and action metaproperties regarding secondary prevention of cardiovascular disease (CVD) and of diagnosis and management of duodenal ulcer (DU). The students were required to draw the task networks in the experiment.

---

1. Goal modeling (high-level: diagnose/may-treat/may-prevent Disease)
   a. Identify the high-level goal in the guidelines' consensus
   b. Specify it as a PROforma plan (e.g., secondary prevention of CVD)
   c. Select Goal-verb: diagnose-diagnosis, treat, prevent (primary/secondary)
   d. Specify the Goal-noun: NDF-RT term for the Disease; when applicable, use post-coordination to specialize the Disease into Disease **due-to** Drug
2. Goal modeling (drug-level: physiological effects of drugs) for drugs that are started
   a. Identify the drug-level goal (e.g., antiplatelet therapy) in the guidelines' consensus, with an example for a specific drug belonging to the drug category (e.g., Aspirin)
   b. Expand the high-level PROforma plan into a task containing a drug-level plan (e.g., antiplatelet drug treatment)
   c. Goal-verb for physiological_effect (PE): examine the OWL restrictions associated with the specific drug or the drug class from the consensus. Look for its physiologic effect. Select the relevant ones among Decreased/Decreased; Inhibition/Stimulation; Diminish/Enhance; Constriction/Dilation). If no relevant physiologic effect exists, choose a "may-treat disease" or a "may-prevent disease" goal
   d. Goal-noun: NDF-RT term for the PE state or for the disease
3. Action modeling (for medications)
   a. Identify the drug-related action in the consensus (e.g., Stop Aspirin)
   b. Specify annotation for the Action-verb: start/stop
   c. Specify annotation for the Action-noun: NDF-RT term for the drug
4. Action modeling (for deciding on diagnosis)
   a. Identify the diagnosis-related action in the guidelines' consensus (e.g., diagnose Duodenal ulcer due-to NSAID)
   b. Specify annotation for the Action-verb: diagnose-diagnosis
   c. Specify annotation for the Action-noun: NDF-RT term for the Disease/Finding; when applicable, use post-coordination to specialize the Disease due-to Drug.

Fig. 4. Guide for creating the declarative goal and action CIG annotations

Empirical Assessment Setup

The empirical assessment took place in December 2018. Ethics approval was granted by the University of Haifa's Ethics Committee. Participation was elective, and the students were told that they could earn up to 3 bonus points for participation and that they could drop out at any time and not submit the assignment. Ten (of fifteen) students started the assignment and nine submitted it. Three hours were allocated to the assignment, but all students had submitted their assignments within two hours. The assignment included starting from an informal consensus document and specifying the guideline in PROforma terms, but not actually doing the encoding using PROforma.

The assignment [12] consisted of drawing the procedural CIGs and specifying the declarative metaproperty annotation for plans' goals and for actions, as in the modeling Guide (Fig. 4). The students were asked to draw and specify two guidelines that involve typical multimorbidities [1]: secondary prevention of DU and diagnosis of secondary osteoporosis. They also received a drawing of a third CIG – treatment of osteoporosis due-to PPI – and were asked to specify its metaproperty values. The specific tasks were to specify the 2 CIGs as task networks with correct choice of task types and correct labeling of tasks, and annotating 3 goals and 2 actions, and for each specifying the verb and noun phrase (3 of which were complex). Thus, the total number of tasks was 12 and they were scored separately for each type of modeling required: 2 repetitions of drawing CIGs, 3 goal verbs, 3 complex goal noun phrase terms, 2 action verbs, and 2 action noun phrase terms.

Figure 5a shows the DU consensus given to the participants. Figure 5b shows the gold standard solution, developed by the knowledge engineers and two clinicians (see acknowledgement). Similarly, Fig. 6 shows the consensus and solution for the diagnosis of secondary osteoporosis guideline and Fig. 7 shows Management of Osteoporosis due to PPI. The consensus documents do not cover the full clinical guideline recommendations and were scoped to include essential components for the empirical evaluation study. The first author of the paper graded the solution against the gold standard. The three authors discussed the grading of all solutions until agreement was reached.

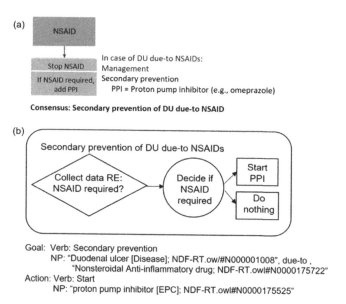

Fig. 5. (a) DU secondary prevention Consensus. (b) PROforma goal-based CIG.

(a)

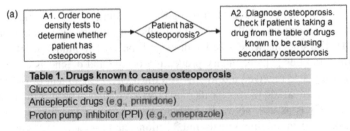

Table 1. Drugs known to cause osteoporosis

Glucocorticoids (e.g., fluticasone)

Antiepleptic drugs (e.g., primidone)

Proton pump inhibitor (PPI) (e.g., omeprazole)

Consensus: Diagnosis of secondary osteoporosis

(b)

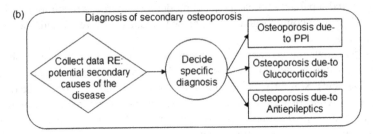

Goal: Verb: Diagnose
        NP: "Osteoporosis [Disease/finding]; NDF-RT.ow/#N000002260"
Action: Verb: Diagnose
        NP: ="Osteoporosis [Disease/finding]; NDF-RT.ow/#N000002260", due-to,
"proton pump inhibitor [EPC]; NDF-RT.owl#N0000175525"

Fig. 6. (a) Diagnosis of secondary osteoporosis Consensus. (b) PROforma goal-based CIG

(a)

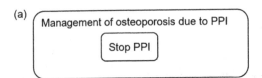

Consensus: Treatment of osteoporosis due-to PPI

(b) Goal: Verb: treat
          NP: ="Osteoporosis [Disease/finding]; NDF-RT.ow/#N000002260", due-to, "proton
              pump inhibitor [EPC]; NDF-RT.owl#N0000175525"

Action: Verb: stop
        NP: "proton pump inhibitor [EPC]; NDF-RT.owl#N0000175525"

Fig. 7. (a) Management of osteoporosis due to PPI Consensus. (b) PROforma goal-based CIG

4   Results

Table 1 (last row) and Fig. 8 present the mean scores of the students (mean of the means) on each modeling task. Table 1 shows additional information. The average score of tasks of each of the 9 students is shown in columns 2–6. The tasks had 2–3 repetitions (number provided in parentheses). The last column shows the total score of each student on all 12 tasks, normalized to 1.

Table 1. Results of specification tasks

	Means					Total score
	Drawing CIG (2)	Goal verb (3)	Goal complex term (3)	Action verb (2)	Action term (2)	
1	1	0.67	0.67	1	1	0.83
2	0.88	1	0.83	1	1	0.94
3	0.88	0.17	0.5	1	1	0.65
4	0.63	1	0.33	1	1	0.77
5	1	1	0.83	1	1	0.96
6	0.38	0.33	0.33	0.5	0	0.31
7	1	1	0.83	1	0.75	0.92
8	1	1	1	1	1	1
9	1	1	0.5	1	1	0.88
avg ± stdev	0.86 ± 0.21	0.80 ± 0.3	0.65 ± 0.23	0.94 ± 0.16	0.86 ± 0.31	0.81 ± 0.2

5   Discussion

The students performed well on the modeling and annotation tasks that are needed for the goal-based integration of CIGs for multimorbidity. The only task on which students did not perform well was modeling of complex clinical terms of the form "Disease due-to Drug" (see correct modeling in Fig. 5b).

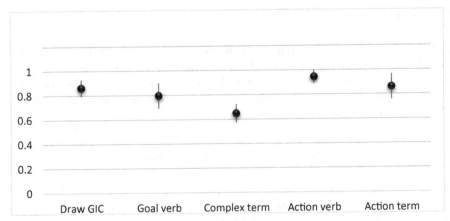

Fig. 8. Results of specification tasks: average score of correct specification (out of 1) and standard errors

We studied the errors made by students. We found that errors belonged to two categories: technical and conceptual. Table 2 summarizes the types of errors and the number of students who made each error type. Specific examples for each error are provided. Note that a certain student can make more than one error type.

Only one student did not make any errors. The total number of errors made by the students were 8 conceptual and 13 technical errors. Four students made conceptual errors and eight students made technical errors. Note that some of the errors which we classified as conceptual may have a technical reason. For example, while writing "Diagnosis of PPI" the student may have meant "arriving at a diagnosis that the cause of Osteoporosis was PPI" and specified it incorrectly due to technical misunderstanding of how to express this relationship.

Certain errors were systematically made by more than one student. These require more attention when teaching students how to represent metaproperty values. Special attention must be paid to explain in detail the clinical decision-making process and to explain the concept of secondary diagnosis of a disease due to a drug adverse effect, which students were not aware of. This probably made them confuse secondary prevention of a disease (related to diagnosis) with secondary diagnosis of the drug that caused the disease, which caused conceptual errors made by 3 students.

Table 2. Error types and quantity

Error description	Example	#st
Conceptual:		4
Confusing between diagnosis and drug	– Instead of management of osteoporosis due-to PPI, wrote management of PPI	2
	– Instead of "Stop PPI" wrote "Stop osteoporosis" (Osteoporosis was due-to PPI) – Instead of "Diagnosis of Osteoporosis" wrote "Diagnosis of PPI"	1
Confusing between diagnosing and treating	– Instead of management of osteoporosis wrote diagnosis of osteoporosis	1
Confusing physiological effect of drug with drug	– Took template of "Physiological Effect has decreased platelet aggregation" and replaced platelet aggregation with PPI: "Physiological effect decreased PPI"	1
Did not aggregate several tasks into same plan	– Instead of modeling one plan of Diagnosis of secondary Osteoporosis with 3 actions of Osteo due-to PPI, Osteo due-to Antiepileptic Osteo due-to Glucocorticoids, had a separate plan for each action	3
Technical:		8
Did not provide specification for part of the consensus	– Did not label all tasks of a CIG	3
	– Did not provide any metaproperty values for a goal	
Did not provide the most specific term	– Wrote "prevention" instead of "secondary prevention"	1
	– Instead of "Prevention of DU due-to NSAID" wrote "Prevention of DU"	6
Selected wrong term	– From NDF-RT chose Osteoporosis, menopausal instead of Osteoporosis	2
	– Chose Calcium gluconate instead of PPI	
Used a specific drug rather than drug group	– Omeprazole instead of PPI	1

This study has limitations. First, the students in this study were information systems majors who were taking a single course of medical informatics, so they are less suitable for CIG modeling tasks than knowledge engineers who have had some experience working in the medical domain. Furthermore, while the experiment shows that modeling and annotation can potentially be done by knowledge engineers, with some acceptable error rate, it does not show how much higher the error rate became by leaving the experts out of the task. Second, the number of participants is very small; hence it is not possible to draw quantitative conclusions and the results should be interpreted as qualitative indications regarding whether using knowledge engineers is a good way to model goal-oriented CIGs.

Even with these limitations, this study has shown that it seems very likely that knowledge engineers with proper short training in medical decision making and CIG modeling, and who have completed several homework CIG specification exercises could reach a good level of proficiency in modeling CIGs and goal-oriented specification. Thus, the extension of the consensus-based CIG elicitation/specification method with goal-based annotations is feasible.

Acknowledgement. The research was funded by grant 906/16 from Israel Science Foundation. We would like to thank Dr. Irit Hochberg and Dr. Raviv Allon for their advice regarding the gold standard for the clinical guidelines used in the study.

References

1. Boyd, C.M., Darer, J., Boult, C., Fried, L.P., Boult, L., Wu, A.W.: Clinical practice guidelines and quality of care for older patients. JAMA **294**(6), 716–724 (2005)
2. Kogan, A., Tu, S.W., Peleg, M.: Goal-driven management of interacting clinical guidelines for multimorbidity patients. In: AMIA Symposium (2018)
3. Fox, J., Rahmanzadeh, A.: Disseminating medical knowledge: the PROforma approach. Artif. Intell. Med. **14**, 157–181 (1998)
4. Shalom, E., Shahar, Y., Lunenfeld, E., Taieb-Maimon, M., Young, O., Goren-Bar, D., et al.: The importance of creating an ontology-specific consensus before a markup-based specification of clinical guidelines. In: Proceeding of the Biennial European Conference on Artificial Intelligence (ECAI), Riva del Garda, Italy (2006)
5. Shiffman, R.N., Michel, G., Essaihi, A., Thornquist, E.: Bridging the guideline implementation gap: a systematic, document-centered approach to guideline implementation. J. Am. Med. Inform. Assoc. **11**, 418–426 (2004)
6. Shiffman, R.N., Dixon, J., Brandt, C., Essaihi, A., Hsiao, A., Michel, G., et al.: The GuideLine Implementability Appraisal (GLIA): development of an instrument to identify obstacles to guideline implementation. BMC Med. Inform. Decis. Making **5**, 23 (2005)
7. Shiffman, R.N., Michel, G., Rosenfeld, R.M., Davidson, C.: Building better guidelines with BRIDGE-Wiz: development and evaluation of a software assistant to promote clarity, transparency, and implementability. J. Am. Med. Inform. Assoc. **19**(1), 94–101 (2012)
8. Shalom, E., Shahar, Y., Taieb-Maimon, M., Martins, S.B., Vaszar, L.T., Goldstein, M.K., et al.: Ability of expert physicians to structure clinical guidelines: reality versus perception. J. Eval. Clin. Pract. **15**(6), 1043–1053 (2009)
9. Kaiser, K., Akkayaa, C., Miksch, A.: How can information extraction ease formalizing treatment processes in clinical practice guidelines? A method and its evaluation. Artif. Intell. Med. **39**(2), 151–163 (2007)
10. U.S. Department of Veterans Affairs. National Drug File – Reference Terminology (NDF-RTTM) Documentation (2015)
11. HL7. Fast Healthcare Interoperability Resources Release 3 Specification (2017). https://www.hl7.org/fhir/overview.html
12. Peleg, M.: PROforma goal modelign tutorial and exam (2018). https://drive.google.com/file/d/1kS6qA8xbRCySxyp1uOpxgGCiJI_Sth3O/view?usp=sharing

Differential Diagnosis of Bacterial and Viral Meningitis Using Dominance-Based Rough Set Approach

Ewelina Gowin[1]([⊠]) [iD], Jerzy Błaszczyński[2], Roman Słowiński[2], Jacek Wysocki[1], and Danuta Januszkiewicz-Lewandowska[3]

[1] Department of Health Promotion, Poznań University of Medical Sciences, Poznań, Poland
ewego@poczta.onet.pl, jawysocki@prof.onet.pl
[2] Institute of Computing Science, Poznań University of Technology, Poznań, Poland
{jerzy.blaszczynski,roman.slowinski}@cs.put.poznan.pl
[3] Department of Oncology, Hematology and Bone Marrow Transplantation, Poznań University of Medical Sciences, Poznań, Poland
1962dj@gmail.com

Abstract. Differential diagnosis of bacterial and viral meningitis remains an important clinical problem, particularly in the initial hours of hospitalization, before obtaining results of lumbar puncture. We conducted a retrospective analysis of the medical records of 193 children hospitalized in St. Joseph Children's Hospital in Poznan. In this study, we applied the original methodology of dominance-based rough set approach (DRSA) to induce diagnostic patterns from meningitis data and to represent them by decision rules useful in discriminating between bacterial and viral meningitis. The rule induction algorithm applied to this end is VC-DomLEM from jRS library. In the studied group of 193 patients, there were 124 boys and 69 girls, and the mean age was 94 months. The patients were characterized by 10 attributes, of which only 5 were used in 5 rules able to discriminate between bacterial and viral meningitis with an average precision of 98%, where C-reactive protein attribute (CRP) appeared to be the most valuable. Factors associated with bacterial meningitis were: CRP level $\geq$ 85 mg/l, or age $<$ 2 months. Factors associated with viral meningitis were CRP level $\leq$ 60 mg/l and procalcitonin level $<$ 0.5 ng/ml, or CRP level $\leq$ 84 mg/l and the presence of vomiting. We established a minimum set of attributes significant for classification of patients with bacterial or viral meningitis. These attributes are analyzed in just 5 rules able to distinguish almost perfectly between bacterial and viral meningitis without the need of lumbar puncture.

Keywords: Viral meningitis · Bacterial meningitis · Dominance-based Rough Set Approach · Decision rules

1 Introduction

Meningitis is an acute inflammation localized in tissues surrounding brain. Infectious meningitis is caused by entry of pathogens into physiologic sterile cerebrospinal fluid.

© Springer Nature Switzerland AG 2019
M. Marcos et al. (Eds.): KR4HC-ProHealth 2019/TEAAM 2019, LNAI 11979, pp. 29–38, 2019.
https://doi.org/10.1007/978-3-030-37446-4_3

The main invasion route is blood from colonized mucous membranes distant sites of infection; sinusitis, pneumonia, otitis media [1]. Fever, headache, changes in mental status, positive meningeal signs, vomiting are the typical signs of meningitis.

Diagnosis of bacterial meningitis is based on a positive culture of cerebrospinal fluid or detection of bacterial genetic material by Polymerase Chain Reaction (PCR), along with typical clinical symptoms (fever, headache, neck stiffness) [1]. A gold diagnostic standard is a cerebrospinal fluid culture. In populations vaccinated against main bacterial pathogens (*N.meningitidis, H. influenzae, S.pneumoniae*) majority of meningitis cases are caused by viruses [2, 3]. There is no single parameter useful for quickly establishing the aetiology of meningitis, however the clinical proper antibiotic treatment must be administrated immediately. This is why a reliable marker, which would be easily and quickly checked, has been search for the diagnosis. However, relying solely on one marker increases the risk of diagnostic error. Moreover, a number of scales to assist the diagnosis of meningitis have been developed, but none of them have been found to have high specificity with 100% sensitivity [4, 5].

Differential diagnosis of bacterial and viral meningitis remains an important unsolved clinical problem, particularly in the initial hours of hospitalization, before obtaining results of lumbar puncture. Classic clinical diagnostic signs have limited value in establishing the diagnosis of meningitis in children [6].

The aim of the undertaken study was to analyse the usefulness of biochemical and hematological parameters in distinguishing between bacterial and non-bacterial meningitis using an artificial intelligence methodology. The preliminary analysis performed on a small group of patients was reported in [7]. In this paper, we extend this analysis by considering a much greater group.

2 Materials and Methods

Our study group consisted of children with clinical manifestation of meningitis. All children were hospitalized at the St. Joseph Children's Hospital in Poznan, Poland. It is one of two infectious disease departments serving the population of children of the Greater Poland Voivodeship. We conducted a retrospective analysis of the medical records from all of the patients hospitalized with meningitis from 2012 to 2018. The bacterial etiology was confirmed either by a cerebrospinal fluid microbiological culture or an identification of the pathogen's DNA using the PCR method. All children were previously healthy, not diagnosed with any immunodeficiencies. They were vaccinated according to the Polish vaccination schedule. The following parameters were analysed: C-reactive protein (CRP) and procalcitonin (PCT) concentration in serum, white blood cells count in peripheral blood. Symptoms present on admission such as fever, seizures, rash, headache, vomiting, duration of symptoms ant patient's age were also analyzed.

In this study, we discovered diagnostic patterns of meningitis data, and represented them by decision rules useful for discriminating between bacterial and viral meningitis. The obtained rules represent cause-effect relationships existing in the data. Prior to inducing rules, we used an extension of rough set theory [8], known as Dominance-based Rough Set Approach (DRSA) [9–13]. The DRSA methodology is able to deal with partially inconsistent data. In our case, inconsistency occurs when two patients have similar data from anamnesis and clinical examinations, while one is classified as bacterial meningitis, and another as aseptic meningitis. The rough sets of patients, corresponding to bacterial and viral cases, are composed of two classical sets each, called lower approximation (composed of consistent patients from bacterial or viral group), and upper approximation (composed of both consistent and inconsistent patients from bacterial or viral group). Then, "*if. . ., then . . .*" decision rules are induced from these approximations, we used VC-DomLEM from jRS library[1]. Rules induced from lower approximations are called certain, and those induced from upper approximations, possible. DRSA was designed for reasoning about ordered data, that is, such that the value sets of condition attributes are monotonically dependent on the order of the decision classes. Consequently, the rules induced from dominance-based rough approximations are monotonic, and their syntax is the following:

- "if $atr_i(patient) \geq v_i$ & $atr_j(patient) \geq v_j$ & . . . & $atr_p(patient) \geq v_p$, then the patient has bacterial meningitis",
- "if $atr_k(patient) \leq v_k$ & $atr_l(patient) \leq v_l$ & . . . & $atr_s(patient) \leq v_s$, then the patient has viral meningitis",

where atr_h is an h-th condition attribute and v_h is a specific value of this attribute discovered from data, that constitute an elementary condition $atr_h(patient) \geq v_h$ or $atr_h(patient) \leq v_h$ belonging to the condition part of a rule, assigning a patient to either bacterial class or viral class, respectively. The afore mentioned syntax of the rules assumes that value sets of all condition attributes are numerical and that the greater the value, the more probable is that the patient develops bacterial meningitis; analogously, this syntax assumes that the smaller the value, the more probable that the patient develops viral meningitis. Numerical attributes with value sets ordered in this way are called gain-type. Value sets of cost-type attributes are ordered in the opposite way; consequently, elementary conditions on cost-type attributes have opposite relation signs. In the case of meningitis data, it is impossible to know a priori if attributes corresponding to anamnesis and clinical examination are gain- or cost-type. For this reason, we adopted the approach described previously in [14] that is, we doubled each original attribute and for the first one we assumed it is of gain-type, while for the second one we assumed it is of cost-type. Such a transformation of data does not affect the truth of discovered cause-effect relationships. Then, the induction algorithm takes decision for rules elementary conditions defined using one or both copies of given attributes.

For instance, in a rule suggesting the assignment of a patient to the bacterial class, there may appear the following elementary conditions concerning attribute, atr_i: $\uparrow atr_i(patient) \geq v_{i1}$ or $\downarrow atr_i(patient) \leq v_{i2}$, $\uparrow atr_i(patient) \geq v_{i1}$ and $\downarrow atr_i(patient) \leq v_{i2}$, which can be summarized as $atr_i(patient) \in [v_{i1}, v_{i2}]$ when $v_{i1} < v_{i2}$, where $\uparrow atr_i$ and $\downarrow atr_i$ are gain-type and cost-type copies of attribute atr_i, respectively. The applied transformation of attributes permits discovering global and local monotonic relationships between anamnesis, clinical examination and class assignment.

For each rule one can calculate its strength, being a ratio of the number of patients matching the condition part of the rule and the number of all patients in the data set, as

---

[1] http://www.cs.put.poznan.pl/jblaszczynski/Site/jRS.html.

well as its coverage, being a ratio of the number of patients matching the condition part of the rule and the number of all patients in the suggested class. In case of our application of DRSA, the rules were induced from the meningitis data transformed in the way described earlier, and structured into lower and upper approximations of bacterial and viral classes of patients. VC-DomLEM induction algorithm [15] was employed to construct decision rule sets. Estimation of attribute relevance in induced sets of rules was performed by measuring Bayesian confirmation. Variable consistency bagging (VC-bagging) [16, 17] was applied in the estimation procedure. Decision rules were induced by VC-DomLEM repetitively on bootstrap samples and then tested on patients who were not included in the samples. Reported results were obtained in a 10-fold cross validation experiment that was repeated 100 times. Let us observe that a rule can be seen as a consequence relation "*if* P, *then* C," where P is rule premise, and C rule conclusion. The relevance of each single attribute in elementary condition of a premise in decision rule may be assessed by the Bayesian confirmation measure which quantifies the contribution of this attribute in rule premise P to correct classification decision of unseen patients [18]. For reasons described previously, we chose confirmation measure denoted by $s(C, atr_i\ P)$, for its easy interpretation as difference of conditional probabilities involving C and atr_i P in the following way: $s(C, atr_i\ P) = Pr(C|\ atr_i\ P) - Pr(C|not\ atr_i\ P)$, where probability $Pr(\bullet)$ is estimated on the testing samples of patients. It quantifies the degree to which the presence of attribute atr_i in premise P, denoted by atr_i P, provides evidence for or against rule conclusion C. In consequence, the attributes being present in the premise of rules that make correct decisions, or attributes absent in the premise of rules that make incorrect decisions, become more relevant.

3   Results

In the studied group, there were 193 patients (124 boys and 69 girls), and the mean age was 94 months. There were 109 children with viral meningitis and 84 with bacterial. VC-DomLEM was able to achieve high classification accuracy on this data set. Overall classification accuracy observed in 10-fold cross validation repeated 100 times was 97.98%, with accuracy in class bacterial meningitis (sensitivity) equal 96.54%, and accuracy in class viral meningitis (specificity) equal 99.08%. We analyzed 10 attributes, of which only 5 were used to generate a minimal set of rules covering all patients from lower approximations of classes. This set contains 5 rules. Moreover, C-reactive protein (CRP) appeared to be the most valuable attribute according to estimated s confirmation measure. Results of this estimation are presented in Fig. 1.

Decision rules generated from the data set of our patients suspected of having meningitis (with fever and positive meningeal signs) are as follows:

1. If CRP level is ≥85 mg/l, then the patient has bacterial meningitis (coverage factor 97.6%).
2. If CRP level is ≥80 mg/l and leukocytes are ≤18 000/μl then the patient has bacterial meningitis (coverage factor 48.8%).
3. If the patient is in first two months of life, then it is bacterial meningitis (coverage factor 2.3%).

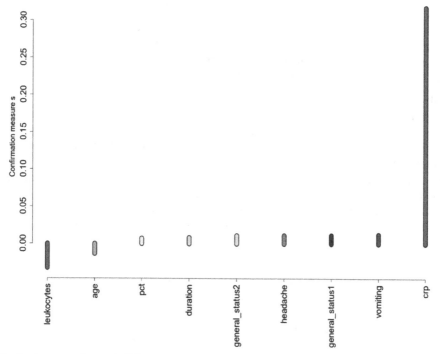

Fig. 1. A comparison of different parameters discriminating between bacterial and aseptic meningitis (pct stands for procalcitonin, and crp for C-reactive protein).

4. If CRP level is ≤60 mg/l and procalcitonin level is ≤0.5 ng/ml, then the patient has viral meningitis (coverage factor 99.8%).
5. If CRP level is ≤84 mg/l and a patient is vomiting, then the patient has viral meningitis (coverage factor 69.7%).

In the group of children with meningitis, inflammatory biomarkers differ statistically significantly depending of the etiology - bacterial or aseptic. Factors associated with bacterial meningitis were: CRP level at least 85 mg/l, or age less than two months. Factors associated with viral meningitis were CRP level not higher than 60 mg/l and procalcitonin level below 0.5 ng/ml, or CRP level not higher than 84 mg/l and the presence of vomiting.

Let us provide an interpretation of obtained rules from a diagnostic perspective:

Rule 1
Patients suspected of having meningitis based on clinical symptoms (fever, meningeal signs) with CRP higher or equal 85 mg/L had bacterial meningitis. This rule identified 82 out of 84 patients with bacterial meningitis (97.6%). The 2 patients not covered had CRP lower than 85 mg/l. All patients with CRP of 85 mg/l or higher had bacterial meningitis. There were no patients with viral meningitis who matched this rule.

Rule 2

If the CRP level is higher than or equal to 80 mg/l and leukocytes are $\leq 18\,000/\mu l$, then the patient has bacterial meningitis. It covered 41 cases (48.8%) of bacterial meningitis and did not cover any patients with viral meningitis. The additional value of this rule was that it covered 2 patients not covered by rule number one.

Rule 3

Suspicion of meningitis in a child within the first two months of life, the etiology is assumed to be bacterial. This rule is based only on the patient's age. In a clinical setting this is reasonable approach: a newborn suspected of a generalized infection, the risk of bacterial etiology is very high, and antibiotics are started immediately. The rule covered two cases of bacterial meningitis (2.38%). There were no patients with aseptic meningitis who matched this rule. The coverage is low, but this is due to the age limit in this rule. In our group there were only two children younger than two months.

Using all three of the above rules together all patients with bacterial meningitis were identified.

Rule 4

When the level of CRP is lower than or equal to 60 mg/l and procalcitonin level is lower than 0.5 ng/ml, the patient is diagnosed as having viral meningitis. This rule covered 108 out of 109 (99.8%) cases of viral meningitis. There were no patients with bacterial meningitis who matched this rule.

Rule 5

If CRP level is ≤ 84 and a patient is vomiting, then the patient has viral meningitis. This rule covered 76 out of 109 (69.7%) patients with viral meningitis. There were no patients with bacterial meningitis who matched this rule.

Using the last two of the above rules together, all patients with viral meningitis were identified.

4 Discussion

Multi-criteria decision analysis is increasingly being used to support healthcare decisions that include many, often non-specific criteria. Criteria (patient data, type of symptom, value of test results and others) are assigned a numerical weight, and decision alternatives, such as the use of a specific treatment, are assessed according to each of the criteria. There are many multi-criteria decision analysis methods and only few works have compared their suitability [19]. Each of the methods has advantages and disadvantages, and a comparison of their suitability for healthcare applications has not been clearly indicated. The authors of this review indicate that deterministic sensitivity analysis is useful in many applications, but more complex approaches are particularly useful when the uncertainty of many parameters must be taken into account simultaneously or when there are complex dependencies.

In our analysis the highest coverage for bacterial meningitis had rule number one. This rule is based on commonly used inflammatory marker. In our study, a normal value of the C-reactive protein concentration appeared to be the most useful inflammation parameter to exclude a bacterial meningitis (high negative predictive value). C-reactive protein is one of acute phase reactants produced by hepatocytes in a response to inflammation. Its production is stimulated by interleukin-1 and interleukin-6 released by macrophages activated by tissue damage, infection (bacterial, viral, fungal) or inflammation. An increase in C-reactive protein concentration in response to generalized inflammation occurs gradually during the first 12 h, reaching maximum level at 48 to 72 h. It has been reported by Nigrovic et al. that C-reactive protein concentrations higher than 100 mg/l is a sensitive marker, but lacking specificity [4].

Oostenbrink et al. proposed a clinical score in which one of criteria suggesting bacterial infection was C-reactive protein level higher than 50 mg/l [5]. In our preliminary study [7], as well as in the present study based on a larger group of patients, all the 11 children with bacterial meningitis had C-reactive protein concentrations higher than 80 mg/l. Data analysed in this study indicated that children with meningitis with C-reactive protein level lower than 80 mg/l are at low risk of having bacterial etiology. Such information obtained before lumbar puncture is helpful in planning further treatment and diagnostic tests.

A high negative predictive value of C-reactive protein concentration, shown in our study, is of great value, because it helps to identify severe bacterial infections at admission. Use of a cutoff C-reactive protein level shown in our study, clearly indicated patients with bacterial meningitis, before lumbar punction was performed. Meta-analysis from 35 studies proposed to use CRP as an additional tool for discriminating bacterial meningitis from viral meningitis, without having evaluated its independent contribution relative to other parameters such as white blood cell count, CSF white cell count, protein, or glucose [20].

In the literature there are examples of usefulness of elevated levels of procalcitonin in diagnosis of bacterial meningitis [21]. Dubos et al. showed that a serum procalcitonin greater than 0.5 ng/mL predicts bacterial rather than aseptic meningitis in children [22]. Gendrel and co-workers based on a study done on 59 children with meningitis showed that measurement of plasma procalcitonin might be of value in the differential diagnosis of bacterial or viral meningitis [23]. Clinical symptoms and signs cannot discriminate between bacterial and aseptic meningitis. Analysis of inflammatory biomarkers will offer additional diagnostic information to distinguish between a bacterial or non-bacterial origin. There are several scaling systems designed for meningitis. But none of them is commonly used. The biggest disadvantage of classical scaling is conversion of clinical data into numeric values. This leads to losing the primary character of the data. Several parameters are added together, the sum of completely different parameters can yield the same results. It discourages the application of this system in daily practice because it does not give doctors the chance to evaluate the results on which the decision was made.

Presented rules support diagnostic process performed by clinicians. The biggest advantage is that application of DRSA methodology does not require data conversion. It enables combination of parametric and nonparametric data, which are commonly used in daily practice. This algorithm helps doctors to distinguish between similar diseases, with different prognosis. In past many of such diseases were diagnosed based on doctors' experience. It is more and more difficult to build the clinical experience among doctors, because thanks to common vaccination programs, the number of bacterial meningitis cases is decreasing. The conversion of clinical data into numerical data is a great problem.

Thanks to the application of DRSA methodology the risk of losing the original nature of the data is minimized. Moreover, the obtained results are definitely more informative, and show how the diagnosis was made.

Final diagnosis of bacterial or viral meningitis can be made after cerebro-spinal fluid analysis. It usually takes up to 48 h to establish aetiology (time for bacteriological culture or molecular tests). Knowledge about possible aetiology, in first hours of hospitalization, before lumbar punction is performed, can change clinical management. Bacterial meningitis is a life-threatening diastase, broad antibiotic treatment must be introduced in a first hour of hospitalization. While viral meningitis is a self limiting diseases, which requires only symptomatic treatment. Instant diagnosis of bacterial meningitis is also important from public health perspective. People who had close contact with patient with meningococcal meningitis should receive chemoprophylaxis, as soon as possible, to prevent further cases of meningitis leading to epidemic infections. Application of generated rules can help in antibiotic stewardship. Due to common use of antibiotics the resistance among bacteria is an increasing problem. So antibiotics must be started only when it is necessary. When it is possible, treatment should be started based on microbiology results. The decision of providing only symptomatic treatment in a child with meningitis of probable viral aetiology, before the bacteriology culture comes back negative, is very challenging. Many children receive empiric broad antibiotic treatment, even if they are in good condition and bacterial aetiology is very unlikely. Nowadays in diagnostic process doctors' can not rely only on one's gut feeling. Having a reliable tool to support the decision-making process provides a large advantage.

Application of presented clinical decision rules could prevent unnecessary antibiotic treatment in aseptic meningitis, with no risk of leaving children with bacterial meningitis without treatment. DRSA, due to its high sensitivity and specificity, seems to be a good tool for determining predictive markers in meningitis. Models thus developed can potentially be used in a number of other disease entities. However, to justify our statements, these models should be tested prospectively on a larger and /or different patient group or a larger multi-center study should be performed on different populations of children to further validate the presented clinical decision rules.

5   Conclusions

Using the Dominance-based Rough Set Approach, we discovered a minimal set of attributes significant for classification of patients with meningitis. This set includes 5 attributes. The set of 5 rules induced from data is using these 5 attributes and correctly reclassifies all patients. It is also useful for prospective decisions for distinguishing between bacterial and viral meningitis before lumbar puncture. As shown in Fig. 1, serum concentration of C-reactive protein appears to be a useful marker of bacterial etiology of meningitis.

References

1. Sáez-Lorens, X., McCracken, G.H.: Bacterial meningitis in children. Lancet **361**, 2139–2148 (2003)

2. Mook-Kanamori, B.B., Geldhoff, M., van der Poll, T., van de Beek, D.: Pathogenesis and pathophysiology of pneumococcal meningitis. Clin. Microbiol. Rev. **24**, 557–591 (2011)

3. Stephens, D.S., Greenwood, B., Brandtzaeg, P.: Epidemic meningitis, meningococcaemia, and Neisseria meningitides. Lancet **369**, 2196–2210 (2007)

4. Nigrovic, L.E., et al.: Clinical prediction rule for identifying children with cerebrospinal fluid pleocytosis at very low risk of bacterial meningitis. JAMA **297**, 52–60 (2007)

5. Oostenbrink, R., Moons, K.G., Derksen-Lubsen, A.G., Grobbee, D.E., Moll, H.A.: A diagnostic decision rule for management of children with meningeal signs. Eur. J. Epidemiol. **19**, 109–116 (2004)

6. Curtis, S., Stobart, K., Vandermeer, B., Simel, D.L., Klassen, T.: Clinical features suggestive of meningitis in children: a systematic review of prospective data. Pediatrics **126**, 952–960 (2010)

7. Gowin, E., Januszkiewicz-Lewandowska, D., Słowiński, R., Błaszczyński, J., Michalak, M., Wysocki, J.: With a little help from a computer: discriminating between bacterial and viral meningitis based on dominance-based rough set approach analysis. Medicine **96**(32), e7635 (2017)

8. Pawlak, Z.: Rough Sets: Theoretical Aspects of Reasoning about Data. Kluwer, Dordrecht (1991)

9. Błaszczyński, J., Greco, S., Słowiński, R., Szeląg, M.: Monotonic variable consistency rough set approaches. Int. J. Approx. Reason. **50**, 979–999 (2009)

10. Greco, S., Matarazzo, B., Słowinski, R.: Rough sets theory for multicriteria decision analysis. Eur. J. Oper. Res. **129**, 1–47 (2001)

11. Słowiński, R., Greco, S., Matarazzo, B.: Rough sets in decision making support. In: Burke, E., Kendall, G. (eds.) Search Methodologies: Introductory Tutorials in Optimization and Decision Support Techniques, 2nd edn, pp. 557–609. Springer, New York (2014). https://doi.org/10.1007/978-1-4614-6940-7

12. Słowiński, R., Greco, S., Matarazzo, B.: Rough set methodology for decision aiding. In: Kacprzyk, J., Pedrycz, W. (eds.) Springer Handbook of Computational Intelligence, pp. 349–370. Springer, Heidelberg (2015). https://doi.org/10.1007/978-3-662-43505-2_22

13. Greco, S., Matarazzo, B., Słowiński, R.: Rough sets methodology for sorting problems in presence of multiple attributes and criteria. Eur. J. Oper. Res. **138**, 247–259 (2002)

14. Błaszczyński, J., Greco, S., Słowiński, R.: Inductive discovery of laws using monotonic rules. Eng. Appl. Artif. Intell. **25**, 284–294 (2012)

15. Błaszczyński, J., Słowiński, R., Szeląg, M.: Sequential covering rule induction algorithm for variable consistency rough set approaches. Inf. Sci. **181**, 987–1002 (2011)

16. Błaszczyński, J., Słowiński, R., Stefanowski, J.: Feature set-based consistency sampling in bagging ensembles. In: European Conference on Machine Learning & Principles of Knowledge Discovery in Databases (ECML/ PKDD 2009). Bled, Slovenia, pp. 19–35, 7–11 September 2009

17. Błaszczyński, J., Słowiński, R., Stefanowski, J.: Variable consistency bagging ensembles. In: Peters, J.F., Skowron, A. (eds.) Transactions on Rough Sets XI. LNCS, vol. 5946, pp. 40–52. Springer, Heidelberg (2010). https://doi.org/10.1007/978-3-642-11479-3_3

18. Błaszczyński, J., Słowiński, R., Susmaga, R.: Rule-based estimation of attribute relevance. In: Yao, J., Ramanna, S., Wang, G., Suraj, Z. (eds.) RSKT 2011. LNCS (LNAI), vol. 6954, pp. 36–44. Springer, Heidelberg (2011). https://doi.org/10.1007/978-3-642-24425-4_7

19. Broekhuizen, H., Groothuis-Oudshoorn, C., van Til, J., Hummel, J., Izerman, M.: A review and classification of approaches for dealing with uncertainty in multi-criteria decision analysis for healthcare decision. Pharmacoeconomics **33**, 445–455 (2015)

20. Gerdes, L.U., Jørgensen, P.E., Nexø, E., Wang, P.: C-reactive protein and bacterial meningitis: a meta-analysis. Scand. J. Clin. Lab. Invest. **58**, 383–394 (1998)

21. Shimetani, N., Shimetani, K., Mori, M.: Levels of three inflammation markers, C-reactive protein, serum amyloid a protein and procalcitonin, in the serum and cerebrospinal fluid of patients with meningitis. Scand. J. Clin. Lab. Invest. **61**, 567–574 (2001)
22. Dubos, F., Lamotte, B., Bibi-Triki, F., et al.: Clinical decision rules to distinguish between bacterial and aseptic meningitis. Arch. Dis. Child. **91**, 647–650 (2006)
23. Gendrel, D., Raymond, J., Assicot, M., et al.: Measurement of procalcitonin levels in children with bacterial or viral meningitis. Clin. Infect. Dis. **24**, 1240–1242 (1997)

Modelling ICU Patients to Improve Care Requirements and Outcome Prediction of Acute Respiratory Distress Syndrome: A Supervised Learning Approach

Mohammed Sayed⑩ and David Riaño⁽✉⁾ ⑩

Universitat Rovira i Virgili, Av Paisos Catalans 26, 43007 Tarragona, Spain
{mgamal.sayed,david.riano}@urv.cat

Abstract. The acute respiratory distress syndrome (ARDS) is a frequent type of respiratory failure observed in intensive care units. The Berlin classification identifies three severity levels of ARDS (mild, moderate, and severe), but this classification is under controversy in the medical community because it reflects neither the care requirements nor the expected clinical outcome of the patients. Here, the database MIMIC III (MetaVision) was used to investigate the similarity of patients within each one of the Berlin severity groups. We also ranked the relevance of common ARDS descriptive features and proposed four alternative classifiers to improve Berlin's classification in the prediction of the duration of mechanical ventilation and mortality. One of these classifiers proved to be significantly better than current proposals and, therefore, it can be considered as a robust model to potentially improve health care processes and quality in the management of ARDS patients in Intensive Care Units (ICUs).

Keywords: Knowledge extraction from health care databases and medical records · Machine learning · Intensive Care unit · Acute respiratory distress syndrome · Mechanical ventilation · Mortality

1 Introduction

Acute respiratory distress syndrome (ARDS) describes an acute respiratory failure that impairs the lungs to correctly exchange oxygen and carbon dioxide. It shows a great variability of incidence that, in average, can range from 17.9 per 100,000 person-years in Europe, to 78.9 per 100,000 person-years in the US [1]. In ICUs, ARDS occurrence was estimated to be 10.4% of all the admissions, and 23.4% of mechanically ventilated patients, according to the LUNG SAVE international multicenter study [2]. In 2012, the ARDS Definition Task Force Group proposed a new classification of ARDS severity that replaced the previous one from 1994 and which was called the *Berlin definition of ARDS*. This definition determines three severity levels of ARDS: mild, moderate, and severe; which are defined for patients with a positive end expiratory pressure (PEEP) of 5 cmH$_2$O or greater, and a respective PaO$_2$/FiO$_2$ ratio of 201–300 mmHg, 101–200 mmHg,

© Springer Nature Switzerland AG 2019
M. Marcos et al. (Eds.): KR4HC-ProHealth 2019/TEAAM 2019, LNAI 11979, pp. 39–49, 2019.
https://doi.org/10.1007/978-3-030-37446-4_4

and ≤ 100 mmHg (see Table 1). PEEP is a measure of the pressure that remains in the airways at the end of the respiratory cycle (i.e., exhalation). In mechanical ventilated patients, it is greater than the atmospheric pressure. PaO2/FiO2 is the ratio of arterial oxygen partial pressure to fractional inspired oxygen. Patients in the above mentioned severity groups showed different mortality ratios [3]: 27% for mild (24–30%, 95% CI), 32% for moderate (29–34%), and 45% for severe (42–48%), with a P-value <0.001. Moreover, mortality prediction of Berlin definition groups outperformed previous ARDS classifications with an AUC (ROC) of 0.577 (0.561–0.593, 95% CI) [3]. In spite of that, a recent publication [4] warns about the risks of the Berlin definition. Precisely, it argues that mild ARDS may be "severe in terms of level of care and outcome". These two health care quality dimensions (i.e., care and outcome) can be measured in terms of the duration of mechanical ventilation in the ICU, and the survival rate, among other clinical parameters.

Table 1. Berlin definition of ARDS severity levels.

PEEP	PaO2/FiO2	Severity
≥ 5 cmH2O	201–300 mmHg	Mild
	101–200 mmHg	Moderate
	≤ 100 mmHg	Severe

MIMIC-III is a large, publicly available database containing de-identified health-related data of approximately sixty thousand admissions of patients who stayed in ICUs of the Beth Israel Deaconess Medical Center in Boston [5]. In MIMIC-III, original data (years 2001–2008) were extended with the MetaVision data (years 2008–2012). MetaVision data includes data of 23,024 follow up interventions on ARDS patients, as described in the Berlin definition.

In order to analyze the duration of mechanical ventilation and the mortality prediction of ARDS patients in ICUs, the clinical features described in [8–10] were selected. These are: age (years), PEEP (cmH$_2$O), PaO$_2$/FiO$_2$, Mean heart rate (beats per minute), Mean respiratory rate (breaths per minute), and Number of ventilation actions. Apart of these, for each patient, we counted with the additional features duration of mechanical ventilation (hours), survival (0 for survival and 1 for death), and the Berlin definition classification (mild, moderate, or severe). While the ones in the first group are considered descriptive features, the ones in the last group are clinical features on the management of the patient.

Sections A-B in Table 2 provide a statistical description of these features in terms of their respective mean values and the 95% confidence intervals (CI). Interesting conclusions drawn from the analysis of these values will be discussed in Sect. 3.

Based on the MIMIC III data, our study was divided in two parts. In the first part, we analyzed the statistical differences of the patient follow up interventions inside each one of the three Berlin severity groups of ARDS. For this purpose, we studied separately each descriptive and clinical attribute in [8–10]. We also investigated the similarity of the patient encounters inside each one of the three Berlin severity groups. With regard to the features, we ranked the most relevant attributes to predict the duration of mechanical ventilation, but also to foresee patient survival. The differences of the attribute relevance among the three severity levels were also analyzed. Finally, we obtained the group of features to develop optimal models of linear regression and logistic regression to predict the duration of mechanical ventilation and survival, respectively. The quality measures used in this process were the root mean square error (RMSE) in the prediction of the ventilation time (which is a quantitative concept), and the area under the ROC curve (AUC) in the prediction of survival (which is a qualitative concept).

In the second part of the study, we developed four alternative types of predictive models representing alternative improved approaches to the Berlin classification, thus contributing to the improvement of the health care and the quality of managing ARDS in ICUs.

The structure of this paper is as follows: after the introduction, Sect. 2 describes the methods followed in the four studies performed. Section 3 presents the results obtained and it provides an interpretation of some of the most relevant ones. Section 4 is deserved to introduce some of the previous works that provide the research context of our work, and Sect. 5 enumerates the most relevant conclusions that we reached.

2 Methods

Four analyses are proposed. The first one is concerning to the values of the descriptive features within each Berlin group for the data in MIMIC III. The second one focuses on the similarity of patients within each Berlin group as a measure of their homogeneity. The relevance of the features is also considered one by one and in groups, for predicting patient needs of ventilation hours and survival in ICU. The last analysis is centered in the proposal of a model that could outperform the predictive quality of the Berlin classification of ARDS patients. All these analyses are detailed in the next sections.

2.1 Analysis of the Descriptive Features

A statistical analysis was performed for all the descriptive features. This analysis considered the mean and the 25% confidence interval (CI) of the values of each feature as contained in the MIMIC III database. The study considered all the patient follow-ups together, but also the follow-ups in each Berlin definition of the ARDS severity levels, separately. That is to say, mild ARDS patients alone, moderate patients alone, and severe patients alone. This study was extended to the clinical features as well. These features are: duration of mechanical ventilation and mortality.

2.2 Analysis of Patient's Similarity

The similarity of the patients inside each Berlin group was also investigated. Three similarity analyses were performed: one considering the descriptive features of the patients, another one considering only the hours of mechanical ventilation, and a third one based exclusively on the mortality rate.

All the descriptive and clinical features were normalized to values in the range 0–1, and the new values used to calculate the similarity between all the patients, but also between patients within the same ARDS severity group. The Euclidean distance was taken to calculate distances between pairs of patients, and the average value of these pairwise comparisons of patients, computed. Similarity was calculated as (1 - distance).

For the first analysis, only the descriptive features were considered in the calculation of the patient similarities. For the second analysis, only the duration of mechanical ventilation is considered for that calculation. In this case, patient similarity is considered to be equivalent to the amount of hours of mechanical ventilation required. Finally, in the third analysis, we considered patient similarity 0 if only one of the two compared patients survived, and 1 if both survived or if both died.

2.3 Relevant Descriptive Features and Feature Groups

In order to determine similarities and differences among the Berlin classification groups, we performed a ranking of the most relevant features to predict the duration of mechanical ventilation of patients within each group. Moreover, we obtained a ranking of the features that better assist to discriminate between ARDS patients who died or survived in the ICU. We used the Relief algorithm [6] to calculate the relevance of the features, and then ordered them in respective rankings. Relief applies an iterative algorithm in which each iteration is used to refine the relevance of all the features by calculating the square differences between a randomly selected case and the nearest cases in the same and in the opposite classes.

The combination of attributes was also considered. Force brute combination of all the possible groups of descriptive features were subject to 10-fold cross validation to assess which group could obtain a better prediction. Specifically, to predict duration of mechanical ventilation, we performed a linear regression as the modelling process, and the root mean square error (RMSE) as the quality indicator. Regarding to predict mortality in ICU, we performed logistic regression and the AUC value.

2.4 Compared Performance of Predictive Models

Four types of models were developed to predict duration of mechanical ventilation (quantitative prediction) and mortality (qualitative prediction). As in the previous section, for the first predictions, we used linear regression to develop the model, and RMSE to measure the predictive quality of the results. On the contrary, for the last models, we used logistic regression to model and the AUC value to assess the quality of the model.

The first type of models was developed considering just the information carried by the Berlin class (i.e., the targeted question was: is it enough to know the Berlin class to develop a robust prediction of the hours of mechanical ventilation and mortality?). For the second type of models, we considered the two features that define the Berlin class. That is to say, the PEEP and PaO_2/FiO_2 values (i.e., the new targeted question was: is it enough if we know the values of PEEP and PaO_2/FiO_2 to develop a robust prediction of the time of mechanical ventilation required and the patient outcome?). The third type of models was defined in terms of all the descriptive features available (see Table 2). Here, the targeted question was: can ARDS descriptive features determine a true duration of mechanical ventilation and a successful prediction of mortality? Finally, we designed a fourth type of models using a gradient boosted machine (GBM) with H2O [7]. This time, the targeted question was: is it possible to use machine learning to improve the prediction of care and patient outcome provided by the Berlin classification for ARDS patients? All the models were tested following a 10-fold cross validation approach.

The analysis with other successful machine learning algorithms such as Light Gradient Boosting Machine (LightGBM) [13], Random Forest (RF) [14], and Support Vector Machine (SVM) [15] were left out of this initial work, and postponed to a latter complementary analysis.

3 Results and Discussion

Table 2 summarizes the results obtained after the application of all the methods explained in Sects. 2.1–2.3. In section A of the table, we can see the number of follow-up interventions on ARDS patients in the study, and their distribution across the Berlin groups (see columns Mild, Moderate, and Severe). The table also shows, in section B, the mean and 95% CI of all the descriptive features considered [8–10]. Again, these values are provided for the follow-ups of all the ARDS patients together, and of the follow-ups in each Berlin group in different columns.

We can observe, in general, that 95% CIs of different severity levels do not overlap for any feature (horizontal comparison). This non-overlapping distribution of values among mild, moderate, and severe cases confirm that any feature, when considered separately, can be a robust classifier of the Berlin classes. For example, if a woman patient with ARDS has a mean heart rate of 93.5 bpm, she is very likely to be in the group of moderate ARDS severity, and the opposite, if a man patient has a mild ARDS, his mean respiratory rate is very likely to be between 19.92 and 20.12 bpm. But this relation between single descriptive feature values and ARD severity levels is not necessarily useful for a robust prediction of patient care requirement and outcome indicators such as the duration of mechanical ventilation and the mortality rate [5]. An exception is observed for the feature ventilation times, whose CI for severe ARDS patients is contained in the CI of moderate cases. This fact and the similar boundaries of the ranges support the idea that severe and moderate ARDS require a similar number of ventilation actions.

The age of the patient decreases with the severity of the Berlin groups. At the moment, we are unable to provide a contrasted explanation of this curiosity. The mean heart rate of mild and moderate ARDS patients are close but differentiated (i.e., there's no overlapping between CIs). This differentiation is more evident for severe cases. The duration of mechanical ventilation grows significantly as the ARDs severity level increases. This represents a more prolonged care for complex cases. As expected, the PaO_2/FiO_2 values between Berlin severity groups are different, due to the definition of these groups in terms of this ratio, as it was explained in the introduction. Mortality rate is also higher for severe patients than for moderate (+4.21%) and for mild (+7.36%) cases. When compared to the results in [3], mortality rates in MIMIC III cases (i.e., 23.58%, 26.93%, and 31.14%) are lower than the ones observed in previous studies (i.e., 27%, 32%, and 45%), respectively. This improvement could be explained by the fact that the population of patients in [3] is distributed as 20% of mild ARDS patients, 50% of moderate ARDS patients, and 28%

of severe ARDS patients, while patients in our study are in the proportions 32% mild, 48% moderate, and 20% severe, as Table 2 shows. Consequently, our survival rates are higher probably because MIMIC III (Metavision) patients are less severe than patients in [3].

Table 2. ARDS Berlin severity levels analysis with mean values and 95% CIs.

	Mild	Moderate	Severe	All
A. ARDS follow-ups	7,429 (32%)	11,026 (48%)	4,569 (20%)	23,024 (100%)
B. Descriptive feature (units) – means and 95% confidence intervals				
Age (years)	61.81, [61.44, 62.18]	60.14, [59.83, 60.45]	54.84, [54.30, 55.38]	59.63, [59.41, 59.85]
PEEP (cmH$_2$O)	7.89, [7.78, 8.01]	9.21, [9.11, 9.32]	12.12, [11.94, 12.31]	9.36, [9.29, 9.44]
PaO2/FiO2	246.51, [245.85, 247.17]	150.09, [149.57, 150.62]	75.68, [75.23, 76.14]	166.4, [165.57, 167.31]
Mean Heart Rate (bpm)	92.82, [92.43, 93.22]	93.64, [93.31, 93.97]	99.34, [98.80, 99.87]	94.51, [94.28, 94.74]
Mean Respiratory Rate (bpm)	20.02, [19.92, 20,12]	21.26, [21.18, 21.34]	23.19, [23.06, 23.32]	21.24, [21.18, 21.30]
Ventilation Times	1.73, [1.69, 1.77]	1.60, [1.57, 1.62]	1.57, [1.53, 1.60]	1.63, [1.61, 1.65]
Duration of ventilation (hours)	194.92, [191.34, 198.50]	217.25, [213.95, 220.54]	234.20, [228.65, 239.74]	213.41, [211.16, 215.66]
Mortality rate (%)	23.78, [23, 25]	26.93, [26, 28]	31.14, [30, 32]	26.75, [26, 27]
C. Internal similarity within each group – means and 95% confidence intervals				
Descriptive features	0.60, [0.59994, 0.60000]	0.60, [0.59992, 0.60007]	0.58, [0.57990, 0.58009]	0.569, [0.56629, 0.57171]
Duration of ventilation	0.914, [0.91398, 0.91403]	0.886, [0.88598, 0.88602]	0.869, [0.86894, 0,86906]	0.905, [0.90498, 0.90502]
Mortality rate	0.638, [0.63787, 0.63813]	0.606, [0.60591, 0.60609]	0.571, [0.57079, 0.57121]	0.61, [0.60992, 0.61008]
D. Feature ranking according to their relevance				
Duration of ventilation	Respiratory rate Age Heart rate Ventilation times PaO2/FiO2 PEEP	Respiratory rate Ventilation times Age Heart rate PaO2/FiO2 PEEP	Respiratory rate Ventilation times Age Heart rate PaO2/FiO2 PEEP	Respiratory rate Ventilation times Age Heart rate PaO2/FiO2 PEEP
Mortality	Age Respiratory rate Heart rate PaO2/FiO2 Ventilation times PEEP	Respiratory rate Age Heart rate PaO2/FiO2 Ventilation times PEEP	Respiratory rate Age Heart rate PaO2/FiO2 Ventilation times PEEP	Respiratory rate Age Heart rate Ventilation times PaO2/FiO2 PEEP
E. Best feature combination to construct a predictive model				
Duration of ventilation	Heart Rate (excluded)	Heart Rate (excluded)	None excluded	None excluded
Mortality	None excluded	Heart Rate (excluded) Ventilation times (excl'd)	PEEP (excluded) Heart Rate (excluded) Ventilation times (excl'd)	None excluded

When the width of CIs is considered, some interesting conclusions arise. For example, CI ranges are narrower for moderate patients than for any other severity group, which means that the similarity between moderate patients is higher than in any other group, for each single feature. We can also conclude that severe ARDS are less homogeneous in terms of the values of all the features, except for PaO_2/FiO_2, whose values are more similar than for mild and moderate ARDS.

The normalized similarity of patient's follow-ups is shown in the section C of the table. Note that the similarity, according to the descriptive features, is not very high for any of the three Berlin groups, but more specifically for severe ARDS patients. A similar result is observed when similarity of patients is measured exclusively in terms of mortality. On the contrary, patients in the same Berlin group have a high mean normalized similarity (87% or above) with regard to the duration of mechanical ventilation. This indicates that patients within each group are heterogeneous with regard to their clinical description and their mortality, but they are quite homogeneous with regard to the required time of mechanical ventilation.

The rankings in the section D of the Table 2 show the relative relevance of the descriptive features. Thus, ventilation times is very relevant to determine the duration of ventilation in moderate and severe ARDS, but not so relevant in mild ARDS. The respiratory rate and the age of the patient appear as the most relevant features in almost all the groups for both, determining the duration of ventilation and predicting mortality. Heart rate is also important to determine mortality of mild, moderate, and severe patients. PEEP is always the less informative feature.

The last section of Table 2 describes the group of features that, when they are used in combination, produce the best predictive models of duration of ventilation and mortality. Two modeling approaches were considered here: linear regression for the quantitative feature duration of ventilation, and logistic regression for the qualitative feature mortality. Note that linear regression and logistic regression are used to detect the group of features that better characterize the prediction. The average heart rate is not necessary to develop the optimal model to predict ventilation duration of mild and moderate ARDS, or to predict mortality of moderate and severe ARDS. Interestingly, all the features are required to predict mortality of mild cases, but heart rate and ventilation times can be excluded of the model to predict mortality of moderate cases, and these two and PEEP are not required for severe cases. This can be interpreted as predicting mortality is simpler as the severity of the patient increases, confirming some of the statements in [4].

Our last results are shown in Table 3. Columns contain the RMSE and the AUC values obtained after a 10-fold cross validation of four alternative modeling methods when confronted to the prediction of the duration of mechanical ventilation and the mortality of a patient, respectively. Model 1 develops these predictions considering only the Berlin group where the patient belongs to. Model 2 predicts based on the PEEP and PaO_2/FiO_2 values of the patient (recall that these two features are the ones used by the Berlin definition to characterize mild, moderate and severe ARDS, see Table 1). Model 3 results from the use of all the descriptive features available to develop a prediction based on linear regression or logistic regression. These features are[1]: age (years), PEEP

---

[1] During the fold-cross validation, the statistical/machine learning method to produce the model may consider not to use all the features, but only some of them.

(cmH_2O), PaO_2/FiO_2, Mean heart rate (beats per minute), Mean respiratory rate (breaths per minute), and Number of ventilation actions. Finally, model 4 applies the GBM of H2O [7] in the prediction. All the descriptive features were allowed in the developing of the models 3 and 4.

Table 3. Predictive models performance.

	Model 1	Model 2	Model 3	Model 4
	(Berlin class)	(PEEP and PaO2/FiO2)	(Descriptive features)	(GBM H2O)
Quality of prediction				
Duration of ventilation (RMSE)	173.682	172.709	172.079	**149.497**
Mortality (AUC)	0.538	0.535	0.640	**0.834**

Note that RMSE measures the error in the predictions, while AUC measures the ability of the predictive model to distinguish between the classes. Therefore, low RMSE and high AUC values are preferred.

From the results in Table 3, we observe that models 1–3 perform very alike with some slight improvement when we move from model 1 to model 2, but more clearly with model 3. However, the best prediction is obtained with model 4, for which the error reduces in 22.582 h (in average) in the prediction of the duration of mechanical ventilation for any ARDS patient, and the AUC increases 0.194, with respect to the second best model.

When these results are compared to previous studies such as [3], where the AUC of the prediction of ARDS mortality is 0.577, we can confirm the great improvement achieved with models 3 and 4. Model 4 is, therefore, a promising tool to predict the needs of mechanical ventilation and the survival expectancy of patients, and consequently, useful to manage ARDS patients in ICUs.

4 Antecedents

The Berlin classification has been in continuous controversy since its initial declaration in 2012 [2]. Berlin definition came to replace the previous one from 1994 [11]. The new definition was simple and more efficient to determine the seriousness of ARDS. It classified the severity of hypoxemia [8]. Part of its simplicity came from the fact that it was based only on two clinical parameters: the positive end expiratory pressure or BEEP, and the ratio of partial pressure arterial oxygen and fraction of inspired oxygen or PaO_2/FiO_2. Some of the drawbacks of this classification can be found summarized in [4] and they concern the misconception of the mild ARDS proposed by the Berlin classification. Precisely, mild cases could be not so mild and even comparable to severe cases, in terms of care requirements and clinical outcome.

Several studies exist on the advances of diagnosis and treatment of ARDS (see review [8]). This review concluded that (1) the Berlin definition addresses limitations of the previous definition [11], (2) the new criteria may contribute to under-recognition of ARDS by clinicians, (3) no pharmacological treatments have been shown effective and therefore (4) current ARDS management must be centered in lung-protective mechanical ventilation to achieve a better outcome. This study underlines two important factors that are central in our approach: duration of mechanical ventilation (as ARDS management), and mortality (as ARDS outcome).

The application of computer-based intelligent data analysis for knowledge extraction has been a common practice in medical informatics. Particularly, the use of the MIMIC II database [16] to extract ARDS knowledge is present in several publications: [12] to analyze the influence in ventilator settings in the development of new ARDS, [9, 17] to predict ARDS in hospitalized patients using physiological signals such as heart rate and breathing rate, or others [18, 19] to study the contribution of ARDS to mortality among ventilated patients. There are some other studies exploiting the extended database MIMIC III [5]: [20] to recognize patients at high risk of ARDS, or [21] to determine the prognostic value of a new parameter (red blood cell distribution width) for critically ill patients with ARDS.

All these studies are mainly focused on generating diagnostic knowledge (e.g., parameters influencing ARDS onset) and preventive knowledge (e.g., parameters to predict ARDS). These present a clear difference with our study which is about the care needs and outcome after ARDS is already diagnosed according to the Berlin definition. Among all these previous works, [9] and [21] are the closer ones to ours. So, [9] describes a study on 2,892 ICU patients in terms of heard rate, breath rate, SpO2, and ABPMean, reaching a sensitivity of 92.3% and a specificity of 33.3% in the prediction of ARD up to 24 h before its occurrence. [21] describes a mortality analysis on 404 patients concluding that the mortality of ARDS patients with a "red blood cell distribution width $\geq 14.5\%$" has an odds ratio equal to 2.56, with a wide 95% CI (1.50–4.37). On the contrary, our study is based on a larger population ($N = 23{,}024$) and reaches conclusions on the best features (and groups of features) to predict the duration of mechanical ventilation and mortality of ARDS patients, and also proposes a highly successful model (which is based on some implicit knowledge derived from the application of machine learning algorithms) to perform these predictions.

5   Conclusions

Acute Respiratory Distress Syndrome (ARDS) is an open issue in ICUs and a medical domain where new knowledge needs to be generated. Even international classifications of this syndrome, which are worldwide accepted, are not free of deep and serious controversy. The Berlin definition that identifies three levels of ARDS severity (mild, moderate, and severe) is precisely defined and very useful, if compared with the previous classification, but still presents some weaknesses at the time of correctly describe care requirements and clinical outcome within each severity class. Our study aims at delving into the understanding of these weaknesses and in the extraction of new knowledge. After the intelligent analysis of 23,024 follow-up interventions of ARDS cases contained in the MIMIC III (MetaVision) database, we reached the following conclusions:

(1) values of physiological features such as PEEP, PaO_2/FiO_2, heart and respiratory rates, and ventilation times, have non overlapping intervals for the three severity levels of the Berlin definition; (2) patients in the same severity group can be very different in terms of their clinical description and mortality, but more similar in terms of the hours of ventilation required; (3) optimal prediction of mechanical ventilation time and mortality for mild patients is more complex and it requires more information (i.e., patient descriptive features) than these same predictions for moderate patients, but predictions for moderate are also more complex and information-demanding than for severe ARDS cases; and (4) it is possible to reach promising predictive models for ARDS duration of mechanical ventilation and mortality with the use of machine learning algorithms without the consideration of the Berlin definition.

Although the models generated and presented in this paper represent a clear improvement in the predictive capacity in ARDS so far, we believe that it is still possible to develop better predictive models about the duration of mechanical ventilation and mortality of patients with ARDS. In order to verify this, we are currently working on the use of the data in MIMIC III concerning ARDS patients to perform a benchmark of alternative machine learning algorithms, such as Light Gradient Boosting Machine (LightGBM) [13], Random Forest (RF) [14], and Support Vector Machine (SVM) [15], among others, to construct predictive models on the duration of mechanical ventilation and mortality in ARDS patients.

Acknowledgements. The authors acknowledge financial support from the RETOS P-BreasTreat project (DPI2016-77415-R) of the Spanish Ministerio de Economia y Competitividad.

References

1. Rezoagli, E., Fumagalli, R., Bellani, G.: Definition and epidemiology of acute respiratory distress syndrome. Ann. Transl. Med. **5**(14), 282 (2017)
2. Bellani, G., et al.: Epidemiology, patterns of care, and mortality for patients with acute respiratory distress syndrome in intensive care units in 50 countries. JAMA **315**, 788–800 (2016)
3. Ranieri, V.M., Rubenfeld, G.D., Thompson, B. T., et al.: Acute respiratory distress syndrome: the Berlin definition. JAMA **307**(23), 2526–2533 (2012). ARDS Definition Task Force
4. Pirracchio, R., Gropper, M.A.: Heterogeneity in intensive care: low severity does not mean low risk! Anesthesiology **130**(2), 190–191 (2019)
5. Johnson, A.E.W., et al.: MIMIC-III, a freely accessible critical care database. Sci. Data **3**, 160035 (2016)
6. Kira, K., Rendel, L.A.: A practical approach for feature selection. In: 9th International Proceedings on Workshop on Machine Learning, pp. 249–256. Morgan Kaufmann Publishers Inc., Aberdeen (1992)
7. Malohlava, M., Candel, A.: Gradient Boosting Machine with H2O, 7th edn. H2O.ai, Inc., Mountain View, CA (2018). http://h2o-release.s3.amazonaws.com/h2o/master/4297/docs-website/h2o-docs/booklets/GBMBooklet.pdf
8. Fan, E., Brodie, D., Slusky, A.S.: Acute respiratory distress syndrome. advances in diagnosis and treatment. JAMA **319**(7), 698–710 (2018)

9. Taoum, A., Mourad-Chehade, F., Amoud, H., Chkeir, A., Fawal, Z., Duchêne, J.: Data fusion for predicting ARDS using the MIMIC II physiological database. In: IEEE 18th International Conference on e-Health Networking, Applications and Services, Munich, pp. 288–292 (2016)
10. Villar, J., et al.: Age, PaO_2/FiO_2, and plateau pressure score: a proposal for a simple outcome score in patients with the acute respiratory distress syndrome. Crit. Care Med. **44**(7), 1361–1369 (2016)
11. Bernard, G.R., et al.: The American-European consensus conference on ARDS. definitions, mechanisms, relevant outcomes, and clinical trial coordination. Am. J. Respir. Crit. Care Med. **49**(3 Pt 1), 818–824 (1994)
12. Jia, X., Malhotra, A., Saeed, M., Mark, R., Talmor, D.: Risk factors for ARDS in patients receiving mechanical ventilation for >48 h. Chest **133**(4), 853–861 (2008)
13. Ke, G., et al.: LightGBM: a highly efficient gradient boosting decision tree. In: Advances in Neural Information Processing Systems, pp. 3149–3157 (2017)
14. Boulesteix, A.L., Janitza, S., Kruppa, J., Konig, I.R.: Overview of random forest methodology and practical guidance with emphasis on computational biology and bioinformatics. Wiley Interdisc. Rev. Data Min. Knowl. Disc. **2**(6), 493–507 (2012)
15. Vapnik, V., Vashist, A.: A new learning paradigm: learning using privileged information. Neural Netw. **22**(5), 544–557 (2009)
16. Lee, J., Scott, D.J., Villarroel, M., Clifford, G.D., Saeed, M., Mark, R.G.: Open-access MIMIC-II database for intensive care research. In: Annual International Conference of the IEEE Engineering in Medicine and Biology Society (2011)
17. Taoum, A., Mourad-Chehade, F., Amoud, H., Fawal, Z.: Predicting ARDS using the MIMIC II physiological database. In: IEEE International Multidisciplinary Conference on Engineering Technology (2016)
18. Taoum, A., Mourad-Chehade, F., Hassan, A., Chkeir, A., Fawal, Z., Duchene, J.: Data fusion for predicting ARDS using the MIMIC II physiological database. In: IEEE 18th International Conference on e-Health Networking, Applications and Services (2016)
19. Fuchs, L., et al.: The effect of ARDS on survival: do patients die from ARDS or with ARDS? J. Intensive Care Med. **34**(5), 374–382 (2019)
20. Wang, T., Tschampel, T., Apostolova, E., Velex, T.: Using latent class analysis to identify ARDS sub-phenotypes for enhanced machine learning predictive performance (2019). https://arxiv.org/abs/1903.12127
21. Wang, B., Gong, Y., Ying, B., Cheng, B.: Relation between red cell distribution width and mortality in critically ill patients with acute respiratory distress syndrome. BioMed. Res. Int. **2019**, 8 (2019). https://doi.org/10.1155/2019/1942078. Article no. 1942078

Deep Learning for Haemodialysis Time Series Classification

Giorgio Leonardi⬤, Stefania Montani(✉)⬤, and Manuel Striani⬤

DISIT, Computer Science Institute, Università del Piemonte Orientale,
Alessandria, Italy
stefania.montani@uniupo.it

Abstract. In this paper, we propose a deep learning approach to deal with time series classification, in the domain of haemodialysis. Specifically, we have tested two different architectures: a Convolutional Neural Network, which is particularly suitable for time series data, due to its ability to model local dependencies that may exist between adjacent data points; and a convolutional autoencoder, adopted to learn *deep* features from the time series, followed by a neural network classifier. Our experiments have proved the feasibility of the approach, which has outperformed more classical techniques, based on the Discrete Cosine Transform and on the Discrete Fourier Transform for features extraction, and on Support Vector Machines for classification.

1 Introduction

End Stage Renal Disease (ESRD) is a severe chronic condition that corresponds to the final stage of kidney failure. Haemodialysis is the most widely used treatment method for ESRD. It relies on an electromechanical device, called haemodialyzer, which, thanks to an extracorporeal blood circuit, is able to clear the patient's blood from metabolites, to re-establish acid-base equilibrium and to remove water in excess. On average, haemodialysis patients are treated for four hours three times a week.

The efficacy of haemodialysis sessions can be assessed on the basis of a few monitoring variables [2], regularly sampled during the session itself (and thus recorded as time series).

Among them, the behavior of the Haematic Volume (HV) variable is extremely important, because it is strictly related to the water reduction rate. Indeed, a correct extraction of the water from the blood is particularly critical to maintain a proper hydration status of the patient. On the other hand, changes in the expected HV shape should be studied, since they can be related to cardiovascular problems occurred to the patient along the session [7,15]. According to the experts, in a good session, the HV fits a model where, after a short period of exponential decrease, a linear decrease of the volume follows. Hypotension episodes, or haemodynamic instability of the patient under control, may influence this kind of behavior; this may result in a different temporal pattern not

© Springer Nature Switzerland AG 2019
M. Marcos et al. (Eds.): KR4HC-ProHealth 2019/TEAAM 2019, LNAI 11979, pp. 50–64, 2019.
https://doi.org/10.1007/978-3-030-37446-4_5

fitting the model, showing for example a linear reduction from the beginning, or sudden changes, or curves and peaks, related to an insufficient water extraction rate [12].

Classifying haemodialysis sessions on the basis of HV evolution over time allows the physician to identify patients that are being treated inefficiently, and that may need additional monitoring or corrective interventions. Therefore, *HV time series classification can lead to an adaptation of the haemodialysis patient management process*, through, e.g., a personalization of the haemodialyzer settings, or the introduction of corrective actions, leading to an overall optimization of patient care.

Time series classification typically requires a dimensionality reduction step, where the original n points measured at the different sampling times are converted to m (with $m << n$) features, able to summarize the time series behavior. Time series features are then provided in input to a classifier. Classical approaches to feature extraction require intensive hand-crafted feature engineering, or are based on the adoption of mathematical transforms, such as the Discrete Fourier Transform (DFT) [1] or the Discrete Cosine Transform (DCT) [14]. Classification can then be performed relying on any classical machine learning technique, such as Support Vector Machines (SVM) [13].

However in recent years, as Artificial Intelligence progresses, we are assisting to the development of an alternative approach to feature learning and classification, which is based on deep learning techniques [9].

In this paper, we present a deep learning approach to HV classification in the domain of haemodialysis. Specifically, we have tested two different architectures: a Convolutional Neural Network (CNN), which is particularly suitable for time series data, due to its ability to model local dependencies that may exist between adjacent data points; and a convolutional autoencoder, adopted to learn *deep* features from the time series, followed by a neural network to complete the classification task.

In the following, we illustrate the proposed architectures and showcase our experiments, where the deep learning solutions have outperformed solutions based on DCT and DFT for features extraction, and on Support Vector Machines for classification.

The paper is organized as follows: in Sect. 2 we present related work; Sect. 3 illustrates the two proposed deep learning architectures; Sect. 4 provides experimental results. Finally, Sect. 5 is devoted to conclusions and future research directions.

2   Related Work

Deep learning architectures are able to stack multiple layers of operations, in order to create a hierarchy of increasingly more abstract *deep* features [9]. These techniques have achieved a great success in computer vision, and also their application to time series data classification is gaining increasing attention [8], with proposals ranging from the application of CNNs [4, 11] to Long Short Term Memory Networks (LSTMs) [10]. Within this research area, autoencoders [17] have also been proposed for feature extraction.

CNNs are a type of deep learning architecture able to extract features by stacking multiple convolution operators. A convolution is an operation which takes a filter and multiplies it over the entire area of the input. Convolution layers are followed by pooling layers, meant to further reduce dimensionality. The convolution+pooling modules can be stacked in the network, providing progressively deeper architectures. The output of the final pooling layer is then flattened, and provided as an input to a fully connected network, outputting the class. A basic CNN architecture is depicted in Fig. 1. Specifically, one-dimensional CNNs are suitable for time series data [16].

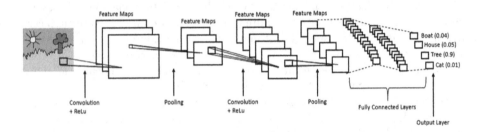

Fig. 1. Basic CNN architecture

Autoencoders, on the other hand, allow to extract deep features in an unsupervised fashion. The main idea behind autoencoders is to reduce the input into a latent space with fewer dimensions and then try to reconstruct the input from this representation. The first step is called encoding, and the second step is the decoding phase (see Fig. 2). By reducing the number of variables which represent the data, we force the model to learn how to keep only meaningful information, from which the input is reconstructable. It can also be viewed as a compression technique. In image and time series classification, convolutional autoencoders are often adopted [17]. In this kind of architecture, the encoding phase uses convolutional layers, followed by pooling layers, meant to further reduce dimensionality. The convolution+pooling modules can be stacked in the network, as described above. The decoding phase, on the other hand, uses upsampling and convolutions. Once the model achieves a desired level of performance recreating the time series, the decoder part may be removed, leaving just the encoder model. This model can then be used to encode input time series to a fixed-length vector, which can be provided as an input for a classifier. An alternative autoencoder architecture, well-suited for temporal data sequences, is the Encoder-Decoder Long Short-Term Memory (ED-LSTM) [3, 10] architecture. Recurrent neural networks, such as the LSTM, are indeed designed to process sequences of input data, and can learn the complex dynamics within the temporal ordering of input sequences as well as use an internal memory to remember information across long input sequences. In the ED-LSTM architecture, an encoder LSTM model reads the input sequence step-by-step. After reading the entire input sequence, an internal representation of the input is learned, and represented as a fixed-length vector. This vector is then provided to the decoder model that interprets it to generate the output sequence. The performance of the model, as usual, is evaluated based on the model's ability to recreate the input sequence. In this paper, we resort to a convolution autoencoder, as described in the next section. We will consider ED-LSTM in our future work.

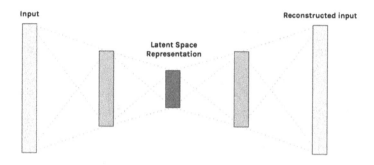

Fig. 2. Basic autoencoder architecture

3 Deep Learning for HV Classification

In this section, we technically describe the two deep learning architectures we have proposed and tested.

3.1 CNN-Based Classification

We have designed a CNN architecture with 4 one-dimensional convolution layers, with a kernel size of 3, Rectified Linear Unit activation function, and 16, 32, 64 and 128 filters respectively. Each convolution layer is followed by a max pooling layer with a pool size of 2. The output of the last pooling layer is then flattened and provided to a fully connected network, composed by two layers: the first one uses the Rectified Linear Unit activation function to obtain a set of 50 output nodes, while the second layer uses the Sigmoid activation function to output a final node, representing the predicted class. The parameters values were set experimentally, and the overall architecture is depicted in Fig. 3.

3.2 Autoencoder-Based Feature Extraction and Classification

Our autoencoder framework exhibits an encoder part (from the input layer to the latent space representation), which extracts features by adopting a CNN. Then, in the decoder part (from the latent space representation to the output

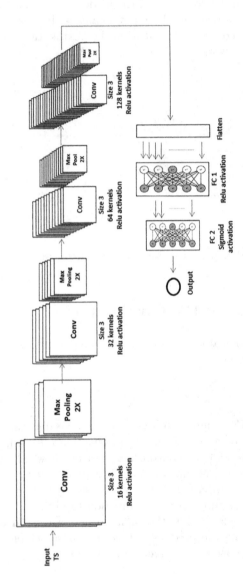

Fig. 3. The proposed CNN architecture for HV classification

layer), we use the extracted features to reconstruct sample signals by convolution and up-sampling. We also use the learned deep features as an input to a neural network classifier, with one hidden layer of $n = \frac{f+c}{2}$ hidden units (being f the number of features and c the number of classes), provided by open source tool Weka [6].

Specifically, for the autoencoder we have adopted an architecture with 3 one-dimension convolution layers with 16, 32 and 64 filters respectively and a kernel size of 3, each one followed by a max pooling layer with a pool size of 2. All the convolution layers are activated by the Rectified Linear Unit function. Subsequently, a flatten layer and a fully connected layer with Rectified Linear Unit activation function were adopted in order to reduce dimensionality to 50 values. The decoder mirrors the architecture of the encoder: a fully connected layer followed by a reshape reorganizes the output of the decoder, furtherly processed by three convolutional layers with 32, 16 and 1 filter respectively and a kernel size of 3. Each convolutional layer is preceded by a 2X up-sampler. The fully connected layer and all the convolution layers of the decoder are activated by the Rectified Linear Unit function. The overall architecture is depicted in Fig. 4.

4   Experimental Results

Our input HV time series were recordings of 240 samples on average, with a sampling time of 1 min. We truncated longer series, and added zeros to extend shorter series. Note, however, that less than 3% of the time points were affected by windowing or extension, and these corrections did not lead to misclassification, since the starting and ending measurements are simply related to initial/final adjustments of the haemodialyzer. We could work on a dataset of 5376 time series, belonging to 74 different patients: 72 series (i.e., 72 different haemodialysis sessions) per patient on average, varying from 1 to 280. Actually, after its onset, ESRD often becomes a life-long disease, especially in older patients, who do not receive kidney transplantation: therefore for some patients we could collect quite a large set of recordings.

Our classification was a binary one, where positive cases represent problematic haemodialysis sessions, while negative cases are close to the ideal model described in the Introduction. Examples of a positive and negative case are shown in Figs. 5 and 6, respectively. The HV in Fig. 5 decreases very slowly since the beginning, suggesting problems in water and metabolites extraction. On the other hand, a very fast decrease characterizes the first part of the series in Fig. 6, followed by a slower, linear decrease: this behaviour corresponds to an efficient session.

Since the label of each time series (i.e., positive or negative) is related to its shape, we performed the labeling process in two steps:

1. Automatic labeling: each time series was de-noised through wavelet transform and its gradient was calculated over time to apply a first temporary label;

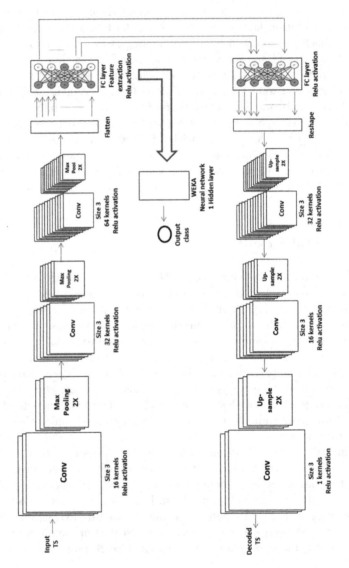

Fig. 4. The proposed autoencoder architecture for HV classification

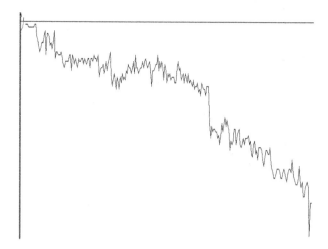

Fig. 5. Example of a positive case

2. Manual validation: the labeled time series were validated by medical experts to confirm or to correct the labels assigned at Step 1.

Indeed, we wanted to be sure about the correct labeling on the basis of medical knowledge. However, interestingly, the manual check operated by medical experts on automatically labeled series identified an extremely limited number of errors. At the end of the process, 3680 negative cases and 1696 positive cases were made available.

All the experiments were performed with a 10-fold cross validation (90% of the time series for the training set, and 10% for the validation set), and we calculated the average classification performance. Both the CNN and the autoencoder-based classifiers were run with 20 epochs for training.

Experiments were conducted by resorting to the TensorFlow tool[1].

The CNN approach provided an average accuracy of 90%, coupled with a Matthews Correlation Coefficient (MCC), a parameter which is particularly suitable to assess the quality of classification when dealing with unbalanced classes, very close to 1 (namely 0.79). The complete results are shown in Table 1, which reports precision, recall, F1-score, specificity, MCC, K-statistics and accuracy. The validation results are provided for each class and as the weighted average by class cardinality, according to the unbalanced distribution of positive and negative cases. Class 0 refers to the positive cases, while class 1 refers to the negative ones. MCC, K-statistics and Accuracy are not related to a single class, therefore we provide them only as overall results.

The plot of loss for each epoch is shown in Fig. 7.

Table 2 also reports the confusion matrix for the CNN-based classifier, for the sake of completeness.

---

[1] https://www.tensorflow.org/.

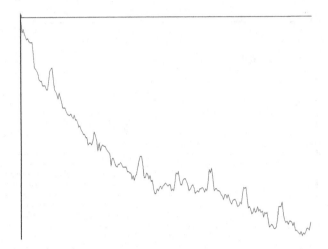

Fig. 6. Example of a negative case

Table 1. Results obtained by the CNN-based classifier

Class	Precision	Recall	F1-score	Specificity	MCC	K-Stat	Accuracy
0 (positive)	0.97	0.73	0.83	0.89			
1 (negative)	0.89	0.99	0.94	0.89			
Weighted average	0.92	0.87	0.89	0.89	0.79	0.77	0.90

Table 2. Confusion matrix obtained by the CNN-based classifier; the elements must be read in columns

	Class 0	Class 1
Class 0	1244	452
Class 1	42	3638

As a further experiment, we also tested a patient-based cross-validation (leave-one-patient-out). The network architecture was learned on all records from all patients except one, and tested on records from that single patient, and this procedure was repeated for all patients. This technique rules out overly optimistic results, that may be obtained when the dataset contains many records from a single patient, and the test is executed on some record of the same patient. The approach also allows one to mitigate the risk of overfitting [5].

As it can be observed in Table 3 (reporting precision, recall, F1-score, specificity, MCC, K-statistics and accuracy), and in Table 4 (reporting the confusion matrix), results were very encouraging in this case as well (accuracy = 80%, MCC = 0.51), even though a bit worse than the ones reported in Table 1. This result supports the hypothesis that the tested deep learning technique is actually performing well, and that the high accuracy should not be interpreted in the light of overfitting problems.

Table 3. Results obtained by the CNN-based classifier with a leave-one-patient-out cross validation

Class	Precision	Recall	F1-score	Specificity	MCC	K-Stat	Accuracy
0 (positive)	0.61	0.70	0.65	0.83			
1 (negative)	0.88	0.83	0.85	0.70			
Weighted average	0.80	0.79	0.79	0.74	0.51	0.51	0.80

Table 4. Confusion matrix obtained by the CNN-based classifier with a leave-one-patient-out cross validation

	Class 0	Class 1
Class 0	1041	652
Class 1	450	3233

Considering the autoencoder-based classification performance, on the other hand, we obtained an average accuracy of 88%, coupled with a MCC of 0.72. The complete validation results are shown in Table 5, while Table 6 reports the confusion matrix. The plot of loss for each epoch is shown in Fig. 8.

Table 5. Results obtained by the autoencoder-based classifier

Class	Precision	Recall	F1-score	Specificity	MCC	K-Stat	Accuracy
0 (positive)	0.81	0.81	0.81	0.91			
1 (negative)	0.91	0.91	0.91	0.81			
Weighted average	0.88	0.88	0.88	0.84	0.72	0.72	0.88

In summary, both deep learning models show very promising results, with the CNN classifier performing generally better than the autoencoder-based one when cross-validating at the time series level. Considering the results per class, however, it can be observed that the autoencoder-based classifier has slightly better recall and specificity than the CNN version in recognizing the positive cases, making it more suitable when the detection of the problematic haemosyalisis

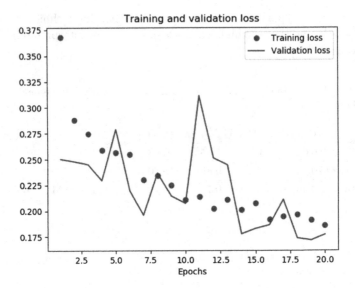

Fig. 7. Loss per epoch of the CNN

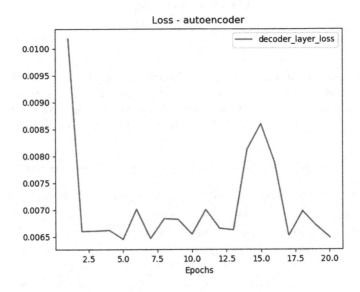

Fig. 8. Loss per epoch of the autoencoder

Table 6. Confusion matrix obtained by the autoencoder-based classifier

	Class 0	Class 1
Class 0	1375	321
Class 1	321	3359

sessions is requested, even if the results can be considered aligned. Interestingly, we obtained very similar results by exploiting, as a classifier, a Support Vector Machine (SVM) with polynomial kernel and automatic search for the best kernel degree.

In order to verify the feasibility of the proposed deep learning approaches, we have compared the results presented above with the ones of a more classical architecture, where we resorted to DCT for feature extraction, and to SVM for classification. DCT operates by decomposing the input into its constituent cosine waves, and returns an ordered sequence of coefficients, where the most important information is concentrated at the lower indices of the sequence itself (energy compaction property). In particular, we extracted the first 50 DCT coefficient for each time series (since we also obtained 50 features through the autoencoder; however, thanks to the energy compaction property, the last 45 coefficients were very close to 0). We provided the coefficients to an SVM model with the same kernel as above (polynomial kernel and automatic search for the best kernel degree). The tests were performed using the open source tool Weka [6]. As reported in Table 7, the SVM using the 50 DCT coefficients obtained poorer results with respect to the CNN and the autoencoder-based classifiers. In particular, this model failed in identifying the positive cases, making it almost useless in a real environment. Furthermore, the very low value of the MCC suggests that this model is not far from a random predictor. The corresponding confusion matrix is shown in Table 8. We also repeated the experiment exploiting only the first 5 DCT coefficients, but results were basically identical (not surprisingly, given that, as already observed, the other DCT coefficients were close to 0).

Table 7. Results obtained by the support vector machine classifier using 50 DCT coefficients

Class	Precision	Recall	F1-score	Specificity	MCC	K-Stat	Accuracy
0 (positive)	0.77	0.10	0.19	0.98			
1 (negative)	0.70	0.98	0.82	0.10			
Weighted average	0.72	0.70	0.62	0.38	0.21	0.12	0.70

Table 8. Confusion matrix obtained by the support vector machine classifier using 50 DCT coefficients

	Class 0	Class 1
Class 0	183	1513
Class 1	52	3628

As a final experiment, we also repeated the latest test by reducing dimensionality by means of the DFT [1], in order to rule out a possible bias related to the choice of the dimensionality reduction technique. DFT decomposes the input into its constituent sine waves, and returns an ordered sequence of coefficients, where the most important information is concentrated at the lower indices of the sequence itself. Therefore, the higher coefficients can be disregarded in this case as well, while the lower ones are kept as features, reducing dimensionality without losing information.

Table 9. Results obtained by the support vector machine classifier using 50 DFT coefficients

Class	Precision	Recall	F1-score	Specificity	MCC	K-Stat	Accuracy
0 (positive)	0.86	0.01	0.01	0.99			
1 (negative)	0.69	0.99	0.81	0.01			
Weighted average	0.74	0.69	0.56	0.32	0.06	0.01	0.69

Table 10. Confusion matrix obtained by the support vector machine classifier using 50 DFT coefficients

	Class 0	Class 1
Class 0	12	1684
Class 1	2	3678

As reported in Table 9, the SVM using the 50 DFT coefficients obtained even worse results than the approach exploiting DCT. The corresponding confusion matrix is shown in Table 10.

5   Conclusions

In this paper, we have proposed a CNN for HV classification in the domain of haemodialysis, as well as a convolutional autoencoder to learn *deep* HV features, followed by a classifier. HV classification will be adopted as a first step towards patient management process optimization.

Our experiments have proved the feasibility of the approach, which has provided an accuracy of 90% in CNN-based classification, coupled with a MCC of 0.79, and an accuracy of 88% in autoencoder-based classification, coupled with a MCC of 0.72. We also repeated the test on the CNN-based architecture by executing a leave-one-patient-out cross validation. Results, although a bit poorer (accuracy of 80% and MCC of 0.51), were still good, thus supporting the hypothesis that overfitting was not influencing the experimental output.

We have compared the proposed approaches to DCT and DFT feature extraction, followed by SVM classification; our deep learning architectures have largely outperformed these more classical solutions.

In the future, given the temporal nature of our input data, we will also consider ED-LSTMs as an alternative to learn deep features.

The overall experimental results will allow us to configure an optimized architecture for our classification task; classification results, in turn, will lead to a personalization and an optimization of the haemodialysis patient management process.

As a final consideration, however, it is worth noting that deep learning architectures operate as black boxes, and do not provide a motivation for misclassified examples, nor a general indication about the suitability of the solution for another application domain. This lack of explainability is a well known limitation of deep learning, and an open research issue, that will need to be carefully considered in the next years.

Acknowledgements. The authors are grateful to Dr. Roberto Bellazzi for having provided medical knowledge.

References

1. Agrawal, R., Faloutsos, C., Swami, A.: Efficient similarity search in sequence databases. In: Lomet, D.B. (ed.) FODO 1993. LNCS, vol. 730, pp. 69–84. Springer, Heidelberg (1993). https://doi.org/10.1007/3-540-57301-1_5
2. Bellazzi, R., Larizza, C., Magni, P., Bellazzi, R.: Temporal data mining for the quality assessment of a hemodialysis service. Artif. Intell. Med. **34**, 25–39 (2005)
3. Chu, K.L., Sahari, K.S.M.: Behavior recognition for humanoid robots using long short-term memory. Int. J. Adv. Robot. Syst. **13**(6), 1–13 (2016)
4. Fan, X., Yao, Q., Cai, Y., Miao, F., Sun, F., Li, Y.: Multiscaled fusion of deep convolutional neural networks for screening atrial fibrillation from single lead short ECG recordings. IEEE J. Biomed. Health Inform. **22**(6), 1744–1753 (2018)
5. Gao, Y., Zhang, X., Wang, S., Zoub, G.: Model averaging based on leave-subject-out cross-validation. J. Econ. **192**, 139–151 (2016)
6. Hall, M., Frank, E., Holmes, G., Pfahringer, B., Reutemann, P., Witten, I.H.: The WEKA data mining software: an update. SIGKDD Explor. **11**(1), 10–18 (2009)
7. Krepel, H.P., Nette, R.W., Akcahuseyin, E., Weimar, W., Zietse, R.: Variability of relative blood volume during hemodialysis. Nephrology, dialysis, transplantation: official publication of the European Dialysis and Transplant Association - European Renal Association, 15, pp. 673–679, May 2000
8. Längkvist, M., Karlsson, L., Loutfi, A.: A review of unsupervised feature learning and deep learning for time-series modeling. Pattern Recogn. Lett. **42**, 11–24 (2014)
9. LeCun, Y., Bengio, Y., Hinton, G.E.: Deep learning. Nature **521**(7553), 436–444 (2015)
10. Mehdiyev, N., Lahann, J., Emrich, A., Enke, D., Fettke, P., Loos, P.: Time series classification using deep learning for process planning: a case from the process industry. Procedia Comput. Sci. **114**, 242–249 (2017)

11. Sani, S., Wiratunga, N., Massie, S., Cooper, K.: kNN sampling for personalised human activity recognition. In: Aha, D.W., Lieber, J. (eds.) ICCBR 2017. LNCS (LNAI), vol. 10339, pp. 330–344. Springer, Cham (2017). https://doi.org/10.1007/978-3-319-61030-6_23

12. Santoro, A., Mancini, E., Zucchelli, E.: Ultrafiltration behaviour with different dialysis schedules. Nephrology, dialysis, transplantation: official publication of the European Dialysis and Transplant Association - European Renal Association, **13**(Suppl. 6), 55–61 (1998)

13. Steinwart, I., Christmann, A.: Support Vector Machines. Springer Publishing Company, Incorporated (2008)

14. Strang, G.: The discrete cosine transform. SIAM Rev. **41**(1), 135–147 (1999)

15. Titapiccolo, J.I.: Relative blood volume monitoring during hemodialysis in end stage renal disease patients. In: Conference proceedings: Annual International Conference of the IEEE Engineering in Medicine and Biology Society. IEEE Engineering in Medicine and Biology Society. Conference, 2010, pp. 5282–5285, August 2010

16. Wang, Z., Yan, W., Oates, T.: Time series classification from scratch with deep neural networks: a strong baseline. In: 2017 International Joint Conference on Neural Networks, IJCNN 2017, Anchorage, AK, USA, 14–19 May 2017, pp. 1578–1585. IEEE (2017)

17. Wen, T., Zhang, Z.: Deep convolution neural network and autoencoders-based unsupervised feature learning of EEG signals. IEEE Access **6**, 25399–25410 (2018)

TEAAM - Workshop on Transparent, Explainable and Affective AI in Medical Systems

Towards Understanding ICU Treatments Using Patient Health Trajectories

Alexander Galozy$^{(\boxtimes)}$, Sławomir Nowaczyk , and Anita Sant'Anna

Center for Applied Intelligent Systems Research, Halmstad University,
Kristian IV:s väg 3, 301 18 Halmstad, Sweden
alexander.galozy@hh.se
http://caisr.hh.se/

Abstract. Overtreatment or mistreatment of patients is a phenomenon commonly encountered in health care and especially in the Intensive Care Unit (ICU) resulting in increased morbidity and mortality. We explore the MIMIC-III intensive care unit database and conduct experiments on an interpretable feature space based on the fusion of severity subscores, commonly used to predict mortality in an ICU setting. Clustering of medication and procedure context vectors based on a semantic representation has been performed to find common and individual treatment patterns. Two-day patient health state trajectories of a cohort of congestive heart failure patients are clustered and correlated with the treatment and evaluated based on an increase or reduction of probability of mortality on the second day of stay. Experimental results show differences in treatments and outcomes and the potential for using patient health state trajectories as a starting point for further evaluation of medical treatments and interventions.

Keywords: Electronic Health Records · Health trajectory · Intensive care treatments · Clustering

1 Introduction

Medical errors, commonly defined as "the failure of a planned action to be completed as intended or the use of a wrong plan to achieve an aim" [24], frequently occur in the Intensive Care Unit (ICU), leading to increased mortality and morbidity. Kohn et al. [24] drew attention to patient safety, garnering much attention from the medical community. Unfortunately, there exists only sparse evidence that the situation has improved significantly [17], with medication errors being relatively common in the ICU (1 to 96.5 per 1000 patient-days) often having severe consequences for the patients. Polypharmacy is common in the ICU setting where medications are prescribed to patients without prior exposure, and conciliation of those prescriptions might not be prioritized, leading to adverse drug reactions [18]. Further, procedures intended to improve the patient's survival may lead to adverse effects or interventions are executed incorrectly, leaving the patient in a more severe condition.

© Springer Nature Switzerland AG 2019
M. Marcos et al. (Eds.): KR4HC-ProHealth 2019/TEAAM 2019, LNAI 11979, pp. 67–81, 2019.
https://doi.org/10.1007/978-3-030-37446-4_6

Much to the detriment of retrospective analysis and treatment management, near misses are rarely or not reported at all, substantially reducing the probability that interventions are modified or reconsidered, leading to avoidable mistakes potentially jeopardizing patient health [22]. Recent advances in AI, Big Data, and rapid digitization of information and collection of Electronic Health Records (EHR) in hospitals might provide new insights into treatment patterns and anomalies helping to identify medication error. EHRs are a systematic consolidation of longitudinal health care data, including the medical history of a patient and are increasingly being used in contemporary healthcare systems. Using this source of routinely collected data provides additional and potentially novel insights into practical treatment patterns, expose errors in treatment practice, and potentially judge treatment efficacy. In this paper, we focus on the issue of treatment efficacy in the ICU.

We propose a basic method to investigate patient health state trajectories and how the change in health state might help in finding treatment patterns associated with an increase or reduction in the probability of mortality. Finding such patterns may provide a starting point for further analysis of the efficacy of treatments in the ICU. For the analysis, we use data from the freely available MIMIC-III medical database [9] in conjunction with SAPS-III and OASIS severity sub-scores, forming a human interpretable health state. Both SAPS-III and OASIS have been used cumulatively to assess the severity of illness and predict hospital mortality. We explore patient trajectories in the subscore feature space to find trajectory similarities among patients and correlate them with administered medications and procedures.

2 Related Work

Previous research focused primarily on in-hospital/out-hospital mortality, readmission, or length of stay prediction in the ICU. This is hardly a surprise since ICU admissions are rather costly and carry additional health risks for patients like infections [27,29] and increased risk of long-term mortality after hospital discharge [28]. Methods and tools have been developed to assess the necessity of a patient to receive intensive care using patient-oriented outcomes such as mortality. Some of the more frequently used mortality prediction models in an ICU setting include APACHE IV [30], SAPS-II [15] and SOFA [26] with overall similar predictive performance [6]. One particular disadvantage of these scores is their calibration issue on ICU data that is different from data they were developed on, leading to overestimation or underestimation of mortality. Especially SAPS-II suffers from poor calibration and efforts have been made to expand the score to better fit the particular ICU data [16].

Most of the severity assessment scores use patient data collected over a short period, usually the first 24 h after patient admission. This methodology does insufficiently capture the evolution of the patient's health state over time, relying on static multivariate statistics, overlooking the usefulness of *health trends* in the ICU setting [12]. Most of the more recent works concerning patient health state and trajectory have focused on modeling time series data based on raw EHR without manual feature engineering, where the patient's health state is represented as the states or hidden representation of latent variable/deep learning models [1, 3, 4, 20, 21], suffering from the interpretability issue of the patients state. Inspecting the representations of patients that are deemed similar by the algorithms is a non-trivial, time-consuming task since inputs to these models can exceed thousands of attributes that are combined in a nonlinear fashion [19]. To the author's knowledge, little investigation was undertaken on using subscores of severity of illness scores directly, which are inherently interpretable, to describe the patient's health state on a static or temporal level. Furthermore, investigations beyond scores indented purpose (outcomes prediction) are rare and constitute a research gap.

3   Methodology

3.1   Health State

We generated a health state of the patient by combining the subscores of SAPS-III and OASIS. Data for subscore computation includes attributes for vital signs recorded at the bedside, daily lab measurements, age at admission, whether elective surgery and mechanical ventilation were performed. Furthermore, we included attributes for measuring the conscious state of patients categorized by the Glasgow Coma Scale [25]. SAPS-III [13] and OASIS [8] rate each of the attributes and compute a final overall score by simple summation of all subscores. The magnitude of each subscore depends on how severely the measurements deviate from a "healthy" state. We computed the subscores for every day in the ICU. The final number of attributes (subscores) amounts to 25. 20 scores from SAPS-III and five scores from OASIS. Attributes in the OASIS computation that are not included in SAPS-III are: Previous in hospital length of stay(days), age(in years) and a binary flag indicating if elective surgery was performed or not.

A GitHub[1] repository is provided by the MIMIC-team, containing complete queries to compute the severity scores used [11]. Since the scores are computed only for the first day of stay, we modified the code to compute the scores for each day in the ICU. The modified queries are available on a separate GitHub repository[2].

3.2   Patient Cohort

For the analysis, we focus on patients with Congestive Heart Failure (CHF). The number of patients included in this cohort amounts to 4,454 with a total of 21,544 ICU stays. Of those patients, 1,919 (43.1%) have a length of stay less or equal to one day, which we excluded from the trajectory analysis. The final number of patients in the CHF cohort amounts to 2,535 with a length of stay of two days

---

[1] https://github.com/MIT-LCP/mimic-code.

[2] https://github.com/caisr-hh/Dayly-SAPS-III-and-OASIS-scores-for-MIMIC-III.

or longer. Patients from all ICUs are considered, potentially ignoring apriori knowledge about patients in specific ICUs in favor of a more general analysis. Further, patients under the age of 16 are not considered, effectively excluding children and neonates. We do this, since both SAPS-III and OASIS are not well calibrated for younger patients, making interpretation of the subscores difficult and potentially misleading. In the data preprocessing step, we excluded patients that have missing lab results.

From the 2,535 CHF patients, we choose a smaller cohort of 108 patients with similar severity subscores on the first day of stay. We define the "general" similarity between patients using the principal component embedding of the original 25-D health state, i.e., patients are considered "similar" if they are located close to each other in the 2-D principal component space. We chose patients with a moderate probability of mortality (around 25% on average), i.e., patients that would need a moderate amount of interventions to keep in stable condition. The 108 patients are chosen from within a grid spanning the first two PCs within the intervals: $PC1 \in [0.8, 1]$, $PC2 \in [-0.2, 0]$. This region acts as a natural "decision point" where treatments would have arguably made a difference in patients' survival since the distributions of people that survived and died have the most overlap, as can be seen in Fig. 2(b) later in the experimental section.

3.3   Patient Trajectory and Treatment Clustering

Health State Trajectories. The basic premise in this study is that patients with similar health states receive similar treatment, and patients may react to similar treatment similarly. For example, Vasopressor administration will increase blood pressure levels. We note that patients might have adverse reactions to treatment where the assumption above of similar reactions to similar treatment might not hold. The ultimate goal of the health state is to capture enough patient-specific information so that reactions to treatment can be represented accurately. Such a health state would effectively "normalize out" individual factors and subsequently provide the basis for "patients with similar health state react to similar treatment similarly".

Provided the assumptions hold, one might find clusters of trajectories and treatments in the data corresponding to the betterment or worsening of the health state, which may indicate adverse reactions, interesting enough to warrant further exploration. We compute the subscore differences between two days of stay for each of the 108 patients and standardize the differences using robust median-shift and interquartile range scaling. Those normalized differences are then clustered using the DBSCAN [5] algorithm.

Treatment Representations Using Doc2Vec. Since procedures and treatments can constitute thousands of codes, finding a suitable data representation without the problem of exploding dimensionality is challenging. To address this problem, we represent the treatment of patients by generating a 64-dimensional

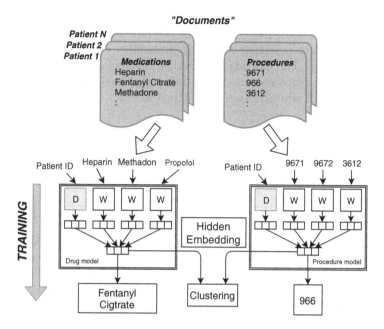

Fig. 1. The Process of training the Doc2Vec model, which generates vector representations of medications and procedures for every patient in the cohort. For each patient, we generate medications and procedures "text documents" containing the descriptions of administered drugs (without dosage) and procedure codes. The model predicts the likely medication/procedure using the current context as a guide. The resulting embeddings are similar for similar contexts.

context vector representation for both performed procedures and administered medications, using the distributed memory model with negative sampling [14]. Those embeddings are powerful since they capture the context of a giving medication or procedure in a sequence of treatments a patient has received on a particular day. Medications or procedures that are used in a similar medical context will have a similar embedding and are close in vector space, allowing a concept of similarity beyond mere code occurrences and overcome this weakness the simple bag of words models have. Raw procedure codes from both ICD9 and MetaVision systems are extracted, aligned in chronological order, and concatenated into "code sentences". The same is done for medication administered, but instead of using the raw drug codes/names which correspond to a specific brand, we use the generic drug name describing the active agent in the medication.

We use the freely available natural language processing library gensim [23] for model implementation. We conducted model training on the full cohort of 2,535 patients and clustered the resulting embedding vectors for the 108 patients using DBSCAN. The whole process of embedding and clustering is shown in Fig. 1.

3.4   Correlating Clusters Patient Mortality

Patient outcomes are measured using the probability output from models for mortality prediction. The mortality prediction models for SAPS-III and OASIS use simple logistic regression models utilizing the final accumulative severity scores. For SAPS-III the model used is defined as [8]:

$$SAPSIII = \frac{1}{1 + exp(-(4.4360 + 0.04726 * (x_{saps})))},$$

and the OASIS model is defined as [10]:

$$OASIS = \frac{1}{1 + exp(-(6.1746 + 0.1275 * (x_{oasis})))},$$

with x_{saps} and x_{oasis} being the accumulative severity scores of SAPS-III and OASIS, respectively. We consider the patient's health improved, if we observe a reduction in the predicted probability of mortality compared to the first day of stay, and worsened otherwise. Assuming patients with similar conditions, such as the CHF cohort investigated, and similar health state on the first day of stay, we investigate patient outcomes by correlating trajectory clusters with treatment clusters.

4   Experiments

Data Visualization. We visualize the patient health state using Principal Component Analysis (PCA) [7], one of the most widely used unsupervised statistical methods for dimensionality reduction of high dimensional data. PCA aims to find a linear orthogonal transformation of correlated variables into linearly uncorrelated so-called principal components. The severity score feature space is complex (requires domain knowledge for interpretation), high-dimensional (25-D), and exhibits highly nonlinear correlations between features. For example, the respiratory rate score depends on mechanical ventilation in a nonlinear fashion, i.e part of the score within specific ranges of respiratory rates are not given for patients on mechanical ventilation. The same respiratory rate can have different scores between ventilated and non-ventilated patients. Due to the nonlinearity, the first two principal components only explain about 30% of the variance in the data, and an additional 17 components would be required to achieve 95% of explained variance.

Nonetheless, the first two components are enough to discover useful ordering among the patients, as can be seen in Fig. 2(a), where patients with a higher probability of mortality are located at high values for both PCs. The right subplot (b) illustrates the relative density distributions of patients who died or survived on their last day of ICU stay. Both severity scores and actual mortality are in relatively good agreement.

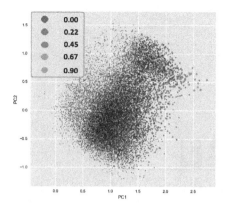
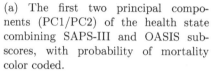

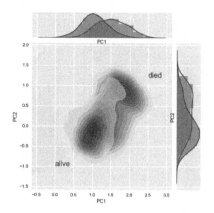

(a) The first two principal components (PC1/PC2) of the health state combining SAPS-III and OASIS subscores, with probability of mortality color coded.

(b) Corresponding principal components of real in-ICU, last day of stay mortality distributions using kernel density estimations with Gaussian kernel(red: died, blue: alive)

Fig. 2. Data visualization using PCA. (Color figure online)

Health state trajectories and procedure/medication embeddings are visualization using a nonlinear dimensionally reduction technique called metric multidimensional scaling (metric MDS) which aims to preserve the inter-point distance between embedding as much as possible [2].

Clustering Two-day Health State Differences. To evaluate trajectories that might correlate with an improved or deteriorated health state of the patient, we performed clustering of the 25-D severity subscores differences. We observe several clusters of points indicating patients with similar health state trajectories. Assuming that the found clusters correspond to similar trajectories of patients regarding their health state starting from similar initial subscores, it is of interest to know how procedures or administered medications correlate with those trajectories and how the trajectories correspond to an increase or decrease of probability of mortality.

To avoid small clusters with only a couple of patients, we chose a threshold of 10 points (patients) that are needed to be considered a cluster. Furthermore, the interpoint distance (ϵ-parameter for DBSCAN) between the points in a candidate cluster needs to be below a certain threshold. Since DBSCAN is highly sensitive to this particular parameter, and we do not know the optimal value apriori, we chose to employ a statistical methodology choosing thresholds based on percentiles. Thresholds that are lower than the 5th, 10th, 15th, and 20th percentile of pairwise Euclidean distances are considered for the values of ϵ. The final ϵ-parameter we chose is the 10th-percentile of pairwise distances. This threshold has been chosen primarily by inspecting the cluster assignments visually

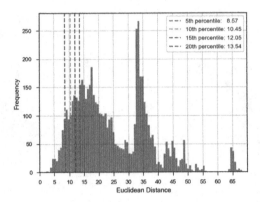

Fig. 3. Distribution of euclidean distances between CHF-patient cohort sub-score differences. Distances for several percentiles are shown.

since unsupervised clustering metrics, such as the Silouhette score, did not show significant differences between the values and were therefore not particularly useful for choosing the optimal value for ϵ. The Euclidean distance distribution and corresponding percentile limits is shown in Fig. 3. The clustering for several different percentile limits is shown in Fig. 4. Points that do not meet the set criteria are considered "noise" points by DBSCAN and not included in any cluster. Patients within a cluster have "similar" trajectories, that is, they have reacted to treatment similarly, while patients not within a cluster have an "individual trajectory" and reacted to treatment in different ways.

Clustering Medication and Procedure Embeddings. The clustering of the context embedding vectors for medications is done similarly to trajectory clustering. The distribution of pairwise cosine distances between context vectors and clustering results for the 20th percentile is shown in Fig. 5. We divided patients into two clusters: Those with "common" drug treatment context, patients in cluster 0, and those whose treatment is more "individual", patients outside any cluster.

Given a similar/individual trajectory and common/individual treatment, we can split the patient group into these four categories to determine the fraction of patients with health states that improved or worsened after the first day. The four categories have potentially interesting implications for treatment efficacy if a difference in outcome between them can be found, such as common adverse reactions to common/individual treatments or patients with unique reactions to common treatments resulting in worsening or betterment of the health state.

The distribution of pairwise cosine distances of the 64-D embedding vectors for medication contexts can be seen in Fig. 5 in conjunction with the resulting clustering using DBSCAN with the 20th percentile of distances as a limit. We discovered a relatively dense cluster. Correspondingly, the distance distribution of the 64-D embedding vectors for procedure contexts and resulting clustering

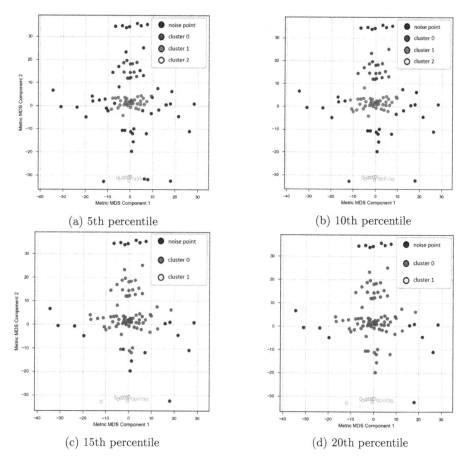

(a) 5th percentile

(b) 10th percentile

(c) 15th percentile

(d) 20th percentile

Fig. 4. Clustering of sub-score differences between first and second day using DBSCAN visualised using metric MDS. We choose a minimum of 10 points (patients) that are required to form a cluster.

with a 10th percentile distance threshold can be seen in Fig. 6. Here we find one cluster of patients with a "common" procedure context.

Correlating Trajectories and Treatments with Outcomes. We split the cohort into patients with similar and individual trajectories, followed by further division into patients with similar and individual treatment. Results are shown in Fig. 7. We turn to patients with similar trajectory first. Since more than one common trajectory has been found, we can split the patients by their cluster assignments. Each cluster exhibits a different percentage of improved health state, with the highest number of 50% in Cluster 0. For patients with individual treatment, we observed a similar pattern with patients in Cluster 0 having improved 75% of the time and patients in Cluster 1 and Cluster 2 having

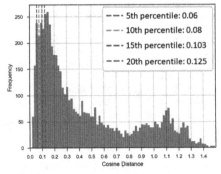

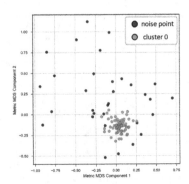

(a) Cosine distances distribution for 64-D document embedding of medications administered within the first 24 hour of stay.

(b) Clustering medication contexts. Threshold: 20th percentile of cosine distances.

Fig. 5. Clustering of first day administered medications context vectors.

improved 50% of the time. One could assume that patients in Cluster 0 have received drug treatment that might have been more effective given the circumstances of their health compared to the other patients, where the health state of most patients worsened. Further analysis is required to make definitive judgments about the reasons why, but this quick analysis provided a starting point. It is also important to note that the number of patients in the category of individual treatment is not high, and we might question the statistical significance of the differences in health state.

We now look into patients with individual trajectories ("noise points"). The total number of patients with individual trajectory amounts to 32, where 13 patients with individual treatment got better 71.6% of the time, while patients

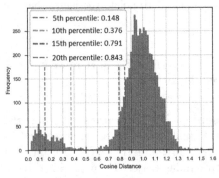

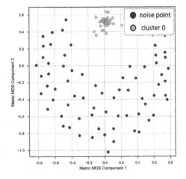

(a) Cosine distances distribution for 64-D document embedding of procedures performed within the first 24 hour of stay.

(b) Clustering procedure contexts. Threshold: 10th percentile of cosine distances.

Fig. 6. Clustering of first day procedure context vectors.

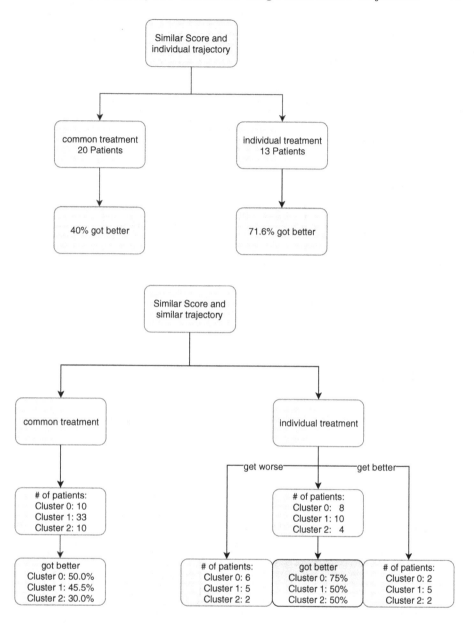

Fig. 7. Medication context

with common treatment got better 40% of the time. Here we see a similar pattern as with patients with common trajectories, suggesting that patients with CHF that received individual drug treatment have their health state improved on average. In contrast, doctors who found it necessary to prescribe drug treatment

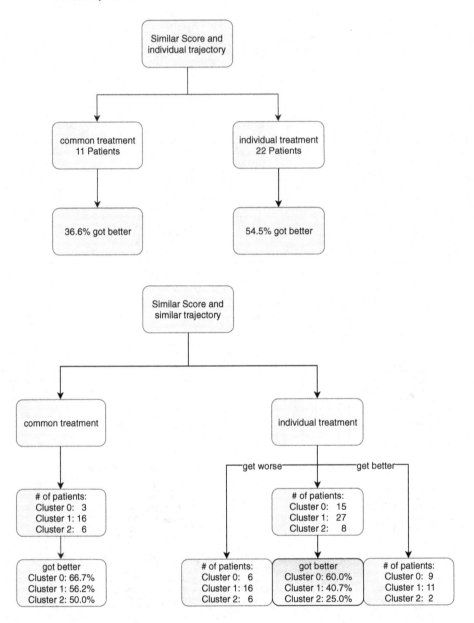

Fig. 8. Procedure context

that is common among the cohort, correlate with an improvement in patients' health state at lower rates than patients with individual treatment.

Similarities for the procedure contexts are analyzed next. Using the 10th percentile cosine distances as a threshold, we observe one cluster of patients with common procedure context, as expected looking at the pairwise cosine distances distribution in Fig. 6. We again divided the patients into the four categories of common/individual treatment and trajectory. The results are illustrated in Fig. 7 for medication contexts and Fig. 8 for procedure contexts. Starting with similar trajectories for procedure contexts, we observed that patients with common treatment got better 43.98% of the time on average, while patients with individual treatment get better 55.97% of the time on average. For common treatments, patients in Cluster 0 improved 66.7%, Cluster 1 56.2% and Cluster 2 50% of the time. We observed a similar ordering for individual treatments with improvements in Cluster 0:60%, Cluster 1:40%, and Cluster 2:25%. Turning to medication contexts, patients with individual trajectories follow a similar trend as in the case of procedure context, where individual treatment resulted in an improved patient's health state at higher rates than patients with common treatment. Patients with individual procedures get better 54.5% of the time, while patients with common treatment got better 36.6% of the time. Patients with similar trajectories and common treatment got better 43.4% of the time, while patients with individual treatment got better 43.98% on average.

5   Conclusion and Future Work

We investigate an interpretable patient health state based on subscore features of severity of illness scores, utilizing expert knowledge. The severity scores rate the physiological, psychological, and procedural characteristics of the patient and may be used to describe a patient's response to treatment and can potentially be used to assess the efficacy of particular treatments. We selected a subset of 108 CHF patients with similar first-day health states, and through the application of DBSCAN we clustered health state trajectories, administered medications and procedures. We investigated patient commonalities among these three dimensions and correlated them with a change in health state. We investigated medication context and procedure contexts separately, ignoring the interactions between those treatment dimensions in affecting the patient's health state and trajectory. Trajectories analyzed in this study are quite short, only considering the first two days of stay. To evaluate treatments and their long term effects, especially for chronic diseases, we recommend investigating longer trajectories. Understanding the pattern found in health state trajectories among patients, given an informative health state representation is found, might further help in understanding underlying causes to the point where individual treatment strategies can be developed more effectively, and harmful interventions avoided to alleviate one of the problems of contemporary health care: Medical error.

References

1. Bajor, J.M., Mesa, D.A., Osterman, T.J., Lasko, T.A.: Embedding complexity in the data representation instead of in the model: a case study using heterogeneous medical data. Manuscript submitted for publication (2018)

2. Buja, A., Swayne, D.F., Littman, M.L., Dean, N., Hofmann, H., Chen, L.: Data visualization with multidimensional scaling. J. Comput. Graph. Stat. **17**(2), 444–472 (2008)
3. Choi, E., Bahadori, M.T., Searles, E., Coffey, C., Sun, J.: Multi-layer representation learning for medical concepts. CoRR abs/1602.05568 (2016)
4. Choi, E., Bahadori, M.T., Sun, J.: Doctor AI: predicting clinical events via recurrent neural networks. CoRR abs/1511.05942 (2015)
5. Ester, M., Kriegel, H.P., Sander, J., Xu, X.: A density-based algorithm for discovering clusters in large spatial databases with noise. In: Proceedings of the Second International Conference on Knowledge Discovery and Data Mining, KDD 1996, pp. 226–231. AAAI Press (1996)
6. Ferreira, F.L., Bota, D.P., Bross, A., Mélot, C., Vincent, J.L.: Serial evaluation of the SOFA score to predict outcome in critically ill patients. JAMA **286**(14), 1754–1758 (2001)
7. Pearson, K.: LIII. On lines and planes of closest fit to systems of points in space. London, Edinburgh, Dublin Philos. Mag. J. Sci. **2**(11), 559–572 (1901)
8. Johnson, A.E., Kramer, A.A., Clifford, G.D.: A new severity of illness scale using a subset of acute physiology and chronic health evaluation data elements shows comparable predictive accuracy. Crit. Care Med. **41**(7), 1711–1718 (2013)
9. Johnson, A.E., et al.: MIMIC-III, a freely accessible critical care database. Sci. Data **3**, 160035 (2016)
10. Johnson, A.E.W.: Mortality prediction and acuity assessment in critical care. Ph.D. thesis, University of Oxford (2014)
11. Johnson, A.E., Stone, D.J., Celi, L.A., Pollard, T.J.: The mimic code repository: enabling reproducibility in critical care research. J. Am. Med. Inform. Assoc. **25**(1), 32–39 (2018)
12. Kennedy, C.E., Turley, J.P.: Time series analysis as input for clinical predictive modeling: modeling cardiac arrest in a pediatric ICU. Theor. Biol. Med. Model. **8**, 40 (2011)
13. Knaus, W.A., et al.: The APACHE III prognostic system: risk prediction of hospital mortality for critically hospitalized adults. Chest **100**(6), 1619–1636 (1991)
14. Le, Q., Mikolov, T.: Distributed representations of sentences and documents. In: Proceedings of the 31st International Conference on International Conference on Machine Learning, ICML 2014, vol. 32, pp. II-1188-II-1196 (2014). www.JMLR.org
15. Le Gall, J., Lemeshow, S., Saulnier, F.: A new simplified acute physiology score (SAPS II) based on a European/North American multicenter study. JAMA **270**(24), 2957–2963 (1993)
16. Le Gall, J.R., et al.: Mortality prediction using SAPS II: an update for French intensive care units. Crit. Care **9**(6), R645 (2005)
17. Leape, L.L., Berwick, D.M.: Five years after To Err Is Human: what have we learned? JAMA **293**(19), 2384–2390 (2005)
18. MacFie, C.C., Baudouin, S.V., Messer, P.B.: An integrative review of drug errors in critical care. J. Intensive Care Soc. **17**(1), 63–72 (2016)
19. Miotto, R., Li, L., Kidd, B., Dudley, J.T.: Deep patient: an unsupervised representation to predict the future of patients from the electronic health records. Sci. Rep. **6**, 26094 (2016)
20. Nguyen, P., Tran, T., Wickramasinghe, N., Venkatesh, S.: *Deepr*: a convolutional net for medical records. IEEE J. Biomed. Health Inform. **21**(1), 22–30 (2017)

21. Pham, T., Tran, T., Phung, D., Venkatesh, S.: Predicting healthcare trajectories from medical records: a deep learning approach. J. Biomed. Inform. **69**, 218–229 (2017)
22. Ravi, P., Vijai, M.N.: Errors in ICU: how safe is the patient? A prospective observational study in a tertiary care hospital. J. Anesth. Clin. Res. **6**(6), 1–7 (2015)
23. Řehůřek, R., Sojka, P.: Software framework for topic modelling with large corpora. In: Proceedings of the LREC 2010 Workshop on New Challenges for NLP Frameworks, pp. 45–50. ELRA, May 2010
24. Kohn, L.T., Corrigan, J., Donaldson, M.: To Err is Human: Building a Safer Health System, vol. 6. National Academies Press, Washington (DC) (2000)
25. Teasdale, G., Jennett, B.: Assessment of coma and impaired consciousness: a practical scale. Lancet **304**(7872), 81–84 (1974)
26. Vincent, J.L., et al.: The SOFA (Sepsis-related Organ Failure Assessment) score to describe organ dysfunction/failure. On behalf of the working group on sepsis-related problems of the European society of intensive care medicine. Intensive Care Med. **22**(7), 707–710 (1996)
27. Wenzel, R.P., et al.: Hospital-acquired infections in intensive care unit patients: an overview with emphasis on epidemics. Infect. Control **4**(5), 371–375 (1983)
28. Williams, T.A., Ho, K.M., Dobb, G.J., Finn, J.C., Knuiman, M., Webb, S.A.R.: Effect of length of stay in intensive care unit on hospital and long-term mortality of critically ill adult patients. BJA: Br. J. Anaesth. **104**(4), 459–464 (2010)
29. Ylipalosaari, P., Ala-Kokko, T.I., Laurila, J., Ohtonen, P., Syrjälä, H.: Intensive care acquired infection is an independent risk factor for hospital mortality: a prospective cohort study. Crit. Care **10**(2), R66 (2006)
30. Zimmerman, J.E., Kramer, A.A., McNair, D.S., Malila, F.M.: Acute physiology and chronic health evaluation (APACHE) IV: hospital mortality assessment for today's critically ill patients. Crit. Care Med. **34**(5), 1297–1310 (2006)

An Explainable Approach of Inferring Potential Medication Effects from Social Media Data

Keyuan Jiang[1(✉)], Tingyu Chen[1], Liyuan Huang[1], Ravish Gupta[2], Ricardo A. Calix[1], and Gordon R. Bernard[3]

[1] Purdue University Northwest, Hammond, IN 46323, USA
huanglydd@gmail.com, {kjiang,chen2694,rcalix}@pnw.edu
[2] Amazon.com, Seattle, WA 98121, USA
rgupt3888@gmail.com
[3] Vanderbilt University, Nashville, TN 37232, USA
gordon.bernard@vanderbilt.edu

Abstract. Understanding medication effects is an important activity in pharmacovigilance in which patients are the most important contributor. Social media, where users share their personal experiences of medication effects, have been recommended as an alternative data source of gathering signal information of suspected medication effects. To discover potential medication-effect relations from Twitter data, we devised a method employing analogical reasoning with neural embedding of Twitter text. The process involves learning the neural embedding from unlabeled tweets and performing vector arithmetic, making it obscure to understand how an inferred relation is derived. To make the process understandable and interpretable and to facilitate the decision making on accepting or rejecting any inferred medication-effect relations, we added explanation(s) to each step of the process. An example of inferred relation is provided to demonstrate the effectiveness of our approach in explaining how the result of each step is derived.

Keywords: Pharmacovigilance · Medication effects · Social media · Analogical reasoning · Explainable machine learning

1 Introduction

Adverse medication effects are one of the leading causes of death in many developed countries [1–4], incurring significant costs to treat the illness caused by the effects. The main goal of pharmacovigilance is to continuously monitor and assess the safety of pharmaceutical products and to promote the safe use of medications. Patients are the primary contributors to pharmacovigilance as they have first-hand personal experience of the effects of medications they take. It has been reported that information shared by patients is different than what healthcare professionals documented: better understanding of adverse experience, better explanation of the nature, significance and consequences, and more detailed information [5].

© Springer Nature Switzerland AG 2019
M. Marcos et al. (Eds.): KR4HC-ProHealth 2019/TEAAM 2019, LNAI 11979, pp. 82–92, 2019.
https://doi.org/10.1007/978-3-030-37446-4_7

Emergency of social media provides a platform enabling patients to share personal medication experiences online more effectively, freely and timely. Numerous efforts have been made in using social media as an alternative data source to discover information of potentially suspected adverse medication effects [6]. However, most of the studies focused on identifying expressions of adverse medication effects or adverse drug reactions (ADRs), and little has been done in understanding the relationships between the expressions of medication and effect in the same context, leading to false positive signals or drawing irrelevant conclusions. Due to the uniqueness of social media, user posts do not necessarily follow the spelling and grammatical rules, making many natural language processing (NLP) tools developed for formal writing perform unsuccessfully, especially with Twitter data. Therefore other solutions need to be sought.

A number of semantic relations do exist in the medical domain, and a list of hierarchical semantic relations has been published by the U.S. National Library of Medicine (NLM) in its Unified Medical Language System® (UMLS®). Many of the UMLS Semantic Relations are related to medication-effect relations, such as *treats*, *causes*, *occurs_in*, *disrupts*, *exhibit*, and *produces*. The SemRep software, also developed by the U.S. NLM, is capable of extracting the predicates from the citations of biomedical literature and mapping them to these normalized semantic relations [10]. Since a predicate is considered as a relation between two biomedical concepts in a subject-predicate-object triple, this requires accurate recognition of the biomedical concepts and predication in the context. The reality is that there are so many different ways to express same biomedical concepts and their similar semantic relations. To gather various ways of expressing the normalized semantic relations, the U.S. NLM even launched an ambitious project of building a repository of semantic predicates extracted from the sentences of all Medline citations based upon the UMLS Semantic Relations [16]. At this writing, the repository contains nearly 94 million predications. It is worth noting that Medline citations are considered formal writings by researchers and clinicians who follow grammatical and spelling rules closely. But for social media data, Twitter data in particular, rules are not followed closely and identifying predicates correctly in tweet text is a challenging task.

To overcome the limitation of being unable to correctly extract predicates directly from the tweet text based upon grammatical rules, we propose to identify semantic relations by finding semantic relations most similar to any known semantic relations. That is, any pair of semantic relations share sufficient similarity is considered semantically similar, indicating that they have similar meanings.

Neural embedding of text is a technique to represent words as dense vectors of real numbers, where the vectors, learned from the words in a large corpus of unlabeled text data, are the weights of a hidden layer of a neural network [7]. This technique has demonstrated state-of-art results in many NLP tasks, including handling similarities of syntactic and semantical relations [7, 13]. For example, it could infer correctly the capital city of a given country based upon a known country and its capital, for the country-capital relation. This power of inference, based upon the similarity of semantic relations, may help in discovering potential medication-effect relations. To discover the potential relationship between each pair of medication and effect, we devised a neural embedding-based method, through relational similarity or analogical reasoning, to infer potential relations from known, reported medication-effect relations. The reasoning process involves several steps including learning neural embedding of tweet text from unlabeled tweets, and manipulating vectors of tweet terms, which can make it obscure to understand and interpret how the inferences are drawn.

Explainability of machine learning in healthcare is crucial, not only in helping make educated decisions but also in understanding how the computer draws the conclusions which can impact the human wellbeing. In particular to pharmacovigilance, the Erice Manifesto calls for openness for audit of decisions in drug safety by all parties involved, transparency of decision making, and transparent evidence-based activities in pharma-covigilance [8]. As a use case of our application, an evaluator may first notice a particular relation inferred by our system. For the evaluator to decide if the inference is acceptable, he or she may want to understand and interpret how the system derives the result, and/or review the actual social media posts related to the inference. In addition, creditability of social media data has been a concern and providing explainability in the process may mitigate or eliminate false statements posted online. To address the need of explainability of our machine learning-based reasoner, we implemented the explanation items in our approach, as described in the following sections.

2   Method

In natural language processing, understanding the semantic relationship between terms is an important task, and being able to discover such relationship can help identify relationship between medical concepts in the medical and healthcare domain. Traditional methods such as dependency tree or syntax parsing [9] and tools like SemRep [10] perform satisfactorily with the formal writing that follows spelling and grammatical rules. When dealing with social media data, these techniques may perform unsatisfactorily because of the fact that spelling and grammatical rules are not well followed in social media posts, especially in Twitter posts where users tend to be creative in coining short text that fits within the limited space.

One of the promising approaches is reasoning through relational similarity in which potential relations between the medical concepts (medication and effect) are inferred from the similar known relations of different concepts. Mikolov and colleagues reported the state-of-art achievements of tasks pertaining to relational similarity with distributional representation of words in a vector space [7]. The underlying mechanism is that similar relations bear similar linguistic regularities, and the similarity between the two relations can be derived by computing the cosine similarity between the two relation vectors, where a relation can be expressed as the offset (vector) of two concept vectors.

Our approach of discovering potential medication-effect relations (hence potential effects) includes the two steps: (1) learning neural embedding of terms from a large corpus of unlabeled tweets related to medication use, and (2) inferring potential medication-effect relations based upon known medication-effect relations for any medications of interest.

2.1 Neural Embedding-Based Analogical Reasoning

Neural embedding of tweet text was learned with the help of Google's word2vec software [11, 13] which trains, from a large corpus of unlabeled textual data, a collection of input weights of a one layer neural network, based upon the occurrence of terms within a window. The outcome is a vector space model in which each term is represented as a dense vector. Each vector embeds the semantic and syntactic representation in the context of co-occurring terms. The word2vec parameters used in our project are skip-gram, window_size = 10, min_count = 5 and dimension = 300.

Analogical reasoning was performed based upon relational similarity. Potential relations were inferred from the similarity to base relations which are known. Mathematically, we have

$$med_{base} : effect_{base} :: med_{potential} : effect_{potential}$$

as two similar relations, where $med_{base} : effect_{base}$ represents the base relation which is known and $med_{potential} : effect_{potential}$ is the inferred relation. For example, we have the following similar relations in our study

$$Toprol\,XL \,:\, chest\,pain \,::\, Depakote \,:\, bad\,dreams$$

where *Toprol XL : chest pain* is the based (known) relation and *Depakote : bad dreams* is the inferred relation. This is to say that the relation of *Depakote : bad dreams* was inferred from the base relation of *Toprol XL : chest pain*, because both relations are similar to each other measured by the similarity between the two. In other words, we have an analogy of "*Depakote* is to *bad dreams* as *Toprol XL* is to *chest pain*," implying that the association between *bad dreams* and *Depakote* is similar to that between *Toprol XL* and *chest pain*.

The goal of analogical reasoning is to find a potential relation most similar to the base relation(s). In the vector space, a relation can be expressed as the offset of two vectors such as $vector(effect_{base}) - vector(med_{base})$. To find the relation most similar to base relations, we can calculate the cosine similarity between $vector(effect_{base}) - vector(med_{base})$ and any $vector(effect_{potential}) - vector(med_{potential})$, and choose the relation with the highest similarity. In implementation, all the possible known relations of $med_{base} : effect_{base}$ except those for $med_{potential}$ were utilized to inferring potential medication-effect relations for $med_{potential}$, to cover more linguistic variations of expressing the same relation and to help improve the confidence of inference.

Base relations, which are pairs of known medication and effect, come from the SIDER database [12], a resource of drug side effects, hosted by the European Molecular Biology Laboratory. SIDER side effect data are from pharmaceutical manufacturers and contain one name for each medication. Other names of the same medications were compiled by this team in order to handle various medication names used in Twitter posts.

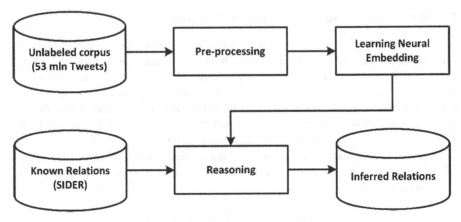

Fig. 1. Data processing pipeline.

The data processing pipeline is illustrated in Fig. 1. A corpus of 53 million unannotated tweets related to medications of interest was collected, and preprocessed to generate
a corpus of 3.6 million "clean" tweets which was used to learn the neural embedding
of tweet text. Vectors in the neural embedding model were used for inferring potential
medication-effect relations from known medication-effect relations.

2.2 Explainability

As can be seen, the above steps involve learning from co-occurrence of textual terms and
vector manipulations, which are not straightforward in interpretation and understanding.
An evaluator, following the steps of our analogical reasoning method, may want to review
and check (1) the instances of relevant Twitter posts and (2) the top candidate relations
inferred. With the inferred candidates, the evaluator may wish to examine how the final
candidate relation was chosen. Furthermore, the evaluator may like to investigate which
known relations were based on to infer the top candidates. And finally, the evaluator may
desire to read the tweets relevant to the base relations. In each of the steps, the evaluator
wants to have an explanation regarding how the result was derived.

Illustrated in Fig. 2 is the flow of explaining the reasoning process as described
above. The illustration can also be viewed as how the evidences of the inference support
each step of the reasoning (from bottom to top). Tweets are used to generate the neural
embedding model and they are foundation of many base relations which are known.
Base relations in turn are used to computing the similarity of other relations which may
become the top candidates of inferred relations. The top most similar relation is chosen
according to the similarity to the base relation(s). After an inferred relation is available,
its related tweets can be examined to confirm or reject the relation.

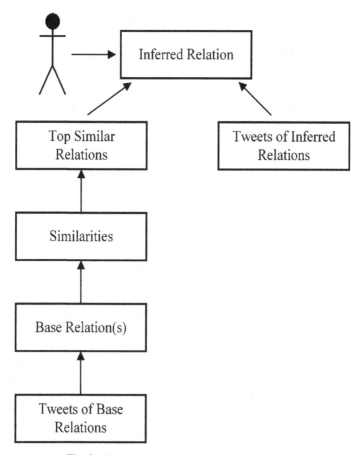

Fig. 2. Flow of explaining the reasoning process.

We define an explanation as an item, either numeric or textual, that provides explanation to the corresponding step in the reasoning process. To make the process explainable, we added explanation(s) to each item in our approach. The added explainable items were based upon our observation and available data at each step. For instance, if an evaluator observed an inferred relation, he or she may desire to know the relevant tweets about the inferred relation and most similar relations yielded by the system, and at this point, both can be readily accessible and helpful in explaining and interpreting the inference. Summarized in Table 1 are items and their corresponding explanations.

When a particular inferred relation is examined, relevant tweets can be presented as the textual evidence of the inferred relation, and/or the candidates with the most similar relations can be reviewed. The decision on which candidate relation was chosen can be explained by the relational similarities. The base relation(s) used to infer the chosen potential relation can be investigated by the known medication-effect pair(s) and relevant tweet text.

Table 1. List of items and their corresponding explainable items and explanation.

Item	Explainable item	Explanation
Inferred relation	(1) Relevant tweets (2) Top similar relations	(1) Textual evidence of inferred relation (2) The choice of the most similar inferred relation
Similar relations	(1) Similarities	(1) The candidates of inferred relations with high similarities
Similarity	(1) Base relations	(1) The base relations (medication-effect pairs) used to derive the candidates
Base relations	(1) Relevant tweets	(1) The raw tweets describing the base relations

2.3 Data

By combining two lists of top 100 drugs (by sales in dollars and by units) listed at drugs.com, a collection of 1,147 medication names was generated by including their generic and brand variations, and these medication names were used as keywords for querying related tweets. A corpus of 53 million tweets was retrieved from twitter.com in June of 2017 with a home-made crawler capable of handling the limitations of Twitter APIs. The free RESTful Twitter Search API returns the data only published in the last 7 days, and has rate limits on how many tweets can be queried within a time window. The free real-time Streaming API requires a long time period to retrieve a large number of tweets needed for learning the neural embedding, and has a limit of the number of keywords that can be used for filtering. Our crawler, designed to collect tweets for a large time span, searches for tweets containing the medication names of interest on twitter.com, and can continue searching for the historic tweets all the way back to the inception of twitter.com. The collected corpus of tweets spans from the inception of twitter.com (March 2006) to the date of retrieval. Another benefit of gathering Twitter data directly from www.twitter.com is to leverage the spam filter implemented by Twitter for its web interface, effectively removing a significant amount of spam tweets and generating a much cleaner collection of results. The raw tweets were preprocessed to remove non-English tweets, duplicates, tweets with URL (which typically are irrelevant promotional tweets), and many punctuations, and to convert tweet text to lower case text. The tweets were also filtered by effect terms from SIDER to ensure that each tweet contains at least a medication name and an effect expression. This treatment helps in reasoning such that both medication and effect terms will be more likely to appear within the context of a given window which in our case is 10, and the expression of their semantic relation is more like to occur within the same context. The remaining 3.6 million "clean" tweets were utilized for learning neural embedding and subsequently performing analogical reasoning.

3 Results

Our reasoning process generated a total of 5,182 potential medicine-side effect relations from a collection of 3,184 unique base relations, as shown in Table 2. Among inferred relations, 1,448 relations are known, meaning that they are found in the SIDER database, and 3,734 relations do *not* exist in the SIDER database. In inferring potential relations, the 3,184 unique base relations were utilized in a total of 78,369 times, indicating that a single base relation may be used multiple times for inferring different potential relations.

Table 2. Statistics of inference.

# of unique base relations	# times of base relations	# inferred relations	# inferred relations known	# inferred relations potential
3,184	78,369	5,182	1,448	3,734

With the involvement of the reasoning process, it is neither obvious nor straightforward to understand how the process derives a particular potential relation. To illustrate how the explainability added to our reasoning process can help understand and interpret the reasoning process, we take an inferred medication-effect relation, *Depakote-bad dreams*, as an example. The explanation of each step is shown in Table 3.

In this table, the italicized text represents the explanations with the actual evidential data: relevant tweets, candidates of most similar relations, similarities, base relation and its relevant raw tweets. For this inferred *Depakote-bad dreams* relation, there are two instances of Twitter posts, providing the textual evidence of the inferred relation. There are three other relations similar to *Depakote-bad dreams*, and they are *Depakote-broken hand*, *Depakote-dyslexics*, and *Depakote-chemical burns*, which are the candidate relations the machine discovered in analogical reasoning or the outcome of vector manipulation (offset and cosine similarity).

Among 4 relation candidates, the *Depakote-bad dreams* relation was chosen because it has the highest similarity (0.362) to the base relation, and all other relations have lower similarities to the base relation.

The single base relation, *Toprol XL-chest pain* served as the source for deriving 4 relation candidates for Depakote. In many cases, there can be more than one base relation, but for Depakote, only this base relation generated a meaningful inference. There are two tweets related to *Toprol XL-chest pain* in the corpus of medicine-related tweets we collected.

Table 3. Items and explanations of inferred medication-effect relation.

Item	Explainable item
Inferred relation *Depakote-bad dreams*	(1) Relevant tweets *(a) New dose of depakote giving me really vivid bad dreams. Ugh. I need something that will give me vivid GOOD dreams LOL* *(b) Thx sweetie. I get awful, vivid nightmares on Depakote. Always had bad dreams but now theyre* (2) Top candidate relations *(a) Depakote-bad dreams* *(b) Depakote-broken hand* *(c) Depakote-dyslexics* *(d) Depakote-chemical burns*
Top candidate relations *(a) Depakote-bad dreams* *(b) Depakote-broken hand* *(c) Depakote-dyslexics* *(d) Depakote-chemical burns*	(1) Similarities *(a) Depakote-bad dreams: 0.362* *(b) Depakote-broken hand: 0.300* *(c) Depakote-dyslexics: 0.275* *(d) Depakote-chemical burns: 0.268*
Similarity *Depakote-bad dreams: 0.362*	(1) Base relations *Toprol XL-chest pain*
Base relations *Toprol XL-chest pain*	(1) Relevant tweets *(a) Thinks it is time to make a big decision. No more Toprol XL. Stinging feelings in my fingers, chest pains, suicidal thoughts, no thanks.* *(b) My med list: Prilosec.levothyroxine.amiodarone.toprol xl.zoloft. This is what a 105 year old takes daily swallowing issues, chest pain meals*

4 Discussions

Explainability has been enhanced by adding explanations to the process of our analogical reasoning. It provides evidential support at every step of the reasoning process for an evaluator to understand and interpret how an inferred potential medication-effect relation was derived, hence to facilitate the decision making on whether to accept or reject the inferred relation. Some explanations such as tweet instances are straightforward and comprehensible, while others such as co-occurrence of words in the same context are indirect. Although not explaining directly the co-occurrence and vector manipulations, it still provides a certain level of explanation that help understand how the reasoning process behaves. Co-occurrence is represented in dense vectors, which do not seem to be easily understandable by the evaluator – a 300 dimensionality vector of real numbers can easily overwhelm most individuals. The result of vector offset is another vector, which again is not easily comprehensible by individual human beings.

Whereas our work presented in this paper mainly focuses on the explainability of our approach, it is worth noting that the inferred potentially relations (or effects) warrant a stringent check with other authoritative sources of medication information to ensure that they have not been reported elsewhere, given the fact that SIDER has not been updated since 2015 and it does not cover many medications on the market. Strong candidates of authoritative sources include (1) www.fdable.com which is a user-friendly web-based interface for querying the data from the FDA Adverse Event Reporting System (FAERS); (2) the FDA dailymed website which allows for searching for the official FDA drug label information; (3) MedlinePlus.gov which is an online information service produced by the U.S. National Library of Medicine (NLM) using the data from the AHFS® Consumer Medication Information; (4) Clinicaltrials.gov which is a registry of clinical trials worldwide and maintained by the U.S National Library of Medicine (NLM); and (5) Pubmed.gov which a search engine of the MEDLINE database of published references and abstracts on biomedical and health sciences, and maintained and hosted by the U.S National Library of Medicine (NLM). Another step that should be involved in our process is to annotate the tweets of inferred relations. Although human annotation is laborious, time-consuming, and perhaps cost-prohibitive process, its outcome can help confirm if any inferred relations were actually presented in the Twitter posts.

One of unique features the SIDER data has is that each concept of medication effect is associated with a Concept Unique Identifier (CUI) of the Unified Medical Language System (UMLS) [14], facilitating the expansion of effect concepts to consumer health vocabulary (CHV) terms [15], and such expansion helps in searching for relevant information containing expressions used by consumers such as the Twitter users, and covering as many variations of linguistic expressions as possible.

At the end, any potentially unreported medication effects may help develop hypotheses to be validated with clinical investigations, and validated hypotheses will help advance medical science and clinical practices.

5 Conclusion

In our effort of identifying potential medication-effect relations from Twitter data, we devised a neural embedding-based analogical reasoning process which infers potential medication-effect relations from known relations. However, the process involves learning neural representation from a large corpus of unannotated tweets and manipulating representational vectors for reasoning. To understand these obscure steps, we added an explanation at each step of our reasoning process, making it explainable and comprehendible to the evaluator who makes the decision on whether to accept or reject an inferred medication-effect relation.

Acknowledgement. Authors wish to thank anonymous reviewers for their critiques and constructive comments that helped improve the final manuscript. This work was supported in part by the US National Institutes of Health Grant 1R15LM011999-01.

Ethics Compliance. The protocol of this project was reviewed and approved for compliance with the human subject research regulation by the Institutional Review Board of Purdue University.

References

1. Pirmohamed, M., et al.: Adverse drug reactions as cause of admission to hospital: prospective analysis of 18 820 patients. BMJ **329**(7456), 15–19 (2004)
2. Lazarou, J., Pomeranz, B.H., Corey, P.N.: Incidence of adverse drug reactions in hospitalized patients: a meta-analysis of prospective studies. JAMA **279**(15), 1200–1205 (1998)
3. Moore, T.J., Cohen, M.R., Furberg, C.D.: Serious adverse drug events reported to the Food and Drug Administration, 1998–2005. Arch. Intern. Med. **167**(16), 1752–1759 (2007)
4. Levinson, D.R., General, I.: Adverse events in hospitals: national incidence among Medicare beneficiaries. Department of Health & Human Services (2010)
5. Härmark, L., et al.: Patient-reported safety information: a renaissance of pharmacovigilance? Drug Saf. **39**(10), 883–890 (2016)
6. Golder, S., Norman, G., Loke, Y.K.: Systematic review on the prevalence, frequency and comparative value of adverse events data in social media. Br. J. Clin. Pharmacol. **80**(4), 878–888 (2015)
7. Mikolov, T., Yih, W.T., Zweig, G.: Linguistic regularities in continuous space word representations. In: Proceedings of the 2013 Conference of the North American Chapter of the Association for Computational Linguistics: Human Language Technologies, pp. 746–751 (2013)
8. Adice International Limited: The Erice manifesto: for global reform of the safety of medicines in patient care. Drug Saf. **30**(3), 187–190 (2007)
9. De Marneffe, M.C., MacCartney, B., Manning, C.D.: Generating typed dependency parses from phrase structure parses. LREC **6**, 449–454 (2006)
10. Rindflesch, T.C., Fiszman, M.: The interaction of domain knowledge and linguistic structure in natural language processing: interpreting hypernymic propositions in biomedical text. J. Biomed. Inform. **36**(6), 462–477 (2003)
11. Google Code Archive, word2vec. https://code.google.com/archive/p/word2vec/
12. Kuhn, M., Letunic, I., Jensen, L.J., Bork, P.: The SIDER database of drugs and side effects. Nucleic Acids Res. **44**(D1), D1075–D1079 (2015)
13. Mikolov, T., Chen, K., Corrado, G., Dean, J.: Efficient estimation of word representations in vector space. In: International Conference on Learning Representations (2013)
14. Bodenreider, O.: The unified medical language system (UMLS): integrating biomedical terminology. Nucleic acids research **32**(suppl_1), D267–D270 (2004)
15. Zeng, Q.T., Tse, T.: Exploring and developing consumer health vocabularies. J. Am. Med. Inform. Assoc. **13**(1), 24–29 (2006)
16. Kilicoglu, H., Rosemblat, G., Fiszman, M., Rindflesch, T.C.: Constructing a semantic predication gold standard from the biomedical literature. BMC Bioinform. **12**(1), 486 (2011)

Exploring Antimicrobial Resistance Prediction Using Post-hoc Interpretable Methods

Bernardo Cánovas-Segura[1]([✉])(iD), Antonio Morales[1](iD),
Antonio López Martínez-Carrasco[1], Manuel Campos[1](iD), Jose M. Juarez[1](iD),
Lucía López Rodríguez[2], and Francisco Palacios[1]

[1] AIKE Research Group, University of Murcia, Murcia, Spain
`{bernardocs,morales,antonio.lopez31,manuelcampos,jmjuarez}@um.es`,
`franciscodepaula@gmail.com`
[2] University Hospital of Getafe, Madrid, Spain
`lucialopezrodriguez@yahoo.es`

Abstract. An accurate and timely prediction of whether an infection is going to be resistant to a particular antibiotic could improve the clinical outcome of the patient as well as reduce the risk of spreading resistant microorganisms.

From a data analysis perspective, four key factors are present in antimicrobial resistance prediction: the high dimensionality of the data available, the imbalance present in the datasets, the concept drift along time and the need for their acceptance and implantation by clinical staff.

To date, no study has looked specifically at combining different strategies to deal with each of these four key factors. We believe interpretable prediction models are required. This study was undertaken to evaluate the impact of baseline interpretable predicting approaches using a dataset of real hospital data. In particular, we study the capacity of logistic regression, conditional trees and C5.0 rule-based models to improve the prediction when they are combined with oversampling, filtering and sliding windows.

Keywords: Interpretable models · Antimicrobial resistance · Concept drift · High dimensionality · Class imbalance

1 Introduction

Antimicrobial ineffectiveness due to resistant bacteria is a major problem increasing the risk of spread to others, becoming a threat for national health systems [18].

Antimicrobial susceptibility tests (ASTs) are helpful tools to identify the effect of antimicrobials on bacterial strains [16]. According to their results, clinicians can prescribe the most appropriate antimicrobial with which to improve the patient's clinical outcome and contribute to reduce the spread of resistant bacteria.

© Springer Nature Switzerland AG 2019
M. Marcos et al. (Eds.): KR4HC-ProHealth 2019/TEAAM 2019, LNAI 11979, pp. 93–107, 2019.
https://doi.org/10.1007/978-3-030-37446-4_8

However, ASTs require days to complete since they need to culture bacteria in laboratory and study their growth. Consequently, to early predict whether a patient is being infected by resistant bacteria is a relevant research topic nowadays.

This work is an extension of the results presented in [7]. In particular, we study the combination of different strategies to develop prediction models for an early identification of patients that would be infected by resistant bacteria. The main objective of this study is to assess the impact of these techniques on different kinds of models within the antimicrobial resistance scenario. We have identified four characteristics of the data available and the models required in this context: the preference for interpretable models, the presence of concept drift, the high dimensionality of datasets and the imbalance present in the class to predict. To the best of our knowledge, there are no studies dealing with these four circumstances as a whole in prediction models for antimicrobial resistance.

In detail, we test the development of logistic regression, conditional trees and C5.0 rule-based prediction models in a dataset with real data to estimate the infection by a strain of *Enterococcus* species resistant to the antimicrobial called *vancomycin*, that is, the prediction of patients infected by *Vancomycin-Resistant Enterococci* (VRE). Furthermore, we design different combinations of oversampling, filtering and sliding windows in order to deal with the aforementioned problems in antimicrobial resistance prediction. The resulting models are compared according not only to their discrimination capabilities but also to their simplicity. To this end, we use both the Area Under the ROC Curve (AUC) and the number of features selected for being part of the model, that is, the number of predictor variables.

2   Methods

2.1   Post-hoc Interpretable Classification Models

According to Lipton's classification [17], model and method properties to comprise interpretations fall into two categories: transparent models (how the method work) and post-hoc explanations (what the model tells). We focus on post-hoc interpretable prediction models, that is, the effect of each predictor and how they are combined to obtain the prediction is easy to understand and evaluate.

We consider that current interpretable models are grouped in three main categories:

- Regression models: the estimation method is intuitive and easy to understand.
- Tree based models: dataset instances are partitioned using a model structure easy to visualize.
- Rule-based models: simple and short IF-THEN statements are considered one of the most simple and effective representations of knowledge.

The purpose of this research work is to illustrate the capacity of interpretable models to solve a specific classification problem in the clinical field. For this reason, in this preliminary study we have selected one algorithm for each category: logistic regression (LASSO), conditional inference trees and rule-based prediction models.

Logistic Regression Model. Among the interpretable models, logistic regression is the most used for developing clinical models [12]. These models follow the next equation:

$$log\left(\frac{\mu}{1-\mu}\right) = \beta_0 + \beta_1 x_1 + \beta_2 x_2 + \ldots + \beta_p x_p \tag{1}$$

where $\mu = P(Y = 1)$, in which Y is the variable whose occurrence is being predicted, $x_1 \ldots x_p$ are the values of the features selected for the model, and $\beta_0 \ldots \beta_p$ are weight variables, usually estimated by means of the maximum likelihood [22].

One of the drawbacks of logistic regression models is that they tend to generate overfitted models [3]. For this reason, we use the *Least Absolute Shrinkage and Selection Operator (LASSO)* technique to cope with this problem [23]. LASSO reduces the weight of some β_i towards 0 during their computation, removing them from the final model. Moreover, the reduction in the number of predictors facilitates the interpretation of the resulting model.

Decision Trees. Another common technique in clinical prediction models are decision trees, since they are generally easy to interpret and use [2]. A tree-like structure is inferred in these models, in which each leaf corresponds to a classification output and the path followed to reach them depends on the values of the predictors.

In this work, we use a Conditional Inference Tree that performs an unbiased variable selection for each split based on statistical tests [13].

Rule-Based Models. Many of the computational tools that are used to assist clinicians in their decisions, named as Clinical Decision Support Systems (CDSSs), are based on *if-then* rules: *if* a certain set of conditions are met, *then* an action is taken or suggested. The development of prediction models in the form of rule-based systems can facilitate their implementation in CDSSs.

Most decision tree models can be implemented as rules. However, there are tree-based algorithms that take into account the particularities of rule-based systems when generating the final model. In this work, we rely on the implementation of the C5.0 decision tree algorithm that allows to directly generate a set of rules instead of a decision tree.

2.2   Concept Drift

The influence of some factors in a specific problem may vary over time. This is the case of antimicrobial resistance, that may be influenced by varying factors such as the capability of bacteria to develop resistance to antimicrobials, seasonal variations in the dissemination of bacteria and changes in clinical protocols of the hospital. The dynamic changes in the distribution and the influence of factors on the target of the prediction is commonly known as *concept drift* [24,27].

There is a wealth of strategies to deal with concept drift, such as using a temporal window with the most recent observations, weighting modern samples when creating the model or maintaining a set of models created from data of different time intervals [11].

In this work, we focus on the sliding window approach. We assume that the latest observations are the most relevant in order to create the prediction model [11,27]. Consequently, a set with only the most recent observations (a window) is used to develop the model, ignoring all the observations previous to a specific timestamp. When new observations are available, the window "moves" forward, incorporating these observations and removing the older ones, and a new model is computed. The sliding window approach is easy to implement, and its effects are easy to understand by the clinical staff. Furthermore, they can be used along with any modelling approach, without requiring any extra adjust in the modelling algorithm.

The size of the sliding window is critical. If large windows are used, an abrupt change on class distribution can be diluted in the amount of data. On the contrary, small windows can produce overfitted or inconsistent models due to the small amount of data.

2.3   High Dimensionality

It is a common issue in data mining of clinical data to have a large number of possible predictors extracted from sources such as patient's clinical records and laboratory test results. It may even happen that the number of predictors outnumbers the number of observations available. This situation, known as *Curse of Dimensionality*, is even more frequent when data from *omics* sciences are available.

The LASSO technique can be seen as a feature selection step for a logistic regression model, and decision trees (and the rule-based models derived from them) also perform a selection of the most relevant predictors during the tree building. However, when high-correlated features are present, which is a common issue in datasets with high dimensionality, additional filters may improve the feature selection process. In order to test this condition in the antimicrobial resistance scenario, we study the effect of using the Fast Correlation-Based Filter (FCBF) [28]. This filter selects the most relevant features and removes those ones that it considers redundant due to their high correlation with a low computational cost.

2.4   Imbalanced Datasets

The difference in the number of positive and negative observations for an outcome of interest is a common issue in clinical datasets. In our setting, the strains that are usually susceptible to antimicrobials are far more common than those with characteristics that provide antimicrobial resistance. Therefore, there are few observations belonging to the *Resistant* class when compared to those of the *Susceptible* class.

The imbalanced datasets can affect the accuracy of most prediction models. Furthermore, the particularities of the dataset, the data mining technique and even the error measure employed to build the model can influence on its final performance [26]. This topic has been frequently discussed in the data mining community and there is a wealth of approaches to deal with it, including the modification of the learning algorithms, changes on the data prior to start the learning process, modifications to the models after their generation, and combinations of the previous approaches [4].

In this work, we study the effect of random oversampling on the model. This technique consists on sampling the observations belonging to the minority class until their number reaches a reasonable proportion to those of the majority class. In this case, we reach to the 1:1 proportion (i.e. there will be the same number of observations of each class in the sampled dataset).

3   Experiment

Our experiments are focused on *Enterococci*, common bacteria of the intestinal tract of humans and other mammals, due to the fact that they may produce severe diseases such as endocarditis, urinary tract infections and bacteraemia [25].

In particular, we focus on *Enterococcus faecium* and *Enterococcus faecalis*. Some enterococcal strains can develop resistance to vancomycin, an antimicrobial used in hospitals for many severe infections. These strains, also known as *Vancomycin-Resistant Enterococci* (VRE), can even transfer the genes responsible for this resistance to other dangerous species, such as *Staphylococcus aureus*, complicating the treatment of patients infected by them [9].

3.1   Dataset

The dataset comprises the information of positive cultures for the aforementioned bacteria from 2010 to 2016 at the University Hospital of Getafe. The data was extracted and prepared using the WASPSS tool (Wise Antimicrobial Stewardship Program Support System), a platform that gathers information from different hospital information systems in order to provide support to the groups in charge of the antimicrobial stewardship within the institution [6,8,20].

Our dataset contains data from a total of 1393 positive *Enterococci* cultures, including both vancomycin-susceptible (1351) and vancomycin-resistant (42) cases. Tables 1 and 2 summarize the features that composed the dataset. They were selected in a two-phase process:

– Firstly, a clinical expert indicated a small set of features (Table 1) that have been related to the prevalence of VRE, such as the hospital ward in which the test was made (i.e. VRE infections are more common in the Intensive Care Unit (ICU) ward), days since the patient left the ICU and previous treatments with antimicrobials.
– Secondly, the dataset was extended with additional information regarding the antecedents of infections and treatments of each patient (Table 2). In particular, the species, genus and family of the microorganisms previously present on patients and the Anatomic, Therapeutic and Chemical (ATC [1]) groups of the antimicrobials administered in the last 90 days were included.

The features consisting on continuous data were discretised in ranges commonly used in clinical practice (e.g. *age* was discretised in ranges such as newborn, paediatric, etc.) and all of them were converted into dummy variables. After the whole process, the dataset was composed of 571 Boolean features plus the class to predict, labelled as *Resistant* or *Susceptible* according to the kind of *Enterococcus* strain found in the observation.

3.2   Experimental Settings

We study the effects of using and combining the aforementioned techniques in the performance of prediction models for antimicrobial resistance. With this aim, we have designed the experiment following a training-validation-test strategy [21]. First, the dataset was split according to the date in which the culture was taken. The data from 2010 to 2015 was used for training/validation and the data from 2016 for testing the generated models. In this way, we expect to reflect the capabilities of the different approaches to deal with the possible drift in data.

Figure 1 depicts the strategy followed during the experiment. Bootstrapping was used, due to the lack of available data, in order to generate 200 different bootstrap samples of the dataset. The standard 10-fold cross validation technique was used to train, validate and tune each model on each bootstrap sample. The resulting model was then tested against the test dataset and its Receiver Operating Characteristic (ROC) curve was calculated.

In particular, the Area Under the ROC Curve (AUC) is used to measure the performance of each model, since it is of common use in clinical prediction models. The complexity of the models is also estimated, since clinical models are intended to be understood and validated by physicians and therefore simpler models are preferred among those with similar performance levels.

There are many complexity measures that are focused on specific modelling techniques, such as the depth of decision trees and the number of rules in rule-based models. However, we consider the number of predictor variables as the complexity measure most appropriate for this experiment. Even though it may not be as precise as other model-specific measures, it can be used to estimate model complexity among the different modelling techniques.

Table 1. Features suggested by an expert clinician that were included in the VRE dataset, along with their distribution in the train/validation and test datasets.

Feature	Values	Dataset	
		Train/Val.	Test
Susceptibility to vancomycin (Class)	Susceptible	96.82%	97.84%
	Resistant	3.18%	2.16%
Culture date	From year	2010	2016
	To year	2015	2016
Gender	Male	58.69%	71.43%
	Female	41.31%	28.57%
Age	Elderly	63.68%	64.94%
	Adult	32.96%	33.33%
	Other	3.36%	1.73%
Patient readmitted in last 90 days	False	58.69%	61.04%
	True	41.31%	38.96%
Days since patient left the ICU	Never at ICU	55.42%	59.74%
	At ICU	25.56%	22.94%
	Other	19.02%	17.32%
Culture type	Exudate	15.23%	20.78%
	Urine	15.40%	19.05%
	Other	69.36%	60.17%
Culture performed after 10 days since admission	True	55.42%	59.74%
	False	44.58%	40.26%
Culture performed within first 72 h since admission	False	76.16%	74.89%
	True	23.84%	25.11%
Hospital ward in which the culture was taken	ICU	25.22%	22.51%
	Surgery	12.74%	12.12%
	Other	62.05%	65.37%
Patient received standard selective decontamination	False	66.95%	66.67%
	True	33.05%	33.33%
Patient received mixed selective decontamination	False	81.15%	76.19%
	True	18.85%	23.81%
Patient treated with antimicrobials in last 90 days	False	66.01%	66.67%
	True	33.99%	33.33%
Patient being treated with cefotaxime	False	79.95%	96.10%
	True	20.05%	3.90%
Patient being treated with tobramycin	False	85.28%	82.25%
	True	14.72%	17.75%
Patient being treated with colistin	False	97.85%	93.94%
	True	2.15%	6.06%
Patient being treated with vancomycin	False	64.46%	64.50%
	True	35.54%	35.50%
Patient being treated with amphotericin	False	98.28%	98.27%
	True	1.72%	1.73%

Table 2. Summary of extra features included in the VRE dataset to study in detail the effect of previous treatments and microorganisms found on each patient. The percentage of patients with a "true" in each feature is also indicated for both the train/validation and test datasets.

Feature	Values	Dataset	
		Train/Val.	Test
Species found in cultures from last 90 days	Coagulase-negative Staphylococci	32.27%	23.81%
	Escherichia coli	25.04%	23.81%
	Other species	69.45%	74.89%
Genus found in cultures from last 90 days	Enterococcus	42.25%	44.16%
	Staphylococcus	42.08%	41.99%
	Other genera	67.30%	72.73%
Family found in cultures from last 90 days	Enterococcaceae	42.25%	44.16%
	Staphylococcaceae	42.08%	41.99%
	Other families	66.87%	72.73%
ATC (level 5) prescribed in last 90 days	Amoxicillin and enzyme inhibitor	41.14%	32.47%
	Meropenem	40.71%	49.35%
	Other level 5 ATCs	87.78%	84.85%
ATC (level 4) prescribed in last 90 days	Third-generation cephalosporins	50.09%	55.41%
	Carbapenems	47.93%	53.25%
	Other level 4 ATCs	91.65%	84.42%
ATC (level 3) prescribed in last 90 days	Other beta-lactam antibacterials	76.59%	74.46%
	Beta-lactam antibacterials, penicillins	58.09%	51.95%
	Other level 3 ATCs	78.92%	77.92%

In the experiments with sliding windows, window sizes from 12 to 42 months were evaluated, moving them in steps of one-month size. Figure 2 depicts an example of the experimental process followed within a bootstrap sample for a sliding window of 12-month size. The last data available for training/validation was used until the window size is reached (e.g. the last 12 months of training data for a window of 12-month size). Oversampling and/or FCBF are applied over this dataset and the model was then trained and tuned based on a 10-fold validation with the resulting data. The best fitted model was used afterwards to predict the resistance in the samples of the next available month of test data and the results were stored. The window was then moved forward, incorporating the predicted month to the training/validation data.

This process was repeated until no more test data was available. The predictions made during the process were then gathered and used to compute the overall AUC.

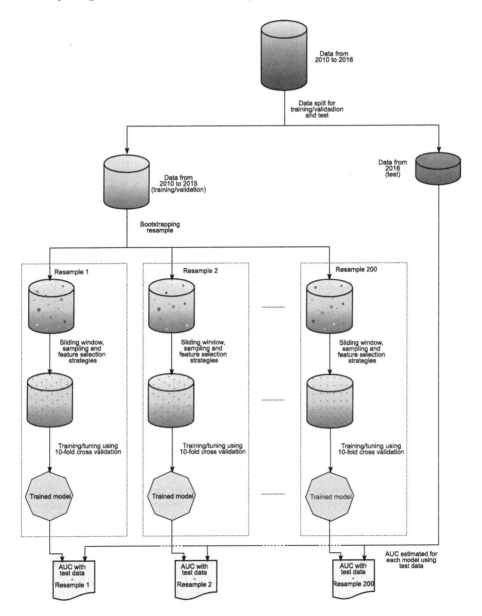

Fig. 1. Schema of the strategy followed to carry out the experiments.

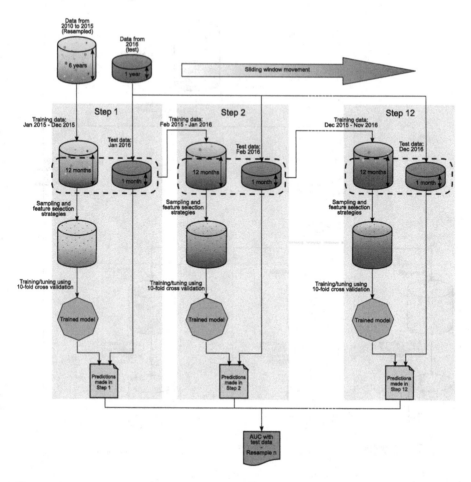

Fig. 2. Schema of the strategy followed to carry out the experiments when using sliding windows (per bootstrapped sample). In this example, we consider a sliding window of 12-month size.

All the experiments were carried out using the R environment[1]. The implementation of logistic regression with LASSO was provided by the package *glmnet* [10]. The parameter λ used by LASSO was fitted for each model during the training/validation step, selecting as final model the one with $\lambda = \lambda_{1se}$, that is, the model whose error was within one standard error of the minimum, as recommended to obtain less overfitted models [10]. The package *caret* [14] was used to train, tune and select the best model for the conditional decision tree (*party* package [13]) and the rule-based C5.0 model (*C50* package [15]). The implementation of FCBF was obtained from the *Biocomb* package [19].

---

[1] R version 3.4.0 from https://cran.r-project.org/.

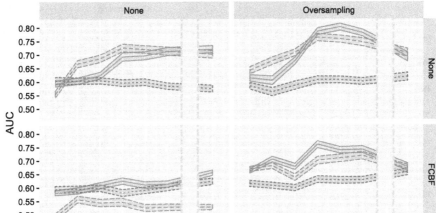

Fig. 3. Mean AUC and the boundaries of its 95% confidence interval for the different combinations of sizes for sliding windows, filtering and sampling strategies. The results over the window size labelled as "none" represent those obtained without applying any sliding window (i.e. using the traditional approach of using all data available for training/validation).

4   Results

Figure 3 shows the mean along with its 95% confidence interval of the AUC obtained with the different combinations of models, concept drift, sampling and feature selection techniques. The best results were achieved by the combination of oversampling, logistic regression and sliding windows of 30 (0.79 mean AUC, C.I. [0.77, 0.80]), 36 (0.80 mean AUC, C.I. [0.79, 0.82]) or 42 months (0.78 mean AUC, C.I. [0.77, 0.79]). These values dropped slightly when also applying FCBF, reaching their maximum value with a sliding window of 30-months length (0.76 mean AUC, C.I. [0.75, 0.77]).

With regard to the complexity of the generated models, Fig. 4 shows the mean number of predictors that were included in them, along with their 95% confidence interval. In this case, the use of FCBF reduces the number of required predictors drastically. In the previously commented cases of high AUC, the models without FCBF were composed of a mean of 62.35, 69.78 and 73.40 predictors, while using this technique reduced them to a mean of 16.28 in the case of a sliding window of 30-month length.

Mean (95% C.I) number of predictors per model

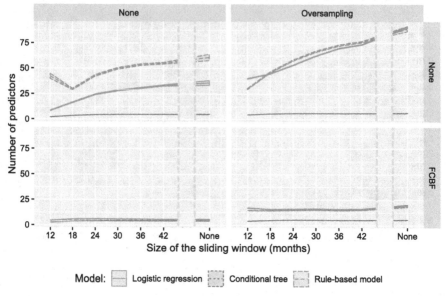

Fig. 4. Mean number of predictors per model and the boundaries of its 95% confidence interval when using different combinations of sizes for sliding windows, filtering and sampling strategies. The results over the window size labelled as "none" represent those obtained without applying any sliding window (i.e. using the traditional approach of using all data available for training/validation).

5 Discussion and Conclusions

In this work, we evaluated different interpretable models and techniques to study the impact of their combination in the prediction of antimicrobial resistance. Logistic regression, decision trees and rule-based models were chosen because of their wide acceptance in the clinical scenario. Among these groups of models, the specific techniques of LASSO, conditional inference trees and C5.0 have been selected because of being well-known and widely used in the data mining community. The same idea was followed when selecting the rest of techniques studied (sliding windows, oversampling and FCBF). Our main intention with this was to expose the problems that arise with each of these baseline techniques in this scenario, so the results could be used as a starting point when selecting and applying more novel interpretable techniques in data mining of antimicrobial resistance.

Our results indicate that the use of oversampling can improve the AUC of models in many circumstances. However, the improvement is more relevant in logistic regression and rule-based models, while in conditional trees it is not so clear. A drawback of oversampling is that the models include more predictors and therefore they are more complex than those generated with the original dataset.

Our results also corroborate that the use of additional filtering techniques is a useful tool in order to reduce model complexity, even when the modelling technique includes a feature selection step (LASSO for logistic regression models and the feature selection at each node in decision trees and the rule-based models derived from them). FCBF was capable to reduce drastically the number of predictors in most cases, yet it had a reduced impact on conditional trees. However, the AUC of the models obtained was reduced slightly. Nevertheless, there can be scenarios, particularly in clinical practice, in which the trade-off between model complexity and performance is welcomed and simpler models with acceptable AUC are preferred.

With regard to concept drift, the use of sliding windows improved the outcomes of the model but only when oversampling was used. The main cause of these results may be the impact on the number of observations for model creation when using sliding windows. Indeed, smaller windows with fewer observations obtained the worst results. However, the fact that windows of size between 30 and 36 months obtained better results than bigger windows corroborate the presence of concept drift within our dataset and encourages the study of similar concept drift techniques in VRE prediction models.

Logistic regression with LASSO obtained the best results in our experiment. However, we do not claim its superiority against other modelling techniques. Despite the fact that a tune of parameters was performed during the train/validation phase, the wealth of possible fine adjustments that can be made (e.g. different split criteria and pruning algorithms in decision trees) makes it difficult to take a grounded conclusion.

Finally, our results of combining oversampling, FCBF and sliding windows with different interpretable models demonstrate that the use of only one technique alone may be not enough to deal with the intrinsic problems of these datasets, and that it is worth considering the combination of different strategies in order to produce the best models with which to predict antimicrobial resistance.

6   Future Work

Even though we used interpretable methods in this work, the evaluation of the usability of the resulting models by clinical staff is still pending.

The results of this work can be used as baseline for comparing novel classifiers and techniques related to imbalance datasets and concept drift [5].

Furthermore, it is well-known that non-interpretable models tend to obtain better prediction results than interpretable ones. In future works we plan to perform a deeper comparative study to quantify the trade-off between accuracy and interpretability of these approaches, as well as the impact of using more advanced classifiers and sampling methods for evolving data in the antimicrobial resistance scenario.

Acknowledgment. This work was partially funded by the SITSUS project (Ref: RTI2018-094832-B-I00), given by the Spanish Ministry of Science, Innovation and Universities (MCIU), the Spanish Agency for Research (AEI) and by the European Fund for Regional Development (FEDER).

References

1. Guidelines for ATC classification and DDD assignment 2018. Technical report, WHO Collaborating Centre for Drug Statistics Methodology, Oslo, Norway (2017). https://www.whocc.no/filearchive/publications/guidelines.pdf. Accessed 28 Aug 2018

2. Adams, S.T., Leveson, S.H.: Clinical prediction rules. Br. Med. J. **344**, d8312 (2012). https://doi.org/10.1136/bmj.d8312

3. Babyak, M.A.: What you see may not be what you get: a brief, nontechnical introduction to overfitting in regression-type models. Psychosom. Med. **66**(3), 411–421 (2004). https://doi.org/10.1097/01.psy.0000127692.23278.a9

4. Branco, P., Torgo, L., Ribeiro, R.P.: A survey of predictive modeling on imbalanced domains. ACM Comput. Surv. **49**(2), 1–50 (2016). https://doi.org/10.1145/2907070

5. Brzezinski, D., Stefanowski, J.: Ensemble classifiers for imbalanced and evolving data streams. In: Last, M., Bunke, H., Kandel, A. (eds.) Data Mining in Time Series and Streaming Databases, Machine Perception and Artificial Intelligence, vol. 83, pp. 44–68. World Scientific (2018). https://doi.org/10.1142/9789813228047_0003

6. Cánovas-Segura, B., Campos, M., Morales, A., Juarez, J.M., Palacios, F.: Development of a clinical decision support system for antibiotic management in a hospital environment. Progress Artif. Intell. **5**(3), 181–197 (2016). https://doi.org/10.1007/s13748-016-0089-x

7. Canovas-Segura, B., et al.: Improving interpretable prediction models for antimicrobial resistance. In: 2019 IEEE International Symposium on Computer Medical Systems (CBMS) (2019)

8. Canovas-Segura, B., et al.: A process-oriented approach for supporting clinical decisions for infection management. In: 2017 IEEE International Conference on Healthcare Informatics (ICHI), pp. 91–100. IEEE (2017). https://doi.org/10.1109/ICHI.2017.73

9. Cetinkaya, Y., Falk, P., Mayhall, C.G.: Vancomycin-resistant enterococci. Clin. Microbiol. Rev. **13**(4), 686–707 (2000). https://doi.org/10.1128/CMR.13.4.686-707.2000

10. Friedman, J., Hastie, T., Tibshirani, R.: Regularization paths for generalized linear models via coordinate descent. J. Stat. Softw. **33**(1) (2010). https://doi.org/10.18637/jss.v033.i01

11. Gama, J., Žliobaitė, I., Bifet, A., Pechenizkiy, M., Bouchachia, A.: A survey on concept drift adaptation. ACM Comput. Surv. (CSUR) **46**(4), 1–37 (2014). https://doi.org/10.1145/2523813

12. Hastie, T., Tibshirani, R.: Generalized additive models. In: Encyclopedia of Statistical Sciences. Wiley, Hoboken (2006). https://doi.org/10.1002/0471667196.ess0297.pub2

13. Hothorn, T., Hornik, K., Zeileis, A.: Unbiased recursive partitioning: a conditional inference framework. J. Comput. Graph. Stat. **15**(3), 651–674 (2006). https://doi.org/10.1198/106186006X133933

14. Kuhn, M.: Building predictive models in R using the caret package. J. Stat. Softw. **28**(5), 1–26 (2008). https://doi.org/10.18637/jss.v028.i05
15. Kuhn, M., Johnson, K.: Applied Predictive Modeling. Springer, New York (2013). https://doi.org/10.1007/978-1-4614-6849-3
16. Leekha, S., Terrell, C.L., Edson, R.S.: General principles of antimicrobial therapy. Mayo Clin. Proc. **86**(2), 156–167 (2011). https://doi.org/10.4065/mcp.2010.0639
17. Lipton, Z.C.: The mythos of model interpretability. CoRR abs/1606.03490 (2016). http://arxiv.org/abs/1606.03490
18. Mayor, S.: First who antimicrobial surveillance data reveal high levels of resistance globally. Br. Med. J. 462 (2018). https://doi.org/10.1136/bmj.k462
19. Novoselova, N., Wang, J., Pessler, F., Klawonn, F.: Biocomb: Feature Selection and Classification with the Embedded Validation Procedures for Biomedical Data Analysis. https://cran.r-project.org/web/packages/Biocomb/index.html. Accessed 28 Aug 2018
20. Palacios, F., et al.: A clinical decision support system for an Antimicrobial Stewardship Program. In: HEALTHINF 2016–9th International Conference on Health Informatics, Proceedings, pp. 496–501. SciTePress, Rome (2016). https://doi.org/10.5220/0005824904960501
21. Ripley, B.D.: Pattern Recognition and Neural Networks. Cambridge University Press, Cambridge (1996). https://doi.org/10.1017/CBO9780511812651
22. Steyerberg, E.: Clinical Prediction Models. Statistics for Biology and Health. Springer, New York (2009)
23. Tibshirani, R.: Regression selection and shrinkage via the lasso. J. R. Stat. Soc. Ser. B (Methodol.) **58**(1), 267–288 (1996). https://www.jstor.org/stable/2346178
24. Tsymbal, A.: The problem of concept drift: definitions and related work. Technical report, Department of Computer Science, Trinity College, Dublin (2004)
25. Van Tyne, D., Gilmore, M.S.: Friend turned foe: evolution of enterococcal virulence and antibiotic resistance. Ann. Rev. Microbiol. **68**(1), 337–356 (2014). https://doi.org/10.1146/annurev-micro-091213-113003
26. Weiss, G.M., Provost, F.: Learning when training data are costly: the effect of class distribution on tree induction. J. Artif. Intell. Res. **19**, 315–354 (2003). https://doi.org/10.1613/jair.1199
27. Widmer, G., Miroslav, K.: Learning in the presence of concept drift and hidden contexts. Mach. Learn. **23**, 69–101 (1996). https://doi.org/10.1007/BF00116900
28. Yu, L., Liu, H.: Feature selection for high-dimensional data: a fast correlation-based filter solution. In: International Conference on Machine Learning (ICML), pp. 1–8 (2003)

Local vs. Global Interpretability of Machine Learning Models in Type 2 Diabetes Mellitus Screening

Leon Kopitar[1]([✉]) [iD], Leona Cilar[2] [iD], Primoz Kocbek[2] [iD], and Gregor Stiglic[2,3] [iD]

[1] Faculty of Mathematics, Natural Sciences and Information Technologies, University of Primorska, Glagoljaska 8, 6000 Koper, Slovenia
leon.kopitar@famnit.upr.si
[2] Faculty of Health Sciences, University of Maribor, Zitna ulica 15, 2000 Maribor, Slovenia
{leona.cilar1,primoz.kocbek,gregor.stiglic}@um.si
[3] Faculty of Electrical Engineering and Computer Science, University of Maribor, Koroska cesta 46, 2000 Maribor, Slovenia

Abstract. Machine learning based predictive models have been used in different areas of everyday life for decades. However, with the recent availability of big data, new ways emerge on how to interpret the decisions of machine learning models. In addition to global interpretation focusing on the general prediction model decisions, this paper emphasizes the importance of local interpretation of predictions. Local interpretation focuses on specifics of each individual and provides explanations that can lead to a better understanding of the feature contribution in smaller groups of individuals that are often overlooked by the global interpretation techniques. In this paper, three machine learning based prediction models were compared: Gradient Boosting Machine (GBM), Random Forest (RF) and Generalized linear model with regularization (GLM). No significant differences in prediction performance, measured by mean average error, were detected: GLM: 0.573 (0.569 − 0.577); GBM: 0.579 (0.575 − 0.583); RF: 0.579 (0.575 − 0.583). Similar to other studies that used prediction models for screening in type 2 diabetes mellitus, we found a strong contribution of features like age, gender and BMI on the global interpretation level. On the other hand, local interpretation technique discovered some features like depression, smoking status or physical activity that can be influential in specific groups of patients. This study outlines the prospects of using local interpretation techniques to improve the interpretability of prediction models in the era of personalized healthcare. At the same time, we try to warn the users and developers of prediction models that prediction performance should not be the only criteria for model selection.

Keywords: Machine learning · Interpretation · Type 2 diabetes mellitus

© Springer Nature Switzerland AG 2019
M. Marcos et al. (Eds.): KR4HC-ProHealth 2019/TEAAM 2019, LNAI 11979, pp. 108–119, 2019.
https://doi.org/10.1007/978-3-030-37446-4_9

1   Background

Type 2 diabetes mellitus (T2DM) is one of the most challenging health problems of the 21st century [21]. The problem is even bigger because of the emergence of T2DM in children, adolescents and young people [31]. T2DM has a negative influence on both healthcare systems and the affected individuals and their families [22]. Thus, there is an urgent need for developing and implementing successful models for detecting those at high risk for development of T2DM and those with impaired fasting glucose (IFG). Moreover, there is a need for developing predictive models for T2DM, which are accurate and can ensure interpretability to gain trust of both service users and healthcare workers.

Prediction performance and interpretability are two of the most critical concepts in modern machine learning modeling. Moreover, interpretability and explainability are two of the key challenges in medical and health care applications of deep learning methods [30]. Interpretability is defined as the ability to explain or present machine learning to the human using understandable terms [7]. Montavon et al. define interpretation as "the mapping of an abstract concept into a domain that the human can make the sense of" and explanation as "the collection of features of the interpretable domain, that have contributed for a given example to produce a decision" [20]. Interpretability of machine learning models is applicable across all types of machine learning, such as supervised learning, unsupervised learning and reinforcement learning [2]. The lack of interpretability in machine learning models can potentially have adverse or even life threatening consequences in different fields of healthcare [2]. Interpretable machine learning techniques can be grouped into global interpretability and local interpretability. Global interpretability is usually used to describe the understanding of how model works with inspection of model concepts, while local interpretability usually refers to explaining each individual prediction [8,19]. There are no clear definitions and ways to measure interpretability. Nevertheless, there are some approaches available for evaluation, such as application level evaluation, human level evaluation and function level evaluation [19]. Other early studies in this field were aiming to address the issue of the trade-off between accuracy and comprehensibility in building ensembles and proposed a novel visual technique for interactive interpretation of the knowledge from the small ensembles consisting of only a few decision trees [27]. Additionally, the researchers also studied local interpretability of machine learning models and tried to propose a metric called operation count in order to measure the relative interpretability of models. They also pointed out that if the number of operations increases the users' accuracy on the local interpretability tasks decreases [25]. If we return to the definition of interpretation and explanation by Montavon et al. we could argue that local interpretability lies much closer to explainability of the model in comparison to more abstract global prediction model interpretability [20].

Most predictive machine learning based models in healthcare provide actionable predictions but in practice they would still need good reasoning to convince healthcare experts in supporting their decisions based on such models. Moreover, healthcare is particularly challenging due to laws and regulations, and medicolegal and ethical requirements [2]. Vellido (2019) stated that it is important to integrate health care experts in the design of data analysis interpretation strategies to improve the model interpretability, if we want to implement the machine learning in clinical and health care practice. Healthcare workers have important role in preventing diseases and health promotion. In the recent years, many clinical prediction models have been developed to identify individuals with T2DM or those at high risk of developing it. Few of those have been using machine-learning techniques, which produce algorithms of greater predictive ability than those developed with multiple logistic regression [23]. But as mentioned before, it is important to observe the interpretability and explainability of the models additional to their predictive performance. Thus, the aim of this paper is to observe the interpretability of the prediction models and explore the possibilities to extract important information on interpretability of the models from the local interpretability techniques, especially in smaller groups of patients that have different characteristics in comparison to the majority of patients. In addition, the focus is mainly placed on the actionable features, since they can be modified during the lifetime and give opportunity to change the course of progress of T2DM.

2   Methods

2.1   Prediction Models and Evaluation

Three different prediction models were used in this paper: Gradient Boosting Machines (GBM) [11], Random Forest (RF) [4] and Generalized linear model (GLM) with Lasso regression [29]. Prediction models were built with an open source machine learning platform *h2o* [1,15]. Performance of prediction models was evaluated using a hold-out validation method (80:20), repeated 100 times. Performance of the models was measured using root mean squared error (RMSE) and mean average error (MAE) metrics.

2.2   Data Sample

Original data consisted of 27,050 records and 111 features. The basic set of features was represented by features from the Finnish Diabetes Risk Score (FINDRISC) [16] questionnaire that is used as a T2DM screening tool in many countries, including Slovenia where the data for this study was collected. The basic FINDRISC set of features consisted of *age, gender, body mass index (BMI), waist circumference, physical activity, daily consumption of fruit and vegetables, a history of antihypertensive drug treatment, a history of high blood glucose,* and *a family history of diabetes.* Only 3,758 records had all FINDRISC survey questions completed. Outliers whose value exceeded or fell outside the 3 × SD interval around a feature mean value ($\overline{X} \pm (3 \times SD)$)) were marked as missing values (NaNs). In the next step, all features with more than 50% missing values were excluded from the analysis. The same procedure was applied to the individual records. Finally, the preprocessed data consisted of 3,723 records, 58 features, and an outcome that represented fasting plasma glucose level (FPGL). All missing values were then imputed using Multiple Imputation by Chained Equations (MICE) method [5]. Bayesian linear regression method was applied over numerical features, logistic regression over dichotomous features and polytomous regression over features with 2 or more levels.

Models were trained and later evaluated on the total of 3,723 patient records with 23 features. This analysis was based mainly on actionable features, whose values can be modified by changing a lifestyle or taking any other action, whilst analysis that are based on non-actionable features cannot reveal potential factors that can be changed in order to the effective prevention of a certain disease. Actionable features cover information about waist circumference, body mass index (BMI), smoking status, evaluation of eating habits and several others, which might have potential negative or positive impact on predictability of FGPL. There were only two non-actionable features included in this study (Age, Gender). The latter features are included in the analyses since they are known to have a significant impact on the predictability of undiagnosed T2DM [3, 16, 26].

2.3   Feature Importance

Feature importance was calculated as the change in loss caused by permutation of feature values for each prediction model separately. Initially, prediction model loss was computed and followed by the randomization of feature values (for each feature separately). In the next step, the model was built using the permuted values to calculate the permuted loss. Feature importance was then obtained as a ratio of permuted and original loss.

$$Feature\ importance = \frac{Permuted\ loss}{Original\ loss}$$

This procedure was then repeated for each feature separately. In the final step, features were ranked by feature importance in the descending order. The feature with the highest feature importance score represents the most influential feature and indicates the global importance of this feature in predicting the outcome [4, 10].

2.4   Local and Global Interpretation

Local feature interpretation was determined according to the Shapley values, later stated as *Phi (Φ) values* [28]. Shapley values were inspired by the coalitional game theory and introduced to machine learning based models' interpretation by Lundberg and Lee [17]. In contrast to the permutation-based method described above where each feature is assessed individually, Shapley values builds on the assessment of combination of features. The predictive performance of every combination of features is calculated with and without the feature we are focusing on. The Φ-value represents a contribution of each feature towards a difference in average predicted value of the model and predicted value for a specific instance [28]. In this paper, we use Φ-values to estimate the local contribution of each feature in predicting FPGL for each instance. Permuted loss based feature ranking described in Sect. 2.3 was used for global interpretation of results. Both, local and global, measures of feature importance were calculated using the Interpretable Machine Learning (iml) library [18] in the R statistical environment [24].

3   Results

Table 1 presents the summary of specific feature values used in this study from the T2DM prediction data. Individuals are divided in three groups based on their FPGL: normal, pre-diabetes and diabetes to allow easier comparison between groups of patients with lower or higher FPGL values.

Table 1. Summary information for T2DM screening dataset.

Feature	Normal FPGL < 6.1 mmol/L (n = 2674, 71.8%)	Pre-diabetes 6.1 ≤ FPGL < 7.0 (n = 788, 21.2%)	Diabetes FPGL ≥ 7.0 mmol/L (n = 261, 7.0%)	p*
Mean (sd) Age	52.7(11.7)	58.5(10.3)	60.9(10.3)	<0.001
Mean (sd) bmi, km/m²	28.5(5.2)	30.3(4.8)	31.9(6.0)	<0.001
Women, %	1582(59.2)	327(41.5)	95(36.7)	<0.001
Smoking status, %				<0.001
1 (non-smoker)	1707(63.8)	439(55.7)	157(60.2)	
2 (smoker)	547(20.5)	174(22.1)	50(19.2)	
3 (former smoker)	410(15.3)	173(22.0)	54(20.1)	
5 (passive smoker)	10(0.4)	2(0.3)	0(0.0)	
Depression (2 weeks), %				<0.001
0 (none)	2290(85.6)	647(82.1)	193(73.9)	
1 (few days)	281(10.5)	105(13.3)	36(13.8)	
2 (more than half of the days)	63(2.4)	21(2.7)	19(7.3)	
3 (almost all days)	40(1.5)	15(1.9)	13(5.0)	
Moderate physical activity (30 min/day), %				<0.001
0 (Yes)	1650(61.7)	434(55.1)	118(45.2)	
2 (No)	1024(38.3)	354(44.9)	143(54.8)	
FPGL (sd), mmol/l	5.3(0.4)	6.4(0.2)	7.9(1.6)	<0.001

*p value of the statistical test performed between the normal, pre-diabetes and diabetes groups, where for continuous values a non-parametric Kruskal–Wallis test was performed, since all features showed significant outliers and for discrete values a chi-squared test was performed.

Table 2. Performance of three machine learning models in prediction of fasting plasma glucose level measured as MAE and RMSE including the 95% confidence intervals.

Metric	MAE	RMSE
GLM	0.573 (0.569 − 0.577)	0.862 (0.846 − 0.878)
GBM	0.579 (0.575 − 0.583)	0.872 (0.856 − 0.888)
RF	0.579 (0.575 − 0.583)	0.871 (0.855 − 0.887)

Initially, we compared the prediction performance of GBM, GLM and RF measured as MAE and RMSE. There were no significant differences in terms of average MAE between the observed methods (Table 2). The confidence interval range of average MAE from 0.569 to 0.583 demonstrates the practical value of separation between patients with normal FPGL and patients with undiagnosed type 2 diabetes.

Since the focus of our experimental setup was on comparison of global and local interpretation results, we first calculated the permutation-based feature importance scores for all features using all three methods. The RMSE was used as a loss metric in feature importance calculations. The results presented in Fig. 1 are based on mean scores from 100 runs of 80:20 hold-out splits of the dataset. The features in Fig. 1 are ordered by their GLM feature importance score as GLM was our baseline model since it offers the highest level of interpretability by observing the regression coefficients.

Observing the results from Fig. 1 it is possible to notice that all three methods strongly agree on the contribution of the age. There are only two more features (gender and BMI) with "positive" contribution in all three compared methods. By "positive" contribution, we mean values above one that indicate higher permuted error in comparison to original error of the model. Permuted error is calculated as an error of the model when randomly permuting the values of a tested feature. To obtain the final score for a specific feature the permuted error is divided by the original error of the model.

To demonstrate the differences between the contributions of features on the global and local level, we additionally observed the local interpretability at the level of individual patients using the Shapley values. This section focuses on three features, where at least the first two of them are usually not used in the undiagnosed type 2 diabetes prediction models – i.e. *smoking status*, *depression* and *physical activity*. If we observe the ranking of smoking status and depression, we can see that they have 'negative' feature contribution on the global interpretability level, while physical activity is even more controversial as it is ranked as fourth and fifth most influential feature by GLM and RF, and one of the least influential features by GBM (Fig. 1).

Figure 2 represents the results of the Shapley values for all patients in relation to the predicted value in each of the three compared machine learning methods. By observing the relation to the predicted value, we observed whether different patterns of local feature importance occur at different predicted risk for specific

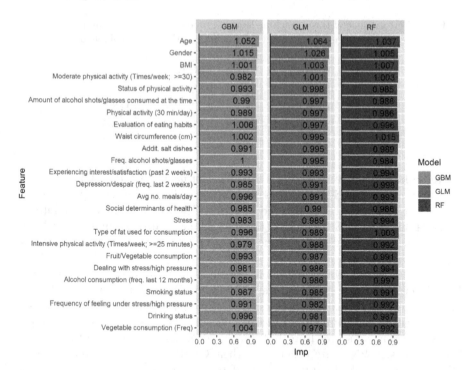

Fig. 1. Feature importance for three prediction models based on feature permutation error.

patients. As it can be seen from Fig. 2, there is no significant trend in terms of local importance of the two features in relation to the predicted risk.

However, interesting patterns can be seen on the y-axis where we plotted Φ-values representing feature importance on the individual level. The results in Fig. 2 show major differences in attribution of local feature importance to individual patients when we compare the three prediction models. In case of depression and smoking status, GBM seems to separate smaller groups of the individuals into very distinct clusters, while GLM based feature importance values mainly reside very close to zero. RF also separates individuals based on feature importance, but much more linearly in comparison to GBM.

It is even possible to observe the two distinct clusters in smoking status and four distinct clusters in depression for GBM, while this is not the case in RF or GLM. The number of clusters corresponds with the number of levels for depression (frequency in the last two weeks) which was measured using a four-level scale ("Not at all", "A few days", "More than half days", "Almost every day"). On the other hand, this is not the case for smoking status that was also measured on a four-level scale ("non-smoker", "smoker", "former smoker" and "passive smoker"). However, it has to be noted that that only an extremely small fraction of participants opted for "passive smoker" as their answer on the smoking status question. The two clusters mainly consist of the participants

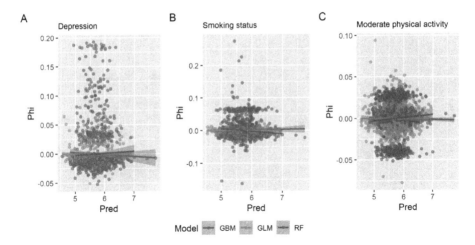

Fig. 2. Comparison of Shapely values (Phi/Φ) for GBM, GLM an RF in relation to the predicted value of fasting plasma glucose level (Pred) for Depression (A), Smoking status (B) and Moderate physical activity (C).

belonging to a group of former smokers on one side and a group of smokers and non-smokers on the other side. In Table 1 it can also be observed that the number of former smokers increases from 15.3% in healthy group to 20.1% in a group of participants with undiagnosed T2DM.

Additional patterns can be observed even in features corresponding to eating habits (Fig. 3). Evaluation of eating habits represented on three-level scale ("Appropriate", "Satisfactory", "Inadequate") is evidently partitioned in three clusters by GLM, while RF does not attribute any local importance value to this feature as measured by Shapley value. It is interesting to note that in the case of GBM, the same feature has a positive impact on FPGL prediction mainly for the patients whose predicted FPGL is below 6 mmol/l. Similarly, feature that indicates an average number of meals per day (three-level scale: "2-times or less", "from 3 to 5-times", "6-times or more") separates cases in two distinct clusters. Since most patients (89.77 %) eat in moderate frequency (3 to 5-times/day), it is likely that for patients who consume 5 meals a day or more, this feature has a higher impact of predicting FPGL in synergy with other features.

As already mentioned, physical activity shows a different pattern where two clusters are formed by the RF with some linearly spread influence on the local interpretability level demonstrated by the GLM. Descriptive summary of feature values in Table 1 shows significant difference between the healthy and participants with undiagnosed T2DM in moderate physical activity. It can be speculated that the 'signal' incorporated in this feature might be picked up from a single or more correlated features in the dataset in case of GBM where no differences in feature contribution on local level were detected in case of physical activity. However, the differences demonstrated in case of the three features analysed on the local level

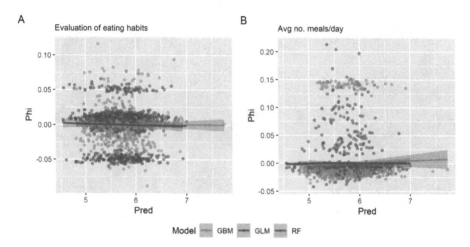

Fig. 3. Comparison of Shapely values (Phi/Φ) for GBM, GLM an RF in relation to the predicted value of fasting plasma glucose level (Pred) for Evaluation of eating habits (A) and Average number of meals per day (B).

point at the differences on both, local and global interpretability level. Therefore, it is important to put greater emphasis on selection of the prediction model also from the interpretability and explainability point of view.

4   Discussion and Conclusions

Our analyses reveal the discrepancies between local and global interpretability based on feature importance metrics for specific groups of patients. Local interpretability offers a better in-depth understanding of a feature importance than a global interpretability alone, hence it can better support health experts at decision making. The results presented in this initial work on comparison of permutation based global ranking of features in comparison to Shapley values based local feature importance scores point at practical implications in the type 2 diabetes mellitus screening example. More specifically, one should be aware that there are groups of patients with features that might not be very influential on the global scale, but might still play an important role for particular individuals. Therefore, it is important to provide such information to healthcare experts who will make decisions based on the prediction models. It is also possible to speculate that proper local interpretability information can significantly increase the trust in prediction model for the healthcare experts, especially in case of models with severely limited interpretability.

Differences in Shapely values between the GBM, GLM and RF models were demonstrated on three examples – smoking status, depression and physical activity. Depression brings an individual to the lack of willingness for selfcare. In this state individuals lose control and begin with extremes such as overeating/undereating or generally speaking malnutrition. Malnutrition is connected to the inadequate and irregular eating Consequently, mental toughness weakens as well, with the lack of a proper social support sedimentary lifestyle strikes in and one might even begin with unhealthy habits they have not had before. It is important to notice that most major prediction model based screening tests such as FINDRISC [16], QDiabetes [13], CANRISK [14] or ADA [3] do not include any of the first two observed features. Even the review studies comparing large number of models report very low number of models that include any of the two observed features, especially in case of depression [6,9]. Observing the global ranking results based on permutation error it is evident that the observed features rank very low or there are big discrepancies in the feature importance scores for the three compared prediction methods. However, when we observe the local importance of all three features it is possible to see large variance in Shapley values indicating large differences in contribution of the three features on the level of individual patients among the GBM, GLM and RF based prediction models. Both ensemble methods, GBM and RF, operates in a different way. The first one is a boosting technique, where the training is based on weak learners. Each weak learner adds up to the overall model performance in a sequential manner. Whereas RF is based on bagging technique, that consists of fully-grown trees where the prediction of overall model is then based on the majority/average voting.

The practical implications of the observed results could include the implementation of modern personalized healthcare information systems where machine learning based prediction models will play an important role in supporting the decision making of the healthcare experts. We assume that local interpretation on the personalized level can significantly increase the trust of healthcare experts towards prediction models. This way we can provide the domain experts with information on features that are important for a particular patient and are perhaps not as important on the global population level. Since some countries already adopted regulations (e.g. General Data Protection Regulation) that place restrictions on automated individual decision making by requiring the right to explanation for each machine-learning based decision, interpretability and explainability of the predictive models are becoming even more important [12]. As already stated this study provides only a limited insight into the differences between the global and local interpretation of the prediction modelling results. Therefore, our future work will focus on detailed identification of characteristics for the identified clusters of patients to support our assumptions laid out in this study.

Acknowledgement. This work was supported by the Slovenian Research Agency grants N2-0101 and P2-0057.

References

1. h2o: R Interface for 'H2O'. R package version 3.22.1.1. Tech. rep. (2019). https://cran.r-project.org/package=h2o

2. Ahmad, M.A., Teredesai, A., Eckert, C.: Interpretable machine learning in health-care. In: Proceedings - 2018 IEEE International Conference on Healthcare Informatics, ICHI 2018, p. 447 (2018). https://doi.org/10.1109/ICHI.2018.00095
3. Bang, H., Edwards, A.M., Bomback, A.S., Ballantyne, C.M., Brillon, D., Callahan, M.A., Teutsch, S.M., Mushlin, A.I., Kern, L.M.: Development and validation of a patient self-assessment score for diabetes risk. Ann. Intern. Med. **151**(11), 775–783 (2009). https://doi.org/10.1059/0003-4819-151-11-200912010-00005
4. Breiman, L.: Random forests. Mach. Learn. **45**(1), 5–32 (2001). https://doi.org/10.1023/A:1010933404324
5. van Buuren, S., Groothuis-Oudshoorn, K.: Mice: multivariate imputation by chained equations in R. J. Stat. Softw. **45**(3), 1–67 (2011). https://doi.org/10.18637/jss.v045.i03. http://www.jstatsoft.org/v45/i03/
6. Collins, G.S., Mallett, S., Omar, O., Yu, L.M.: Developing risk prediction models for type 2 diabetes: a systematic review of methodology and reporting. BMC Med. **9**(1), 103 (2011). https://doi.org/10.1186/1741-7015-9-103
7. Doshi-Velez, F., Kim, B.: Towards a rigorous science of interpretable machine learning. Tech. rep. (2017). http://arxiv.org/abs/1702.08608
8. Du, M., Liu, N., Hu, X.: Techniques for Interpretable Machine Learning. Tech. rep. (2018). http://arxiv.org/abs/1808.00033
9. Fijacko, N., Brzan, P.P., Stiglic, G.: Mobile applications for type 2 diabetes risk estimation: a systematic review. J. Med. Syst. **39**(10), 124 (2015). https://doi.org/10.1007/s10916-015-0319-y
10. Fisher, A., Rudin, C., Dominici, F.: Model class reliance: variable importance measures for any machine learning model class, from the "Rashomon" Perspective. arXiv (2018)
11. Friedman, J.H.: Greedy function approximation: a gradient boosting machine. Ann. Stat. **29**(5), 1189–1232 (2001)
12. Goodman, B., Flaxman, S.: European union regulations on algorithmic decision-making and a "Right to Explanation". AI Mag. **38**(3), 50–57 (2017). https://doi.org/10.1609/aimag.v38i3.2741
13. Hippisley-Cox, J., Coupland, C.: Development and validation of QDiabetes-2018 risk prediction algorithm to estimate future risk of type 2 diabetes: cohort study. BMJ Clin. Res. ed. **359**, j5019 (2017). https://doi.org/10.1136/bmj.j5019
14. Kaczorowski, J., Robinson, C., Nerenberg, K.: Development of the CANRISK questionnaire to screen for prediabetes and undiagnosed type 2 diabetes. Can. J. Diab. **33**(4), 381–385 (2009). https://doi.org/10.1016/S1499-2671(09)34008-3
15. Landry, M., Bartz, A., Aiello, S., Eckstrand, E., Fu, A., Aboyoun, P.: Machine learning with R and H2O: seventh edition machine learning with R and H2O by Mark Landry with assistance from Spencer Aiello, Eric Eckstrand, Anqi Fu, & Patrick Aboyoun. Tech. rep. (2018). http://h2o.ai/resources/
16. Lindström, J., Tuomilehto, J.: The diabetes risk score: a practical tool to predict type 2 diabetes risk. Diabetes Care **26**(3), 725–731 (2003). https://doi.org/10.2337/diacare.26.3.725
17. Lundberg, S., Lee, S.I.: An unexpected unity among methods for interpreting model predictions (2016). http://arxiv.org/abs/1611.07478
18. Molnar, C.: iml: an R package for interpretable machine learning. J. Open Source Softw. **3**(26), 786 (2018). https://doi.org/10.21105/joss.00786
19. Molnar, C.: Interpretable machine learning. a guide for making black box models explainable (2019). https://christophm.github.io/interpretable-ml-book

20. Montavon, G., Samek, W., Müller, K.R.: Methods for interpreting and understanding deep neural networks. Digital Signal Proc. **73**, 1–15 (2018). https://doi.org/10.1016/J.DSP.2017.10.011

21. Narayan, K.V.: Type 2 diabetes: why we are winning the battle but losing the war? 2015 Kelly West Award lecture. Diabetes Care **39**(5), 653–663 (2016). https://doi.org/10.2337/dc16-0205

22. Ogurtsova, K., et al.: IDF diabetes atlas: global estimates for the prevalence of diabetes for 2015 and 2040. Diabetes Res. Clin. Pract. **128**, 40–50 (2017). https://doi.org/10.1016/j.diabres.2017.03.024

23. Olivera, A.R., et al.: Comparison of machine-learning algorithms to build a predictive model for detecting undiagnosed diabetes - ELSA-Brasil: accuracy study. Sao Paulo Med. J. **135**(3), 234–246 (2017). https://doi.org/10.1590/1516-3180.2016.0309010217

24. R Development Core Team: R: A Language and Environment for Statistical Computing. R Foundation for Statistical Computing (2016). https://doi.org/10.1007/978-3-540-74686-7

25. Slack, D., Friedler, S.A., Scheidegger, C., Roy, C.D.: Assessing the local interpretability of machine learning models (2019), http://arxiv.org/abs/1902.03501

26. Štiglic, G., Fijačko, N., Stožer, A., Sheikh, A., Pajnkihar, M.: Validation of the finnish diabetes risk score (FINDRISC) questionnaire for undiagnosed type 2 diabetes screening in the Slovenian working population. Diabetes Res. Clin. Pract. **120**, 194–197 (2016). https://doi.org/10.1016/j.diabres.2016.08.010

27. Stiglic, G., Mertik, M., Podgorelec, V., Kokol, P.: Using visual interpretation of small ensembles in microarray analysis. In: Proceedings - IEEE Symposium on Computer-Based Medical Systems, vol. 2006, pp. 691–695. IEEE (2006). https://doi.org/10.1109/CBMS.2006.169

28. Štrumbelj, E., Kononenko, I.: Explaining prediction models and individual predictions with feature contributions. Knowl. Inf. Syst. **41**(3), 647–665 (2014). https://doi.org/10.1007/s10115-013-0679-x

29. Tibshiranit, R.: Regression shrinkage and selection via the Lasso. J. R. Statist. Soc. B **58**(1), 267–288 (1996)

30. Alfredo, V.: The importance of interpretability and visualization in machine learning for applications in medicine and health care. Neural Comput. Appl. 1–15. https://doi.org/10.1007/s00521-019-04051-w

31. Zimmet, P.Z., Magliano, D.J., Herman, W.H., Shaw, J.E.: Diabetes: a 21st century challenge. Lancet Diabetes Endocrinol. **2**(1), 56–64 (2014). https://doi.org/10.1016/S2213-8587(13)70112-8

A Computational Framework Towards Medical Image Explanation

Xuwen Wang[1] , Yu Zhang[2], Zhen Guo[1], and Jiao Li[1(✉)]

[1] Institute of Medical Information and Library, Chinese Academy of Medical Sciences and Peking Union Medical College, Beijing 100020, China
li.jiao@imicams.ac.cn
[2] Genertec Universal Medical Group Company Limited, Beijing 100000, China

Abstract. In this paper, a unified computational framework towards medical image explanation is proposed to promote the ability of computers on understanding and interpreting medical images. Four complementary modules are included, such as the construction of Medical Image-Text Joint Embedding (MITE) based on large-scale medical images and related texts; a Medical Image Semantic Association (MISA) mechanism based on the MITE multimodal knowledge representation; a Hierarchical Medical Image Caption (HMIC) module that is visually understandable to radiologists; and a language-independent medical imaging report generation prototype system by integrating the HMIC and transfer learning method. As an initial study of automatic medical image explanation, preliminary experiments were carried out to verify the feasibility of the proposed framework, including the extraction of large scale medical image-text pairs, semantic concept detection from medical images, and automatic medical imaging reports generation. However, there is still a great challenge to produce medical image interpretations clinically usable, and further research is needed to empower machines explaining medical images like a human being.

Keywords: Medical image explanation · Medical Image-Text Joint Embedding · Medical Image Semantic Association · Hierarchical Medical Image Caption · Medical imaging reports generation

1 Introduction

Medical images provide rich information for assisting doctors in disease screening, early diagnosis, treatment decision making and prognosis evaluation. With the rapid growth of digital medical image data and the remarkable progress of artificial intelligence, the interdisciplinary research of medical imaging and advanced intelligent technologies has become the key development objective of imaging omics [1].

Advanced intelligent technologies, such as computer vision, natural language understanding and deep learning, showed excellent performance in medical imaging applications, e.g., medical image classification and recognition, positioning and detection, organ and lesion segmentation [2]. However, during the imaging examination, radiologists not only recognize abnormal lesions from medical images, but also describe their findings

© Springer Nature Switzerland AG 2019
M. Marcos et al. (Eds.): KR4HC-ProHealth 2019/TEAAM 2019, LNAI 11979, pp. 120–131, 2019.
https://doi.org/10.1007/978-3-030-37446-4_10

and impressions with natural language, and write clinically understandable imaging reports according to the imaging diagnostic guidelines. Clear, accurate and readable descriptions in imaging reports are the basis of semantically lossless communication between patients and doctors from different departments.

At present, the research of computer-aided medical image understanding mainly focus on the limited image labelling or annotation. It is more challenging for computers to read and interpret imaging findings reasonably like a human being. For one thing, the visual features of medical images with different sources, modes and parameters vary greatly, and the uncertainty and fuzziness of medical images increase the difficulty of image interpretation. For another thing, medical expertise is required to explain imaging findings, especially for the unobserved symptom or a disease in transformation. So, how to enhance the ability of medical image understanding and explanation is of great significance for promoting human-machine interaction and collaboration in the field of medical imaging.

By integrating multimodal data mining and natural language processing technologies, such as medical image concept detection, medical image caption prediction, imaging report generation, etc., biomedical and information science researchers tried to reveal the insights of medical images based on available annotated medical image corpora.

Medical Image Corpora. A multimodal corpus containing medical images and their natural language description, such as annotations, semantic concept labels, captions and reports, is important for medical image explanation. Several open-access medical image datasets, e.g., Chest X-ray8 [3], OpenI [4] and LIDC-IDRI [5] have been released to support the data-driven research on medical image analysis. To enhance the machine learning methods on medical image interpretation, the CLEF Cross Language Image Retrieval Track (ImageCLEF) released multiple large scale datasets containing medical images with related concepts and captions derived from biomedical literature [6–9]. On the basis of ImageCLEFcaption 2018 collection, our image semantic group built an improved ImageSem dataset for the medical image concept detection task [10].

Medical Image Labelling. Supervised learning methods are often employed to annotate medical images based on manual labeled datasets, in which structured or semi-structured medical concepts are used as the semantic labels (e.g., disease, location, lesion and organs) [11]. ImageCLEF launched ImageCLEFcaption evaluation tasks for large-scale medical image concept detection and medical Image caption prediction, the participants generally applied deep learning methods to predict semantic concepts or captions for medical images [6–9]. Wang et al. combined a transfer learning-based multi-label classification model and an image retrieval-based topic modelling method to identify multiple semantic concepts from medical images based on a reconstructed concept detection dataset [10].

Medical Image Caption. The Encoder-Decoder framework is popular used for predicting image captions [12–14]. By introducing visual attention mechanism, multiple captions can be predicted for different regions of images [15–17]. Hasan et al. proposed an attention-based deep learning framework for medical image caption prediction [18], they also classified images based on the modality, e.g. CT scan, MRI etc. to generate better captions.

Imaging Report Generation. Medical imaging reports often describe the content of images sequentially, e.g., the body structure, normal appearance, abnormal or suspicious abnormal appearances. Generating medical imaging reports contributes to facilitate the human-machine interactive diagnosis practice. Some researchers tried to generate medical imaging reports automatically with medical image labelling and image caption technologies. Zhang et al. generated semi-structured pathological reports of five clinical topics [19]. Jing et al. established a multi-task learning framework for joint prediction of labels and sentences, and generated English medical imaging reports [20]. Wang et al. proposed the TieNet network to classify X-ray chest radiographs and generate simple English reports [21].

Despite the progress in the research of medical image analysis, there is still a great room for clinically understandable medical image explanation [22]. First, the current study of medical image labelling was limited to a small amount of labels with respect to low-level visual features, but a reasonable medical image representation is still needed to capture the semantic association based on the relevance of multi-modal data. Second, most current work used a small number of keywords as "semantic seeds" to generate sentences and paragraphs, which are lack of interpretability for radiologists and clinicians. Third, the clinical usability of medical image explanation has not been verified or evaluated, especially in Chinese intelligent-assisted diagnosis scenarios.

In this study, we investigate the problem of promoting the ability of computers to better understand and describe medical images, and propose a unified computational framework towards medical image explanation, which integrates state of art technologies for multimodal semantic analysis, from building multimodal knowledge representation, to discovering association factors of medical images, then predicting understandable natural language descriptions for medical images, finally, generating Chinese imaging reports and carrying out a usability verification.

This paper is organized as follows: Sect. 2 is the overview of the medical image explanation framework, we also summarize the methods applied to each function module. Section 3 describes our preliminary experiments to verify the feasibility of the proposed framework. Section 4 makes a brief conclusion and discuss the further work.

2   Framework of Medical Image Explanation

In this section, we introduce the framework of medical image explanation, which is designed according to the process of image reading and interpretation, including four complementary modules: (1) learning a Medical Image-Text Joint Embedding (MITE) on the basis of large-scale medical images and relevant texts; (2) modeling the Medical Image Semantic Association (MISA) based on the MITE multimodal knowledge representation; (3) predicting explainable Hierarchical Medical Image Caption (HMIC); (4) developing a language-independent medical imaging reports generation prototype system by integrating HMIC model with transfer learning method. We also evaluate the feasibility of the prototype system by human-machine interaction experiments. Figure 1 shows the workflow of proposed framework.

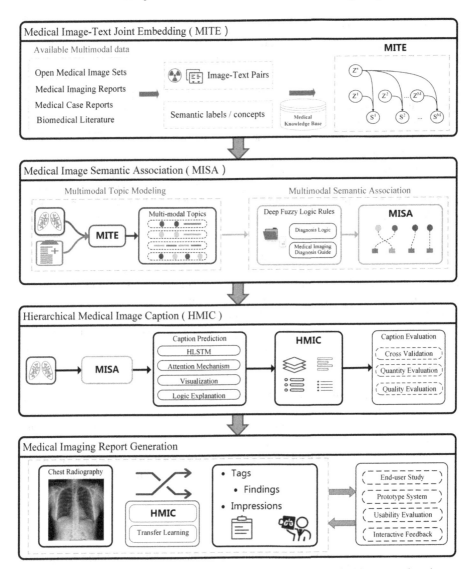

Fig. 1. Overview of the unified computational framework for medical image explanation

2.1 Medical Image-Text Joint Embedding

In a realistic imaging examination, the description of the imaging manifestations written by the radiologists is strictly in accordance with the imaging display, which shows objective consistency and relevance between the medical image and the text. Specifically, "normal findings" usually describe the tissues, structures and organs, and exclude the possible lesions, while "abnormal findings" focus on the detailed description of lesion, such as position and distribution, number and size, shape and edge, density and evenness, surrounding conditions, functional changes, etc.

Learning generalized medical "image-text" joint representation is an important basis for capturing high-quality multimodal semantic features. To explore the multimodal semantic relevance, we refer to the fusion representation theory of multimodal data and construct the Medical Image-Text Joint Embedding (MITE) based on open access medical images, medical imaging reports, case reports and scientific descriptions from biomedical literature.

First, multimodal medical data were preprocessed and normalized, and then medical "image-text" pairs as well as semantic labels were extracted. Second, different from the formal multimodal data representation methods that only focus on common elements, we consult the idea of the partitioned variational autoencoder model proposed by Hsu et al. [23], and learned the Medical Image-Text Joint Embedding (MITE) that represent both common elements of multi-modal space and the elements related to the single-modal space. Medical knowledge bases were also introduced to provide normative descriptions.

2.2   Medical Image Semantic Association

In this study, it is assumed that medical images with similar visual features (e.g., lesion, morphology, edge, peripheral conditions, etc.) have similar high-level semantic descriptions of normal, abnormal, or suspected abnormal manifestations. Therefore, the latent semantic association between medical images can be viewed as the measurement of cross-modal topical relevance. The Medical Image Semantic Association (MISA) model is constructed based on the MITE representation.

First, medical images and corresponding descriptions are represented as vectors by the MITE. Second, the distribution of multi-modal semantic topics of medical images can be modeled using the topic model theory, as suggested in [12]. For a given medical image, the multimodal samples with similar neighborhood structure were found and the similarity of multimodal topics were calculated. Third, using the multimodal topic distribution as high-level semantic feature descriptors, deep fuzzy logic rules [24, 25] were designed according to the diagnosis logic in the medical imaging diagnosis guide for summarizing and interpreting the abnormal appearance in medical images.

2.3   Hierarchical Medical Image Caption

A typical imaging report wrote by radiologists contains orderly comprehensive description in accordance with the image display, such as the body structure, normal appearance, abnormal or suspicious anomaly areas. The descriptions about positive and negative symptom are crucial for diagnosis or differential diagnosis. Linguistically, it often include "Findings" and "Impression/Diagnosis", in the form of phrases, sentences and paragraphs. The "Findings" often contain multiple sentences about normal or abnormal expressions, and provide important evidences for the "Impression". The latter consists imaging diagnosis or suggestions with different semantic tendencies, such as negative, positive or suspicious, and provides diagnostic evidence to clinicians.

We predicted semantically related topics for multimodal medical images based on the MISA model, and introduced the multi-modal topics as a restraint to the language generation model. Hierarchical medical image captions (HIMC) associated with a particular region of medical images were generated with the attention mechanism automatically, including keywords, sentences and paragraphs granularity.

To better understanding and tracing the imaging manifestations, we employed the visualization method of neural network features [26, 27] to interpret the process of medical image caption generation visually and logically. Then we carried out the professional manual evaluation and analysis, as well as the quantitative and qualitative evaluation of multimodal topic modelling and image caption prediction.

2.4 Medical Imaging Report Generation

Radiologists often spend a lot of time to write imaging reports, most of which contain similar descriptions of normal appearances. They also have a need to quickly review past imaging data and locate similar case images and reports. So, we selected the explanation of chest radiography under the intelligent-assisted diagnostic scenarios as a specific issue.

By integrating the HMIC model and the transfer learning method, we designed a language-independent imaging report generation prototype system that can assist radiologists in writing imaging reports. The evaluation of the clinical usability of machine generated imaging reports can be performed via human-machine interaction introduced into the imaging examination workflow.

3 Preliminary Experiments

To verify the feasibility of the proposed framework, we carried out some preliminary experiments, such as collecting a large-scale medical image-text dataset as the foundation of multimodal knowledge representation, identifying semantic concepts from medical images, and developing a medical imaging report generation prototype system.

3.1 Collecting Large Scale Medical Image-Text Pairs

The high-quality dataset of medical image-text pairs provides the basis for the construction of medical image-text joint embedding. In this section, we collected a multimodal dataset from the open access medical imaging reports, case reports, PubMed scientific literature and other medical image descriptions. Table 1 shows the main open access data sources contribute to the experimental dataset. A total of 7,778,235 medical "image-text" pairs were automatically extracted, pre-processed and normalized.

Figure 2 shows an example of medical images and related descriptions extracted from a biomedical literature, which talks about a patient suffering the dissecans disease. It can be observed that, different images are connected with texts from corresponding image captions, context and the surrounding texts. Semantic concepts were also labelled automatically using the Metamap tool [28], the concepts in red boxes represent the same semantic labels from different medical images. A local biomedical image and text retrieval system was then constructed based on the image-text pairs using the open source search engine LIRE [29].

Table 1. Open access data resources for collecting medical image-text pairs

Datasets	Data sources	Data type and amount
ImageCLEFcaption (2017–2019)	http://www.imageclef.org/	406,928 radiology images and related concepts and captions
ChestX-ray14	https://nihcc.app.box.com/v/ChestXray-NIHCC	30,805 patients with 112,120 chest X-ray, 14 disease labels
LIDC/IDRI	https://wiki.cancerimagingarchive.net/display/Public/LIDC-IDRI	1,018 cases with chest CT images and annotation of pulmonary nodules
LUNA16	https://luna16.grand-challenge.org/home/	888 cases with chest CT images and annotation of lesions
Data Science Bowl 2017	https://www.kaggle.com/c/data-science-bowl-2017/data	1,000 chest CT images
Stanford Imaging Datasets	http://langlotzlab.stanford.edu/imaging-datasets/	1,000 chest X-ray, 831 skeleton tumor cases, 4,000 mammograms.
TCIA	https://www.cancerimagingarchive.net/	35,000 case reports
IU Chest X-ray	https://openi.nlm.nih.gov/faq.php	7,470 chest X-ray and 3,955 imaging reports
OpenI	https://openi.nlm.nih.gov/	5,000 case reports
PubMed	https://www.ncbi.nlm.nih.gov/pmc/	1,828,575 archives

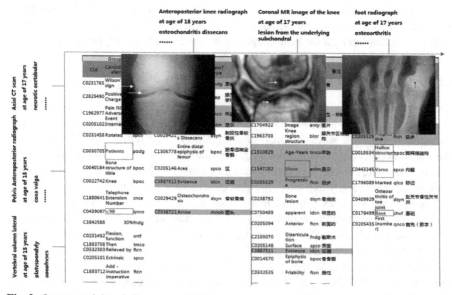

Fig. 2. Images and descriptions extracted from open access medical images and related texts, the red box is the semantic label annotated automatically using the UMLS terms. (Color figure online)

3.2 Identifying Semantic Concepts from Medical Images

Identifying semantic concepts from medical images contributes to promoting the efficiency of medical image analysis. We proposed a two-stage model to detect semantic concepts from large-scale medical images, including the medical image pre-classification based on different body parts (e.g., "abdomen", "chest", "head and neck" and "skeletal muscle"), and the transfer learning-based multi-label classification (MLC) model [30]. For a given medical image, the computer firstly determine which body part the given image belongs to. After the pre-classification step, multiple labels will be predicted by the multi-label classification model (the Inception V3 model trained on the corresponding subset). Different post-processing strategies were also employed, such as filtering low-frequency concepts, selecting top N concepts, or concepts with score above a specific threshold, etc.

Experiments were conducted based on the ROCO dataset [9], and the two-stage concept detection method achieved a best F1 Score of 0.2235, indicating that the pre-classification based on different body parts contributes to the preferable performance on detecting semantic concepts from large-scale medical images. Figure 3 shows an example of concept detection results. The concepts predicted by the two-stage MLC model matched three labels (in red) with the ground truth, while the unmatched concepts (such as C0102410983129, Lung) was also meaningful to the given image.

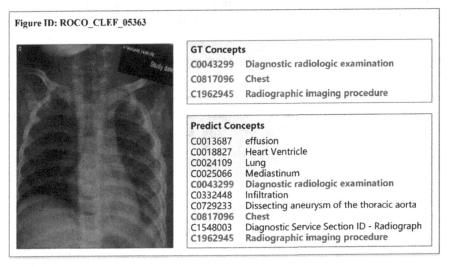

Fig. 3. An example of concept detection based on the ROCO dataset. The GT concepts were ground truth concepts, while the Predict Concepts were results of the proposed model. (Color figure online)

3.3 Medical Imaging Reports Generation

By integrating the medical image concept detection and image caption prediction method, a medical imaging report generation prototype system was implemented to identify chest lesions and generate imaging reports [31]. We preliminarily verified the performance of the prototype system based on the IU Chest X-ray dataset which was available from OpenI [32].

Table 2 shows the comparison of our initial experimental results (ImageSem) with state of art medical imaging report generation models: CMU [20] and TieNet [21]. The evaluation metrics are BLEU [33], METEOR [34], ROUGE [35], and CIDER [36]. Although the multimodal knowledge representation and the multimodal semantic association mechanism have not been introduced to the current system, its performance was close to the state of art models.

Table 2. The performance of medical imaging report generation based on the IU Chest X-ray dataset

Method	BLEU1	BLEU2	BLEU3	BLEU4	METEOR	ROUGE	CIDER
CMU	0.517	0.386	0.306	0.247	0.217	0.447	0.327
TieNet	0.286	0.160	0.104	0.074	0.108	0.226	–
ImageSem	0.342	0.216	0.146	0.1	0.142	0.301	0.317

Table 3 shows an example of the qualitative analysis of medical imaging report generation. It can be observed that there are multiple sentences describing normal appearance in the given image, but the sentences were not perfectly aligned with the abnormal regions, indicating a great room for improving the reasonability of automatic imaging report generation.

Table 3. An example of the medical imaging report generation by ImageSem based on the IU Chest X-ray dataset

Image	Sentence1	Sentence2	Sentence3	Sentence4	Sentence5	Sentence6
Predicted sentences	no acute cardiopulmonary abnormality	no acute cardiopulmonary abnormality	the heart and lungs have xxxx xxxx in the interval	the heart is normal in size	the lungs are clear	the heart silhouette is normal in size and contour
Original reports	No acute cardiopulmonary abnormalities. The heart is normal in size and contour. There is no mediastinal widening. The lungs are clear bilaterally. No large pleural effusion or pneumothorax. The xxxx are intact.					
Predicted labels	normal, degenerative change, opacity, tortuous aorta, cardiomegaly, chronic granulomatous disease, thoracic vertebrae, atelectasis, atelectases, adipose tissue					
Original Labels	Normal					

The above preliminarily experiments provide an initial verification of the feasibility of the proposed medical image explanation framework. However, it can be seen that the description and explanation of medical image using existing common technologies has not been resolved perfectly. In the following work, further research is needed on medical image-text embedding and medical image semantic association, so as to effectively improve the reliability of medical image interpretation. Furthermore, readable Chinese imaging reports can be generated by transfer learning and optimized HMIC model. To evaluate the real feasibility of the proposed framework, end-user studies will also be carried out under the medical imaging diagnosis scenario, and the evaluation of the generated medical image explanation should be performed by professional radiologists via online interaction.

4   Conclusion

This paper proposed a unified computational framework towards medical image explanation. To simulate the process of radiologists reading medical images, four complementary modules were designed by building the medical "image-text" joint embedding based on large-scale medical image-text pairs, establishing the medical image semantic association model based on the joint embedding, predicting hierarchical medical image captions and interpreting the caption generation process visually and logistically, and finally output readable medical imaging reports.

This study contributes to better understanding and interpreting medical images, and provides data foundation for public need of quick access to medical images and reports of similar cases, which is also conducive to online education and research. However, there is still a great challenge to describe and explain medical images with natural language like a human being. Therefore, further research is still needed, such as modelling the semantic association of medical images more effectively, predicting medical image descriptions understandable and reliable to radiologists and clinicians, and generating readable imaging reports that are usable in clinical image-assisted diagnostic scenarios.

Acknowledgments. This study was supported by the Non-profit Central Research Institute Fund of Chinese Academy of Medical Sciences (Grant No. 2018-I2M-AI-016, Grant No. 2017PT63010 and Grant No. 2018PT33024); the National Natural Science Foundation of China (Grant No. 81601573 and Grant No. 61906214).

References

1. Interagency Working Group on Medical Imaging Committee on Science, National Science And Technology Council, Roadmap for medical imaging research and development, 12 (2017)
2. Ma, Q., Kong, D.: A new variational model for joint restoration and segmentation based on the Mumford-Shah model. J. Vis. Commun. Image Represent. 53, 224–234 (2018)
3. Wang, X., Peng, Y., Lu, L., et al.: ChestX-ray8.: hospital-scale chest X-ray database and benchmarks on weakly-supervised classification and localization of common thorax diseases. In: IEEE CVPR 2017, pp. 2097–2106 (2017)

4. Demnerfushman, D., Kohli, M.D., Rosenman, M.B., et al.: Preparing a collection of radiology examinations for distribution and retrieval. J. Am. Med. Inform. Assoc. Jamia **23**(2), 304–310 (2016)
5. Iii, S.G.A., Mclennan, G., Bidaut, L., et al.: The lung image database consortium (LIDC) and image database resource initiative (IDRI): a completed reference database of lung nodules on CT scans. Med. Phys. **38**(2), 9–15 (2011)
6. Eickhoff, C., Schwall, I., Garca íSeco de Herrera, A., Müller, H.: Overview of ImageCLEFcaption 2017 - the image caption prediction and concept extraction tasks to understand biomedical images. In: CLEF 2017 Working Notes. CEUR Workshop Proceedings, CEUR-WS.org, Dublin, Ireland (2017)
7. Garca íSeco de Herrera, A., Eickhoff, C., Andrearczyk, V., Müller, H.: Overview of the ImageCLEF 2018 caption prediction tasks. In: CLEF 2018 Working Notes. CEUR Workshop Proceedings, CEUR-WS.org, Avignon, France (2018)
8. Pelka, O., Friedrich, C.M., Garca íSeco de Herrera, A., Müller, H.: Overview of the Image-CLEFmed 2019 concept detection task. In: CLEF 2019 Working Notes. CEUR Workshop Proceedings, CEUR-WS.org, Lugano, Switzerland (2019). ISSN 1613-0073
9. Pelka, O., Koitka, S., Rückert, J., Nensa, F., Friedrich, C.M.: Radiology objects in COntext (ROCO): a multimodal image dataset. In: Stoyanov, D., et al. (eds.) LABELS/CVII/STENT -2018. LNCS, vol. 11043, pp. 180–189. Springer, Cham (2018). https://doi.org/10.1007/978-3-030-01364-6_20
10. Wang, X., Zhang, Y., Guo, Z., Li, J.: Identifying concepts from medical images via transfer learning and image retrieval. Math. Biosci. Eng. **16**(4), 1978–1991 (2019)
11. Shin, H., Roberts, K., Lu, L., et al.: Learning to read chest X-rays: recurrent neural cascade model for automated image annotation. In: Computer Vision and Pattern Recognition, pp. 2497–2506 (2016)
12. Zhou, C., Mao, Y., Wang, X.: Topic-specific image caption generation. In: Sun, M., Wang, X., Chang, B., Xiong, D. (eds.) CCL/NLP-NABD -2017. LNCS (LNAI), vol. 10565, pp. 321–332. Springer, Cham (2017). https://doi.org/10.1007/978-3-319-69005-6_27
13. Krause, J., Johnson, J., Krishna, R., Li, F.: A hierarchical approach for generating descriptive image paragraphs. In The IEEE Conference on Computer Vision and Pattern Recognition (CVPR) (2017)
14. Liu, C., Wang, C., Sun, F., et al: Image2Text: a multimodal image captioner. In: ACM multimedia, pp. 746–748 (2016)
15. You, Q., Jin, H., Wang, Z., et al: Image captioning with semantic attention. In: Computer Vision and Pattern Recognition, pp. 4651–4659 (2016)
16. Liang, X., Hu, Z., Zhang, H., Gan, C., Xing, E.P.: Recurrent topic-transition GAN for visual paragraph generation. In: The IEEE International Conference on Computer Vision (ICCV) (2017)
17. Xu, K., Ba, J., Kiros, R., et al.: Show, attend and tell: neural image caption generation with visual attention. In: International Conference on Machine Learning, pp. 2048–2057 (2016)
18. Hasan, S.A., Ling, Y., Liu, J., Sreenivasan, R., Anand, S., Arora, T.R., Datla, V., Lee, K., Qadir, A., Swisher, C., Farri, O.: Attention-based medical caption generation with image modality classification and clinical concept mapping. In: Bellot, P., et al. (eds.) CLEF 2018. LNCS, vol. 11018, pp. 224–230. Springer, Cham (2018). https://doi.org/10.1007/978-3-319-98932-7_21
19. Zhang, Z., Xie, Y., Xing, F., McGough, M., Yang, L.: MDNet: a semantically and visually interpretable medical image diagnosis network, pp. 3549–3557 (2017)
20. Jing, B., Xie, P., Eric, X.: On the automatic generation of medical imaging reports. In: Conference 2018, CVPR, pp. 2577–2586, Melbourne, Australia (2018)
21. Wang, X., Peng, Y., Lu, L., et al: TieNet: text-image embedding network for common thorax disease classification and reporting in chest X-rays. In: Conference 2018, CVPR (2018)

22. Kisilev, P., Walach, E., Barkan, E., et al.: From medical image to automatic medical report generation. IBM J. Res. Dev. **59**(2/3), 2:1–2:7 (2015) https://doi.org/10.1147/JRD.2015. 2393193
23. Hsu, W., Glass, J.: Disentangling by partitioning: a representation learning framework for multimodal sensory data, p.1805. arXiv (2018)
24. Angelov, P.P., Gu, X.: Deep rule based classifier with human-level performance and characteristics. Inf. Sci. **463–464**, 196–213 (2018)
25. Gu, X., Angelov, P.P.: Semi-supervised deep rule-based approach for image classification. Appl. Soft Comput. **68**, 53–68 (2018)
26. The Building Blocks of Interpretability Homepage. https://distill.pub/2018/building-blocks/. Accessed 30 Sep 2019
27. LUCID Homepage. https://github.com/tensorflow/lucid. Accessed 30 Sep 2019
28. MetaMap Homepage. https://metamap.nlm.nih.gov/. Accessed 30 Sep 2019
29. Lux, M., Chatzichristofis, S.A.: Lire: Lucene image retrieval: an extensible Java CBIR library. In: Proceedings of the 16th ACM International Conference on Multimedia. British Columbia, Canada (2008)
30. Guo, Z., Wang, X., Zhang, Y., Li, J.: ImageSem at ImageCLEFmed caption 2019 task: a two-stage medical concept detection strategy. In: CLEF 2019 Working Notes. CEUR Workshop Proceedings, CEUR-WS.org, Lugano, Switzerland (2019)
31. Zhang, Y.: Automatic generation of medical imaging report generation based on deep learning, Peking Union Medical College (2019)
32. Demner-Fushman, D., Antani, S., Simpson, M., et al.: Design and development of a multimodal biomedical information retrieval system. J. Comput. Sci. Eng. **6**(2), 168–177 (2012)
33. Papineni, K., Roukos, S., Ward, T., et al.: Bleu: a method for automatic evaluation of machine translation. In: Proceedings of the 40th Annual Meeting on Association for Computational Linguistics, pp. 311–318 (2002)
34. Denkowski, M., Lavie, A.: Meteor universal: language specific translation evaluation for any target language. In: Proceedings of the Ninth Workshop on Statistical Machine Translation, pp. 376–380 (2014)
35. Lin, C.: Rouge: a package for automatic evaluation of summaries. In: Text Summarization Branches out: Proceedings of the ACL-04 Workshop, vol. 8, Barcelona, Spain (2004)
36. Vedantam, R., Zitnick, C.L., Parikh, D.: Cider: consensus-based image description evaluation. In: Proceedings of the IEEE Conference on Computer Vision and Pattern Recognition, pp. 4566–4575 (2015)

A Computational Framework for Interpretable Anomaly Detection and Classification of Multivariate Time Series with Application to Human Gait Data Analysis

Erica Ramirez[1], Markus Wimmer[2], and Martin Atzmueller[1(✉)]

[1] Department of Cognitive Science and Artificial Intelligence, Tilburg University,
Warandelaan 2, 5037 AB Tilburg, The Netherlands
{e.m.ramirezhernandez,m.atzmuller}@uvt.nl
[2] Orthopedic Surgery, Rush University Medical Center,
1611 W. Harrison Street, Chicago, IL 60612, USA
markus_a_wimmer@rush.edu

Abstract. Sensor-based methods for human gait analysis often utilize electromyography capturing rich time-series data. Then, for transparent and explainable analysis interpretable methods are of prime importance. This paper presents analytical approaches in a framework for interpretable anomaly detection and classification of multivariate time series for human gait analysis. We exemplify the application utilizing a real-world medical dataset in the biomechanical orthopedics domain.

1 Introduction

Human gait has been widely studied even though its measurement and analysis continue to be challenging. There are different options for sensor-based analysis, e. g., capturing gait data using accelerometers or marker based tracking, and identifying muscle firing patterns with electromyography (EMG). Here, analysis and interpretation is typically rather complex, e. g., [33]. Then, transparent, explainable and interpretable methods for data analysis are of prime importance.

This paper presents a computational approach based on interpretable analytics methods for human gait analysis. Our contributions are as follows: (1) We present an analytics framework integrating interpretable anomaly detection and classification of multivariate time series for human gait data analysis; for that, we abstract time series into symbolic representations being simple to interpret, for a human-in-the-loop analytics approach. (2) We exemplify the application of the proposed approach utilizing a real-world medical dataset in the biomechanical orthopedics domain of total knee replacement (TKR) subjects, provided by the Arthritis & Orthopedics Institute of Rush University Medical Center.

The rest of the paper is structured as follows: Sect. 2 discusses related work. After that, Sect. 3 outlines the proposed framework and the respective

© Springer Nature Switzerland AG 2019
M. Marcos et al. (Eds.): KR4HC-ProHealth 2019/TEAAM 2019, LNAI 11979, pp. 132–147, 2019.
https://doi.org/10.1007/978-3-030-37446-4_11

approaches. Next, Sect. 4 discusses our results. Finally, Sect. 5 concludes with a summary and outlines interesting directions for future work.

2 Related Work

Below, we first discuss time series clustering and classification, before we discuss approaches for anomaly detection in the time series context.

2.1 Time Series Clustering and Classification

Time series (TS) clustering is an unsupervised data mining technique that groups together homogeneous time series based on a similarity measure, which helps to gain insight into the mechanism that generates the time series, cf. [1,19,27] for a survey. For performing time series classification, a vast number of methods based on specific types of features have been proposed, e. g., [7,10,15,18,20]. Bangall et al. [10] perform an experimental evaluation of 37 different techniques grouped by the mechanism used for extracting the relevant features. In particular, in real life applications, time series data is recorded from multiple channels at the same time, which is an issue for many classifiers because of the high dimensionality. Capturing the interplay of the different signals and using it for gaining relevant information from the data represents a challenge. In this context, several single time series techniques are used after different feature transformation procedures. However, novel algorithms have also emerged, among them Weasel + Muse, which builds multivariate feature vectors using symbolic Fourier approximation (SFA) which are then discretized into symbolic words [28].

Our clustering and classification approach is based on similar ideas, while we utilize additional symbolic representations for interpretable analysis, e. g., cf. [4, 21]. This is complemented by anomaly detection methods which make use of the interpretable symbolic representation.

2.2 Time Series Anomaly Detection

For time series, anomaly detection includes the analysis not only of outliers but also of structural anomalies. The structural anomalies are subsequences of the time series generated from the same process as the others, but usually corresponding to the process' irregularities. Among the different techniques for discovering the structural anomalies, discord discovery has shown to be effective in experiments conducted over different datasets [11]. The first implementation of this concept was HOT-SAX, initially introduced by Keogh et al. [16], which consists of finding the maximally different subsequences to all the rest of the time series subsequences in an effective and efficient manner. For achieving this, the time series is initially transformed into a set of words through quantization using sliding windows and symbolic aggregate approximation (SAX). Later, the search for the most unusual subsequence is performed comparing each word with the rest of the time series using Euclidian distance. However, HOT-SAX has some limitations including that a predefined subsequence size must be indicated; additionally, all the discovered anomalies are assumed to have the same size, which is contrast to many real-life applications.

To overcome these limitations, some techniques have been proposed. Senin et al. [29], proposed a technique that discovers anomalies of different lengths using grammar induction to find a hierarchical structure to uncover irregularities. For that, symbolic transformation techniques using SAX are applied to build grammars. Based on these the rare rule anomaly (RRA) is proposed. RRA works in a similar form as HOT-SAX in the sense that it uses distance measures to evaluate the most different subsequence from the subsequences of the time series. However, its main difference relies on the mechanism in which the subsequences were originally generated. In HOT-SAX they are extracted through the sliding window technique, while in RRA the subsequences are extracted from the inferred grammar and correspond to the subsequences that were not covered by any rule in all the rules. In our proposed approach for anomaly detection, we combine both HOT-SAX and RRA into an ensemble method, considering anomalies with a large overlap in order to support the validation of the proposed anomalies.

3   Method

Below, we first provide an overview on the proposed framework for multivariate time series analysis. Then, we briefly describe the applied dataset. After that, we discuss the approaches for anomaly detection and classification in detail.

3.1   Overview

The proposed approach for interpretable anomaly detection and classification of multivariate time series is shown in Fig. 1. It depicts a computational framework

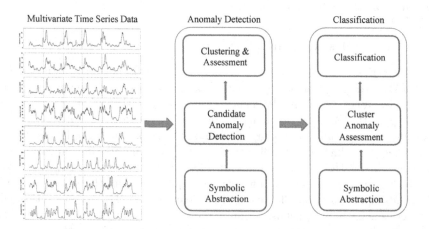

Fig. 1. Analytics framework for interpretable anomaly detection and classification of multivariate time series enabling transparent analysis with a human-in-the-loop.

for such analysis of human gait which is transparent, relying on interpretable methods for anomaly detection and classification.

The process consists of two main steps, which the time series data is provided to (here, we do not include common preprocessing steps on the signals such as, e. g., normalization). First, we identify anomalies using anomaly detection based on discords. In order to identify common anomalies, these are then clustered, and assessed by a human expert in a human-in-the-loop approach, i. e., in an interactive semi-automatic manner. Finally, the obtained anomalies, together with the time series data, are passed to the classification step, where the anomalies can be assessed in context, i. e., by either including or excluding them from analysis and classification. It is important to note, that when data and anomalies are processed and abstracted, e. g., using symbolic abstraction, during assessment the "raw data" can also be inspected if needed, as proposed by the "Mining and Analysis Continuum of Explaining" [9] – providing different abstraction levels for assessment, e. g., (multivariate/collective) anomalies, symbolic patterns, and the original data, i. e., the raw signal information, facilitating the human-in-the-loop approach.

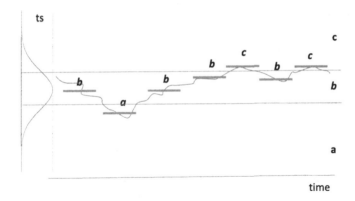

Fig. 2. Piecewise aggregate approximation employed by, e. g., SAX, for interpretable feature reduction by utilizing symbolic abstraction of time series data.

Central to the interpretable analysis methods is symbolic abstraction of the data, in order to make it easier to understand via feature reduction. One exemplary method for that is the piecewise aggregate approximation (PAA), cf. Fig. 2, employed in the SAX transformation, also similar to the technique employed by the symbolic fourier approximation (SFA) transformation employed by the Weasel+Muse algorithm for mutlivariate time series classification. Segments of a time series are mapped to an alphabet which can subsequently be processed to words, which – due to their symbolic nature – facilitate analysis and interpretation, in order to allow also explanation, e. g., by detailed inspection in a "drill-down" approach [9,18], as discussed above. For the human-in-the-loop this serves both as a summary, data abstraction, and interpretable representation, which is also suitable for generating patterns that are simple to interpret.

In the medical domain, for the interpretation of EMG data analysis and interpretation is typically rather complex, e. g., [33]. In particular, this refers to the preprocessing and standardization of the time series data as well as the specific signal interpretation. In particular, for EMG data normalization of the signals and cross-subject comparison is difficult to implement using standard approaches. Therefore, symbolic abstraction of the raw data is often useful for enabling cross-subject analysis and also supporting data normalization. For example, normalization of EMG signals to the maximum voluntary contraction for inter-trial and inter-patient comparison is a recommended practice in gait analysis, however, this method has many limitations, especially in pathologic populations. Therefore, alternative methods continue to be proposed but there is still a lack of consensus on the best approach [33]. The transformation of the time series into SAX words for the discord discovery and the multivariate pattern analysis allows the comparison between subjects. In addition some of the features chosen, for example, for the Random Forest classifier (as described below) are non-amplitude dependent and are suitable for analysis of raw EMG signals. Also, since the transformation is performed in a transparent manner, appropriate "traces" of the processing can then also be supplied for explanation, e. g., [9] for a detailed discussion and summary of such "reconstructive explanations". In addition, important features can be directly inspected [7], as a prerequisite for deriving diagnostic profiles [8].

3.2   Dataset

The applied dataset (provided by Rush University Medical Center) contains de-identified information of 25 patients with a replaced knee joint (so-called cruciate retaining knee prosthesis – divided into high functional and low functional subgroups) and 7 healthy participants of a control group; their gait and EMG data were recorded from three successful trials at the participants' self-selected normal speed [24]. Surface electromyography signals were recorded at a sampling rate of 1200 Hz; the EMG signals were collected from eight lower limb muscles, including the tensor fasciae latae vastus medialis, rectus femoris, vastus lateralis, biceps femoris, semimembranosus/semitendinosus, medial gastrocnemius, and lateral gastrocnemius. For the control group of participants, the EMG data were collected from the same lower limb muscles except that the lateral gastrocnemius was replaced by the tensor fasciae latae [2]. Each trial generates an EMG record that corresponds to a time series of 6000 ms and between 3 to 5 gait cycles of different length could be identified by trial. For further details on the dataset and experimental setup we refer to [2]. The EMG data set was provided with an initial preprocessing of the individual signals. Each signal was band-pass filtered in a range from 20 to 450 Hz, rectified, and smoothed using root mean square calculations over a 50-ms window [2]. In addition, an extra column marks the starting and ending point of each gait cycle within the trial, which can then be used for generating the respective instances for analysis. For a detailed discussion, we refer to [2].

3.3 Anomaly Detection

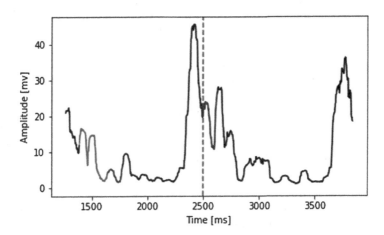

Fig. 3. Time series including two gait cycles of the trial. The red vertical lines correspond to the start/end of a gait cycle. In red, one of the discovered discords that was chosen after eliminating its self-match neighbors (cccaabb, 1384). In blue, two time series segments which have the same SAX word/pattern representation (cccaaac, 1645, 2498). (Color figure online)

In order to enhance interpretability of the results, we applied symbolic representations of the time series for detecting the anomalies, which can then also be mapped back to the time series format. Figure 3 shows an example. In addition, as a mechanism for supporting the validation of the anomalies, two different algorithms for identifying the discords were used, HOT-SAX and RRA, and only the common ones were considered as the discords of the respective signal.

The first method used to discover the anomalies was HOT-SAX, which detects the more rare subsequences as the one with the largest distance to the others. Before comparing the subsequences, the piecewise aggregate approximation (PAA) is applied, transforming the time series to a symbolic representation; for the current research, the size of the subsequences was established as seven. Next, an array of SAX words is generated from new subsequences created by sliding a window of length n across the time series and discretizing them into words through the PPA/SAX approximation. The size of the sliding window was defined after testing different lengths and the window size that reports discords with a higher overlapping between HOT-SAX and RRA corresponds to the 10% of the gait-cycle length average. Finally, the comparison of the subsequences was performed using the Euclidian distance metric, and the ten most unusual subsequences were returned; it is worth to highlight that the discovered anomalies in a signal have equal length and equivalence to the window size. The second technique used for finding the discords was RRA, which initially converts the time series to the PPA/SAX representation. After that, the algorithm generates a grammar by replacing any repeated two adjacent symbols by new symbols called rules. Finally, RRA performs an evaluation for finding the subsequences whose Euclidian distance to their nearest non-self-match is the largest. RRA was evaluated with the same window size parameter established for HOT-SAX. Since for RRA the window size does not determine the final length of the discords, the resulting anomalies per time series were of different sizes. Finally, after running both algorithms, the resulting time series discords have different lengths and starting points; common anomalies to both techniques were selected, where the starting point' distance is less than the smaller window size.

To identify a possible set of common anomalies among the patients, discords from different patients, but belonging to the same muscle, were grouped using hierarchical clustering with dynamic time warping as the dissimilarity measure. Before applying this procedure, the anomalies were z-normalized and set to the same size using linear interpolation. Finally, the effect of each flat cluster on the gait uniqueness patterns was evaluated by removing the cluster discords from the EMG signals and running the classification with the kNN algorithm. The cluster that maximized the accuracy after being removed from the signals and had the larger amount of discords was selected as the group that could reflect similarities among the patients. It is worth noting that not all the cluster anomalies were eliminated; only those with an overlapping percentage between RRA and HOT-SAX over 50%. Finally, this process was performed over each muscle and each of the TKR groups (complete, high functional, low functional group).

3.4   Classification

The first classification task was focused on evaluating the gait uniqueness patterns among the TKR patients. Firstly, the classification of individual subjects was performed over the complete TKR group; afterwards, the dataset was segmented into high and low functional groups. Moreover, to measure the influence of the discords in the classifiers' performance, all the experiments were conducted before and after removing the complete set of discords and the subsets selected in the clustering procedure. The second classification task was oriented to measure the capacity to distinguish the EMG signals of the control group from the signals of the two TKR subgroups. Again, to measure the influence of the discords, all the experiments were conducted before and after removing the complete set of discords and the subset selected in the clustering procedure.

For learning the classifier(s), the dataset was initially split into two partitions, the training set and the test set comprising 75% and 25% of the data respectively. Then, cross-validated grid search or k-fold cross-validation, depending on the algorithm implementation, were used in the evaluation of the hyperparameters and in the features filtering strategies. For both cross-validation techniques, the training set was used to perform a three-fold cross-validation. Even though, some strategies for oversampling the dataset were attempted, in most of the cases it led to lower performance. However, in the multivariate case, oversampling was used, since the internal validation procedure could not be modified and only through oversampling, the performance of the classifier could be tuned.

Feature Extraction. For EMG signals, there are different features that could be considered. Some studies have used basic statistical measures such as the median, media, and variance, and other ones have calculated more elaborated features such as the Fourier and wavelet transform coefficients. In the current research, the first step for generating the features was to apply the FRESH algorithm [12,13] to the raw signals, which generated on average more than 400 statistically relevant features for each time series. Furthermore, different FRESH features were selected depending on the classification task: gait unique patterns or evaluation between the groups. After, reviewing the features that were extracted in at least half of the muscles, it is worth noting that the common features include not only some basic calculations like the mean, median, and standard deviation, but also specific time series domain like the absolute energy of the time series and the Fourier coefficients. It is also relevant that there is a different subset of features that apply when the time series is complete and when the anomalies have been removed. For instance, the number of peaks and length are not more statistically relevant after the discords removal; however, other features become relevant as the first location of minimum and the value count of zeros. The last one could be considered an effect of the zero-padding approach. The difference in the filtered features is also dependent on the TKR group under analysis.

After feature extraction, the number of variables was over 400, but as the data set has only 304 samples when comparing TKR patients and the control group and only 256 samples when analyzing the gait unique patterns, the number of features became larger than the number of samples, which could compromise the effectiveness of the classifiers. As a strategy for reducing the number of features we applied feature selection using feature importance using the random forest model; the number of trees and importance thresholds were tuned with the three-fold cross-validation procedure. In particular, the random forest model allows for a simple yet effective evaluation of the feature importance even in the presence of a large set of features, in order to facilitate interpretation.

Classification Methods. One of the most commonly used as the benchmark in different comparative studies is the k-nearest neighbors (kNN) algorithm in combination with different distance measures. We applied this algorithm in combination with the Euclidean distance metric; the optimal number of neighbors was determined as $k = 1$ in the experiments. Furthermore, over the relevant filtered features an additional random forest classifier was applied to each muscle. The random forest classifier was selected based on the study by Kelecs and Suba [14], which suggests that for classifying EMG signals of patients with different muscle disorders the Random Forest algorithm performs better among other decision tree-based classifiers. This method was evaluated with the number of trees experimentally determined as optimal when filtering the relevant features.

Additionally, for the multivariate analysis the Weasel + Muse algorithm was applied to pairs of muscles, based on the co-contracting muscle combinations used in previous analyses of the same dataset [2], see Table 1. Co-contracting muscle pairs are muscles that work against each other; while they hinder movement and lower efficiency, they increase stability. In addition, for dimensionality reduction, PAA was also used; in this case, the number of segments was determined as 50, which generated a sequence similar in length to the testing datasets' configurations provided with the implementation of the algorithm. For handling imbalanced classes, the SMOTE oversampling procedure was applied over the training set, with the number of neighbors set to one; this parameter was also restricted by the dimensions of the dataset that in the gait uniqueness pattern analysis left the training set with only two samples in the smaller class.

For evaluation, both the binary as well as multiclass accuracy were applied, respectively, for the two-class and the multiclass case, cf. [32] for a detailed discussion on those specifics.

Table 1. Co-contraction muscle combinations

Muscles	Muscles names
S2-S5	Vastus medialis - bicep femoris
S2-S6	Vastus medialis - semimembranosus/semitendinosus
S2-S7	Vastus medialis - medial gastrocnemius
S3-S5	Rectus femoris - bicep femoris
S3-S6	Rectus femoris - semimembranosus/semitendinosus
S3-S7	Rectus femoris - medial gastrocnemius
S4-S5	Vastus lateralis - bicep femoris
S4-S6	Vastus lateralis - semimembranosus/semitendinosus
S4-S7	Vastus lateralis - medial gastrocnemius

4   Results

In the following, we outline our results concerning anomaly detection, and subsequent classification in a univariate and multivariate manner, both concerning individual gait classification as well as distinguishing between case and control groups of total knee replacement (TKR) for both the high functional and low functional subgroups.

4.1 Anomaly Detection

The search for the ten more unusual subsequences along the 72 trials generated 5760 discords, which after filtering to the common to HOT-SAX and RRA were reduced to 3891, an average of 7 anomalies per trial, equivalent in average to the 17% of the signal. Using single visual inspection as the time series has low regularity, the anomalies are not obvious, cf. Fig. 4). However, the symbolic representation facilitates inspection of the discords, together with the abstraction into words, which makes the candidate anomalies more interpretable.

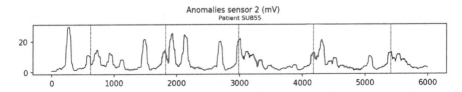

Fig. 4. Discords visualization in the time series. In red the common discords to HOT-SAX and RRA. The X axis represents the time. The y-axis represents the signal's amplitude in mV. The blue vertical lines correspond to the start/end of a gait cycle (Color figure onlione)

Overall, the percentage of overlap between both algorithms gives support to the discovered anomalies, which along the complete dataset reported an overlapping of at least half of the discord length in the 79.5% of the discords. This can also be observed by considering more than one time series, cf. Fig. 5. This percentage is also relevant because was used to perform an additional filter before removing the anomalies from the dataset. Finally, the configuration of the length and position of the discords provided by the RRA algorithm were used in the classification and clustering tasks.

After having obtained the single anomalies – as candidate anomalies – anomaly clustering was performed. The evaluation of different thresholds for creating the flat clusters generated several groups; from them, for each patients' group and muscle one cluster was selected as the set that could represent similarities among the patients. Even though, the cluster anomalies belong to several patients and trials, and the discords' amplitude and location are different, the shape similarity prevails, cf. Fig. 5. Additionally, the clusters generated within the complete TKR group includes anomalies of 12 patients, corresponding to 48% of the group, but when the analysis is separately performed for the high and low functional groups the clusters include a higher percentage of their population, 66% and 85% respectively. This result is in line with the idea of higher similarity within the anomalies in the subgroups than in the complete TKR group.

4.2 Classification

In relation to the experimental settings, the accuracy in the gait unique patterns evaluation increased after the segmentation of the TKR group in high and low functional groups, respectively. Table 2 summarizes the results for the high functional group.

While the accuracy of the classification averaged over all muscles was similar (random forest: 85%), looking at the TKR subgroups vs. the control group, the low functional groups' results indicated a slightly higher differentiation among the EMG signals of the patients, when removing all anomalies. Using the cluster anomalies, it can be observed that for many muscles the removal of the anomalies increases the accuracy scores – pointing at a common set of anomalies for those cases, cf. Table 2. Regarding the applied features, these contain some common features like the Fourier coefficients, but there is also a different subset of features that apply when the TS is complete and when the anomalies have been removed. The analysis of the relevant features then can also lead to a better understanding of the time series and for potentially improving specific domain algorithms for enhancing the time series comprehension.

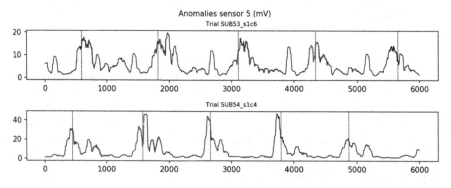

Fig. 5. Example of the EMG signals (muscle 5) of two trials from different patients. In blue and red, the anomalies. In red, the cluster anomalies that maximize the classifier accuracy after being removed from the signals. The Y axis represent the signal's amplitude in mV. The dashed vertical lines correspond to the start/end of a gait cycle. (Color figure online)

For inspection, especially the interpretable approach provided by the symbolic representation which can of course always be related to specific examples of the time series, as well as the transparent classification method given by kNN and random forest facilitated the human-in-the-loop approach, for the discussion with the medical domain experts. When analyzing pairs of muscles, the accuracy scores are also better after splitting the TKR group. In addition, when comparing the best individual muscle's results obtained with the random forest classifier against the multivariate analysis, in at least 60% of the cases the multivariate analysis has a better performance, cf. Table 3 for the high functional group showing the top 5 combinations of the muscles.

Furthermore, it is also interesting to observe that the muscle with the lowest score over all the experiments is the muscle S3, for example, but in the experiment testing the high functional group, its accuracy increases after the cluster anomalies' removal. Again, the interpretability using the symbolic representation facilitated by the alphabet/word representation allows a quite abstract view on the time series (and anomalies) which then can be translated to the specific time series in a "drill-down" view. Also, the applied classifiers can be inspected in detail. Here, the interpretability of kNN and the random forest classifier can be seen as providing different perspectives. While the kNN classifier enables the interpretation of a specific instance in the context of its (most similar) neighbors, the random forest classifier enables to get a view on the overall importance of the specific features, supporting feature interpretation and selection. In the human-in-the-loop approach then both classifiers can complement each other in the respective different phases of analysis, which can also be iterated.

Table 2. Accuracy score: gait unique patterns of the high functional group.

Muscle	Complete time series		w/o anomalies		w/o cluster anomalies	
TS	kNN	Random forest	kNN	Random forest	kNN	Random forest
S1	0.70	0.94	0.48	0.70	0.70	0.94
S2	0.64	0.91	0.45	0.70	0.67	0.85
S3	0.48	0.88	0.27	0.70	0.55	0.94
S4	0.76	0.97	0.39	0.85	0.72	0.79
S5	0.64	0.91	0.33	0.70	0.67	0.79
S6	0.67	0.82	0.39	0.58	0.70	0.88
S7	0.79	0.97	0.27	0.70	0.79	0.85
S8	0.64	0.88	0.21	0.58	0.61	0.76

The column *w/o anomalies* shows the accuracy scores after removal of the complete set of anomalies; *Without cluster anomalies* indicates the scores after removal of the subset of anomalies selected in the clustering process.

Focusing on the effect of the anomalies on the gait unique patterns of the TKR patients, the results indicate that the complete set of anomalies include differentiating elements; there is also a subset of anomalies shared among the patients. On the one hand, as expected, after the removal of the complete set of anomalies the discriminating power decreases approximately 10%, This effect is likely related to the reduction of the data points of the time series, at a rate of about 17% per trial. Interestingly, on the other hand, it was possible to find subsets of anomalies shared among the patients' trials, which once removed increased the accuracy in the classification task, as also observed for the individual muscles. cf. Table 3.

Table 3. Accuracy scores: multivariate analysis (pairs of muscles) for control vs. high/low functional groups. We include the top-5 results for the respective individual combinations.

Muscles	Control vs. High functional			Control vs. Low functional		
TS-TS	Complete	w/o anomalies	w/o cluster anomalies	Complete	w/o anomalies	w/o cluster anomalies
S2-S5	0.96	0.92	0.98	0.91	0.98	0.98
S2-S6	0.94	0.92	0.98	0.96	0.96	0.98
S2-S7	1.00	1.00	1.00	1.00	0.98	1.00
S3-S5	0.94	0.94	1.00	0.93	0.93	1.00
S4-S5	0.96	0.94	0.98	0.89	0.91	1.00

The column *w/o anomalies* shows the accuracy scores after removal of the complete set of anomalies; *w/o cluster anomalies* indicates the scores after removal of the subset of anomalies selected in the clustering process.

5   Conclusions

A challenging task when analyzing anomalies in big and/or complex time series datasets is to provide insights that cover the relevant analytical questions and are understandable to humans. Such computational sensemaking [3,4] in complex data is difficult while it can provide further extended human inference based on the signal inspection. EMG data, for example, provides a lot of information, however, it is rather difficult to interpret. Typically, that requires a high level of domain expertise, the use of expensive technology and a high consumption of time. The proposed approach presents a human-centric mechanism for discovering anomalies using the consensus from two algorithms, integrating the advantages from both – accuracy of HOT-SAX, and length variability of signal anomalies in real-life datasets of RRA. This results in a human-machine approach for interpretable anomaly detection and classification of multivariate time series for human gait analysis, utilizing both symbolic representations, the integration of an interpretable ensemble-approach for anomaly detection, and transparent classification. Thus, raw signals can be abstracted to an integrated data representation, to be then refined to patterns which provide a more comprehensive view on the data, also facilitating the implementation in anomaly detection and classification models, e. g., [5,7]. For the individual methods included in that framework, a human-in-the-loop approach is enabled, in order to provide transparent validation. We have illustrated that in the application of the presented approach on a real-world dataset.

It is important to note, that the integration of the anomaly detection approach and the cluster selection within the classification task provide an additional step for gaining intuition about the effect of the anomalies, specifically the similarities in the anomalies among classes. In addition, the posterior use of the multivariate time series classification allows for evaluating the interplay of the signals; at the same time, it enables a more robust approach when evaluating the effect of the anomalies in the signal. These two elements could be of particular interest in the analysis of complex time series datasets in general, including those from the medical domain. Even though, the proposed approach presents a simple mechanism for finding and evaluating the anomalies' effects, it does not substitute the need for a deeper and contextual analysis in the expertise domain. With the TKR dataset, the multivariate analysis includes the interplay of antagonist muscle activation patterns, however the relationship of the EMG anomalies over other gait parameters requires further research. Ultimately, these technologies will help to identify low-functional and high-functional patients early and help to tailor surgery and rehabilitation programs to their specific needs.

For future work, we aim to tackle those challenges, considering human-centered artificial intelligence approaches, e. g., by developing suitable explicative machine learning and data science methods [3,4,23], extending the human-in-the-loop approaches further. In addition, we aim to extend the medical analysis towards second-opinion systems [25,26], the generation of diagnostic profiles [6,8,17], and advanced decision support [22,30,31] – ultimately towards the implementation into medical surgery and rehabilitation programs.

References

1. Aghabozorgi, S., Shirkhorshidi, A.S., Wah, T.Y.: Time-series clustering-a decade review. Inf. Syst. **53**, 16–38 (2015)
2. Ardestani, M.M., Malloy, P., Nam, D., Rosenberg, A.G., Wimmer, M.A.: TKA patients with unsatisfying knee function show changes in neuromotor synergy pattern but not joint biomechanics. J. Electromyogr. Kinesiol. **37**, 90–100 (2017)
3. Atzmueller, M.: Onto explicative data mining: exploratory, interpretable and explainable analysis. In: Proceedings of the DBDBD 2017. TU Eindhoven, Netherlands (2017)
4. Atzmueller, M.: Declarative aspects in explicative data mining for computational sensemaking. In: Seipel, D., Hanus, M., Abreu, S. (eds.) WFLP/WLP/INAP -2017. LNCS (LNAI), vol. 10997, pp. 97–114. Springer, Cham (2018). https://doi.org/10.1007/978-3-030-00801-7_7
5. Atzmueller, M., Baumeister, J., Hemsing, A., Richter, E.-J., Puppe, F.: Subgroup mining for interactive knowledge refinement. In: Miksch, S., Hunter, J., Keravnou, E.T. (eds.) AIME 2005. LNCS (LNAI), vol. 3581, pp. 453–462. Springer, Heidelberg (2005). https://doi.org/10.1007/11527770_61
6. Atzmueller, M., Baumeister, J., Puppe, F.: Semi-automatic learning of simple diagnostic scores utilizing complexity measures. Artif. Intell. Med. **37**(1), 19–30 (2006)
7. Atzmueller, M., Hayat, N., Schmidt, A., Klöpper, B.: Explanation-aware feature selection using symbolic time series abstraction: approaches and experiences in a petro-chemical production context. In: Proceedings of the IEEE International Conference on Industrial Informatics. IEEE, Boston (2017)
8. Atzmueller, M., Puppe, F., Buscher, H.P.: Profiling examiners using intelligent subgroup mining. In: Proceedings of the 10th International Workshop on Intelligent Data Analysis in Medicine and Pharmacology, Aberdeen, Scotland, pp. 46–51 (2005)

9. Atzmueller, M., Roth-Berghofer, T.: The mining and analysis continuum of explaining uncovered. In: Bramer, M., Petridis, M., Hopgood, A. (eds.) SGAI 2010, pp. 273–278. Springer, London (2010). https://doi.org/10.1007/978-0-85729-130-1_20

10. Bagnall, A., Lines, J., Bostrom, A., Large, J., Keogh, E.: The great time series classification bake off: a review and experimental evaluation of recent algorithmic advances. DMKD **31**(3), 606–660 (2017)

11. Chandola, V., Mithal, V., Kumar, V.: Comparative evaluation of anomaly detection techniques for sequence data. In: Proceedings of the ICDM, pp. 743–748. IEEE (2008)

12. Christ, M., Braun, N., Neuffer, J., Kempa-Liehr, A.W.: Time series FeatuRe extraction on basis of scalable hypothesis tests. Neurocomputing **307**, 72–77 (2018)

13. Christ, M., Kempa-Liehr, A.W., Feindt, M.: Distributed and Parallel Time Series Feature Extraction for Industrial Big Data Applications. arXiv preprint arXiv:1610.07717 (2016)

14. Keleş, S., Subaşı, A.: Classification of EMG signals using decision tree methods. In: Proceedings of the International Symposium on Sustainable Development (ISSD) (2012)

15. Keogh, E., Kasetty, S.: On the need for time series data mining benchmarks: a survey and empirical demonstration. Data Min. Knowl. Disc. **7**(4), 349–371 (2003)

16. Keogh, E., Lin, J., Fu, A.: Hot sax: efficiently finding the most unusual time series subsequence. In: Proceedings of the ICDM. IEEE (2005)

17. Lakany, H.: Extracting a diagnostic gait signature. Pattern Recogn. **41**(5), 1627–1637 (2008)

18. Le Nguyen, T., Gsponer, S., Ilie, I., O'Reilly, M., Ifrim, G.: Interpretable time series classification using linear models and multi-resolution multi-domain symbolic representations. Data Mining Knowl. Discov. 1–40 (2019)

19. Liao, T.W.: Clustering of time series data – a survey. Pattern Recogn. **38**(11), 1857–1874 (2005)

20. Masiala, S., Huijbers, W., Atzmueller, M.: Feature-Set-Engineering for Detecting Freezing of Gait in Parkinson's Disease using Deep Recurrent Neural Networks. CoRR abs/1909.03428 (2019)

21. Merino, S., Atzmueller, M.: Behavioral topic modeling on naturalistic driving data. In: Proceedings of the BNAIC. JADS, Den Bosch (2018)

22. Miller, R.A.: Medical diagnostic decision support systems – past, present, and future: a threaded bibliography and brief commentary. J. Am. Med. Inform. Assoc. **1**(1), 8–27 (1994)

23. Nalepa, G.J., van Otterlo, M., Bobek, S., Atzmueller, M.: From context mediation to declarative values and explainability. In: Proceedings of the IJCAI/ECAI Workshop on Explainable Artificial Intelligence (XAI 2018). IJCAI, Stockholm (2018)

24. Ngai, V., Wimmer, M.A.: Kinematic evaluation of cruciate-retaining total knee replacement patients during level walking: a comparison with the displacement-controlled ISO standard. J. Biomech. **42**(14), 2363–2368 (2009)

25. Puppe, F.: Systematic Introduction to Expert Systems: Knowledge Representations and Problem-Solving Methods. Springer, Heidelberg (2012). https://doi.org/10.1007/978-3-642-77971-8

26. Puppe, F., Atzmueller, M., Buscher, G., Huettig, M., Lührs, H., Buscher, H.P.: Application and evaluation of a medical knowledge-system in sonography (SonoConsult). In: Proceedings of the 18th European Conference on Artificial Intelligence (ECAI 2008), pp. 683–687 (2008)

27. Rani, S., Sikka, G.: Recent techniques of clustering of time series data: a survey. Int. J. Comput. Appl. **52**(15) (2012)

28. Schäfer, P., Leser, U.: Multivariate Time Series Classification with WEASEL+ MUSE. arXiv preprint arXiv:1711.11343 (2017)
29. Senin, P., et al.: Time series anomaly discovery with grammar-based compression. In: Proceedings of the International Conference on Extending Database Technology, pp. 481–492 (2015)
30. Shortliffe, E.H.: Computer programs to support clinical decision making. JAMA **258**(1), 61–66 (1987)
31. Shortliffe, E.H., Sepúlveda, M.J.: Clinical decision support in the era of artificial intelligence. JAMA **320**(21), 2199–2200 (2018)
32. Sokolova, M., Lapalme, G.: A systematic analysis of performance measures for classification tasks. Inf. Process. Manag. **45**(4), 427–437 (2009)
33. Tabard-Fougère, A., Rose-Dulcina, K., Pittet, V., Dayer, R., Vuillerme, N., Armand, S.: EMG normalization method based on grade 3 of manual muscle testing: within and between day reliability of normalization tasks and application to gait analysis. Gait Posture **60**, 6–12 (2018)

Self-organizing Maps Using Acoustic Features for Prediction of State Change in Bipolar Disorder

Olga Kamińska[1,2], Katarzyna Kaczmarek-Majer[1(✉)], Karol Opara[1],
Wit Jakuczun[2], Monika Dominiak[3,4], Anna Antosik-Wójcińska[3],
Łukasz Święcicki[3], and Olgierd Hryniewicz[2]

[1] Systems Research Institute, Polish Academy of Sciences,
Newelska 6, 01-447 Warsaw, Poland
{o.kaminska,k.kaczmarek,karol.opara}@ibspan.waw.pl
[2] Britenet Group, Karolkowa 30, 01-207 Warsaw, Poland
wit.jakuczun@wlogsolutions.com, olgierd.hryniewicz@ibspan.waw.pl
[3] Department of Affective Disorders, Institute of Psychiatry and Neurology,
Sobieskiego 9, 02-957 Warsaw, Poland
{swiecick,aantosik}@ipin.edu.pl
[4] Department of Pharmacology, Institute of Psychiatry and Neurology,
Sobieskiego 9, 02-957 Warsaw, Poland
mdominia@wp.pl

Abstract. Bipolar disorder (BD) is a serious mental disorder characterized by manic episodes of elevated mood and overactivity, interspersed with periods of depression. Typically, the psychiatric assessment of affective state is carried out by a psychiatrist during routine check-up visits. However, diagnostics of a phase change can be facilitated by monitoring data collected by the patient's smartphone. Previous studies concentrated primarily on the phase detection formulated as a classification task. In this study, we introduce a new approach to predict the phase change of BD patients using acoustic features and a combination of the Kohonen's self-organizing maps and random forests. The primary goal is to predict the forthcoming change of patient's state. We report on preliminary results that confirm the existence of a relation between the outcome of unsupervised learning (clustering) and the psychiatric assessment. Next, we evaluate the out-of-sample accuracy to predict the patient's state with random forests. Finally, we discuss the potential of unsupervised learning for monitoring BD patients.

Keywords: Acoustic features · Data stream clustering · Bipolar disorder · Phase change prediction · Smartphone data

This work was partially financed from EU funds (Regional Operational Program for Mazovia) - a project entitled "Smartphone-based diagnostics of phase changes in the course of bipolar disorder" (RPMA.01.02.00-14-5706/16-00).

M. Marcos et al. (Eds.): KR4HC-ProHealth 2019/TEAAM 2019, LNAI 11979, pp. 148–160, 2019.
https://doi.org/10.1007/978-3-030-37446-4_12

1   Introduction

Bipolar disorder (BD) is a mental disorder that affects more than 2% of the world's population [8]. It is a chronic and recurrent disease having a serious impact on psychosocial functioning, cognition and the quality of life [2]. BD is characterized with episodic fluctuations between mood phases ranging from depression, through mixed and euthymic, to manic episodes. Detection and treatment of early symptoms of episode recurrence is crucial since it reduces the conversion rates to full-blown illness, decreases the symptoms severity and reduces the treatment costs.

1.1   Smartphone as a Diagnostic Tool

Widespread of smartphone technology allows for a real-time patient monitoring in naturalistic settings [9]. Consequently, smartphone apps become an increasingly effective tool for the assessment of BD patients' affective state and early detection of a phase change [7,10,13]. Changes in patient's voice signal captured by acoustic features and behavioral activities obtained by monitoring the smartphone usage are suggested as potential sensitive measures of changing course of affective states in bipolar disorder and may become valid markers of an affective state in BD patients [5,10,16]. Especially, the smartphone-based diagnostics using voice features could be game changing in terms of patient mental state monitoring [3]. Acoustic features are regarded as sensitive and accurate measures of mood shifts [1] and have high diagnostic potential [17], as they are not only symptomatic of both cognitive and psychomotor retardation [3] but also convey information about the speaker's emotions [12]. Furthermore, contrary to the statistics on the phone calls, the acoustic features are objective and largely independent from BD patient's personal characteristics or preferences.

1.2   BD Phase Change Detection and Prediction

Smartphone-based systems for BD monitoring typically try to solve a classification problem – detection of the disease phase. However, even though the data collection is performed during the everyday life of a patient, the amount of labeled data is reduced only to days around the psychiatric assessment, and thus, very limited. To overcome this bottleneck, we pursue an alternative approach. We use unsupervised learning technique, which finds groups (clusters) in acoustic data for each patient without taking the assessments into account. This allows us to use the whole dataset for learning rather than constraining it only to a few days before and after the visit to the psychiatrist. Unsupervised learning techniques seem adequate, since they allow for the identification of novelties, anomalies and changes for newly collected data. We show that the automatically detected clusters are related to the psychiatric assessments about the BD phase.

The practical goal is the development of an algorithm to detect and predict the early symptoms of the phase change in BD patients. This could make patients and clinicians more aware of the situation and open options for early intervention.

1.3 Novelty

The novelty of this paper consists in the application of the Kohonen's self-organizing maps using acoustic features for the phase change detection and prediction in bipolar disorder. The proposed approach is preliminarily validated by a comparison of the clusters learned using acoustic features with the results of the psychiatric assessment.

2 Methods

In this research, we developed a multivariable prediction model using combination of the unsupervised and supervised learning. The workflow of the proposed approach is presented in Fig. 1. Data were gathered during an observational study by a BDmon app installed on smartphones of bipolar disorder patients.

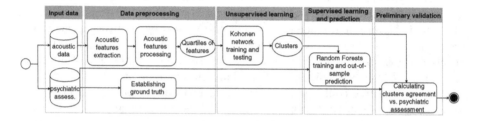

Fig. 1. The workflow diagram

Data preprocessing consisted mainly of the preparation of the acoustic features and establishing of the ground truth for the psychiatric assessment. The ground-truth for the analyses is assumed to be 7 days before the visit with the psychiatric assessment and 2 days after [10]. Then, we train and test the Kohonen's self-organizing map. Next, we use the resulting clusters as source of data for the selected supervised learning algorithm – the random forests. Finally, the degree of agreement between clusters is calculated to evaluate the adequacy of the learned clusters with respect to the psychiatric assessment. Due to the high between-patient variability, we opted for the patient-dependent model rather than for the general one. This concerns both, the clustering and prediction algorithms presented in this study.

2.1 Observational Study

The observational study was conducted in the Department of Affective Disorders, Institute of Psychiatry and Neurology in Warsaw and in the centre specializing in the clinical trials Prosen Net. Sample for the observational study includes patients diagnosed with bipolar disorder according to ICD-10 classification. The study participants were enrolled from both inpatient and outpatient settings.

To conduct the observational study a dedicated smartphone app called BDmon was developed and installed on patients' smartphones. It works in the background to record both daily statistics on calls and text messages and acoustic features of the patient's voice during phone calls. The psychiatric state of each study participant was assessed every two months or more frequently, if requested, by a patient or a doctor.

The psychiatric assessment was based on the Hamilton Depression Rating Scale (HDRS-17), Young Mania Rating Scale (YMRS), Clinical General Impression Scale (CGI-BD) and Beck Depression Inventory (BDI). Note that these scales contain questions closely related to the speech features, e.g., question 8 on the HDRS-17 scale (retardation: slowness of thought, speech, and activity) and question 6 on the YMRS scale (speech: rate and amount). The mental state of the study participants was also evaluated fortnightly via phone-based interactions with a clinician.

2.2 Processing of Acoustic Data

The sound signal is obtained directly from the microphone to avoid recording of the interlocutor's speech. The voice signal is processed in real time to extract its physical descriptors, which are transferred to a secure server and stored in a database for analyses. The cached data are permanently deleted from the phone after feature extraction. Therefore, sensitive data do not leave the patient's phone, and voice parameters sent to the server do not allow for the identification of the patient's identity.

Preprocessing of acoustic data affects wide-spread of smartphone-based assessments [6]. Within this research, the voice signal is divided into short 10–20 ms frames, in which it is approximately stationary. An adopted version of openS-MILE library [4] was used to collect the extended Geneva Minimalistic Acoustic Parameter Set (eGeMAPS) for Voice Research and Affective Computing, the ComParE Acoustic Feature Set as well as some other attributes. These parameterizations are relatively rich and include i.a. time-domain descriptors (zero crossing rate, amplitude statistics, signal energy), spectral features (distribution of energy, mel-cepstral coefficients, fundamental frequency and its harmonics), voice quality (jitter, shimmer, harmonics to noise ratio) and prosodic features (voicing probability, normalized loudness).

Finally, 12 features were manually selected for further analysis based on domain knowledge and the resemblance of their distribution to the Gaussian one, namely: spectral slope in the ranges 0–500 Hz and 500–1500 Hz, energies in bands 0–650 Hz and 1000–4000 Hz, alpha ratio – ratio of the energy in band 50–100 Hz to the energy in band 1000–5000 Hz, spectral roll-off point – the frequency below which 25% of the spectrum energy is concentrated, harmonicity of the spectrum, maximal position of the FFT spectrum, Hammarberg index, entropy of the spectrum, modulated loudness (RASTA), and zero-crossing rate.

For every day, the recordings were aggregated by five-number summary consisting of quartiles (0, 0.25, 0.5, 0.75, 1) of all the acoustic features. This aggregation reflects the characteristics of the entire distribution of values from the last three days. It reduces the noise of the median as well as the lower and upper quartiles at the same time keeping the potentially informative extremes of the distribution. Finally, to increase the stability of the features we smoothed the daily aggregates in time domain by applying the moving average of three days.

2.3   Clustering

The daily aggregates of the acoustic features of the patient's voice were subject to clustering using self-organizing map algorithm known also as Kohonen network [14]. For each patient, we performed clustering of the daily aggregates (quartiles) of theirs voice features using the *kohonen* package from the CRAN repository for R language, [19].

One of the features of the self-organizing maps is the preservation of neighborhood between the clusters in the two-dimensional space. In this study, we used rectangular map topology of dimensions 3×1, which was intended to identify the two most distant affective states – mania and depression and euthymia in between. The fourth affective state, mixed, is in its nature a combination of both, manic and depressive symptoms, and as confirmed with our preliminary experiments, it is more adequately represented as a mixture of depression and mania within the 3×1 Kohonen network, than as an additional dimension of a map, e.g., 4×1. In the future, we plan to compare the performance of the selected approach – Kohonen network with the state-of-the-art clustering approaches for the BD phase change detection.

2.4   Prediction of a State Change

Next, we verified the ability to predict the forthcoming cluster of the self-organizing map with some supervised learning approach. For the start, the random forest algorithm was chosen to classify the state of patient in the third day after the last date of measurement. We used implementation available in the CRAN repository in *caret* package, [15]. In the future we plan to try also other classifiers.

The performance of the random forest was evaluated with the out-of-sample state change prediction accuracy. A single step accuracy of the state prediction is set to 1, if the predicted state is the same as state assessed by the clustering algorithm and to 0 otherwise. The resulting out-of-sample state change prediction accuracy is the arithmetic mean of the one-step-ahead predictions. The same voice features are used as predictors as in our unsupervised learning approach. Three-days prediction horizon is introduced to avoid data leakage due to the moving average smoothing of the daily aggregates during acoustic features preprocessing. In the future, the cross-validation scenarios will be considered.

2.5   Agreement Between Clusters and Psychiatric Assessments

Both, the automatically extracted clusters and psychiatric assessments result in the assignment of the smoothed daily aggregates to some groups. To assess the predictive potential of clustering, we need to know to what extent these groups are similar to each other. In other words, we need to check if the clusters are related to the BD phases rather than some other, irrelevant characteristics of the patient's speech.

Quantification of the similarity of two different groupings of a single dataset is often based on pairs of observations. This follows from the fact that reasonable groupings do not necessarily correspond to each other in one-to-one manner. It is likely to be the case in our task, due to four reasons. First, most patients did not go through all BD phases during the study period. Therefore, the clustering algorithm cannot extract the symptoms of the unseen phases (e.g. depression) but will instead try to find groups within the observed data (e.g. split manic states into hypomania and full-blown mania). Second, heterogeneity of symptoms in the mixed state may lead to splitting the data corresponding to this phase among different clusters. Third, strongly outlying data points can disturb unsupervised learning methods with predefined number of clusters. Finally, the cells within the 3×1 self-organizing map can arrange in two orders, i.e. depression – euthymia – mania or mania – euthymia – depression.

To measure the degree of agreement between clusters, we extract the data around every pair of visits and assign them to clusters trained on the remaining data. Therefore, we aim at comparing two groupings of the same data (daily aggregates), one done by the clustering algorithm and the other by psychiatric assessments extrapolated to 7 days before and 2 after the visit. For concordant groupings, every pair that is in one group according to the first division should also be in one group according to the second division. On the other hand, the pairs which are in distinct groups under one clustering should also be in distinct groups under the other. This idea underlines several clustering similarity measures, such as Rand index. In this paper, we follow a similar approach. For every pair of the visits, assessments can be either concordant or discordant. However, clusters are assigned on a finer scale (daily) than assessments, therefore our measure is slightly modified.

To compare the similarity between the distributions of the clusters we first omit days that are missing e.g. due to the lack of phone calls. Next, for the days around either visit we compute a vector representing the frequencies of each cluster. Let c_t denote a cluster which was assigned to on day t to a particular patient. Frequencies of the i-th cluster for days around the visit on day t_v are given by:

$$f_{t_v,i} = \frac{\sum_{t=t_v-7}^{t_v+2} I\{c_t = i\}}{\sum_{t=t_v-7}^{t_v+2} I\{c_t \text{ is not missing}\}} \tag{1}$$

where I is the indicator function taking value one if the predicate in curly brackets is true and zero otherwise.

Then, we compare the distributions f_{t_A} and f_{t_B} for two visits A and B with the normalized absolute difference

$$a_{t_\text{A},t_\text{B}} = 1 - \frac{1}{2} \sum_{i=1}^{3} |f_{t_\text{A},i} - f_{t_\text{B},i}| \qquad (2)$$

obtaining a relative agreement measure $a_{t_\text{A},t_\text{B}}$ between the cluster distributions for two visits. This measure ranges from zero for distributions without common elements to one for the same distributions. The agreement between clusters is evaluated in experiments. For each patient, all possible pairs of visits are considered as a testing scenario.

3   Preliminary Results

3.1   Prediction of a State Change

First, we present the results of the random forest out-of-sample prediction of cluster changes learned by the unsupervised learning algorithm. The training set comprises of the first 9 months of the observational study from January to September 2018. The testing set comprises of the last three months of the observational study from October to December 2018.

In total, data of 31 patients were considered in the numerical summary. However, due to the high amount of missing data and withdrawal of some patients, the out-of-sample prediction was possible only for 10 patients, who actively used their smartphones during the testing period. In Table 1, the resulting out-of-sample state change prediction accuracy is presented.

Table 1. Random forests out-of-sample state change prediction accuracy

Patient ID	Prediction accuracy
2582	0.67
4923	1.00
5656	0.70
5659	0.70
5736	1.00
5768	0.65
6601	0.69
6754	0.88
8292	1.00
9829	0.91
Mean	**0.82**
SD	**0.14**

The mean prediction accuracy of the forthcoming cluster is rather high and amounts to 0.82 ($\pm$ 0.14). Moreover, we observed that the actual ratio of changes of the clinically confirmed affective states is much lower than the ratio of cluster changes, which suggests oversensitivity of the predictive model. Handling of this issue remains an open problem for future investigations.

3.2   Agreement Between Clusters and Psychiatric Assessments

The validity of clusters learned using acoustic features for the smartphone-based data was evaluated with regard to the psychiatric assessments. Although the data was collected continuously during the everyday life of a patient, only the records obtained 7 days before the visit and 2 days after have psychiatric assessment assigned. The sample of 31 patients available for this study is reduced to patients who have at least one pair of assessments with at least 2 data points available around each of them (within the time frame of -7 to $+2$ days). Then, for every patient, all combinations of pairs of available assessments are evaluated with formula (2). As a result, 97 pairs of visits are considered in the analysis. We refer to them as the testing scenarios. Within each of these scenarios, the self-organizing map is trained on all the data of a given patient except for the period from 7 days before to 2 days after visits A and B. The 10 days surrounding the considered testing visits are regarded as testing data within this scenario. Table 2, gathers detailed results for patients with highest number of non-missing smartphone-based data around psychiatric assessments.

Table 2 presents the sequential identifiers of visit considered in the testing scenario (Visit A, Visit B), the outcomes of the psychiatric assessment of either visit of the testing scenario (Assessment A, Assessment B), the resulting degree of grouping agreement and the number of data points in the compared vectors of clusters (Valid days A, Valid days B). For instance, in the first row of Table 2 the patient's state is assessed as euthymia during both visits of the testing scenario. Out of the ten days surrounding visit A, the data were available only for two and thus, only two clusters were available for comparison. On the other hand, acoustic data were collected every day around visit B leading to 10-element vector of clusters. The agreement calculated for this patient based on the vectors of clusters and formula (2) is 1.0.

In Fig. 2, the summary about the average degree of agreement between clusters averaged over all possible pairs of visits (testing scenarios) is presented.

The highest agreement, of approximately 0.8, is observed for vectors of clusters corresponding to visits with the following assessments: depression – depression, euthymia – euthymia. The lowest agreement of 0.2 was observed for data corresponding to assessments: mixed – euthymia.

Generally, we notice that the agreement between cluster distributions is higher for concordant medical assessments than for discordant ones. This is a promising result that allows us to pose the hypothesis that the unsupervised learning leads to groupings having diagnostic potential.

Table 2. The degree of agreement between clusters learned by the self-organizing map and psychiatric assessment based on pairs of visits

Patient ID	Visit A	Visit B	Assessment A	Assessment B	Grouping agreement	Valid days A	Valid days B
1472	2	3	mania	mixed	0.7	9	10
1472	2	4	mania	mixed	0.7	9	6
1472	3	4	mixed	mixed	0.6	10	6
2004	1	2	euthymia	euthymia	0.0	3	10
2004	1	3	euthymia	depression	0.3	3	10
2004	2	3	euthymia	depression	0.7	10	10
2582	2	3	mixed	mania	0.8	10	10
2582	2	4	mixed	euthymia	0.5	10	6
2582	2	5	mixed	depression	0.5	10	10
2582	3	4	mania	euthymia	0.4	10	6
2582	3	5	mania	depression	0.4	10	10
2582	4	5	euthymia	depression	0.7	6	10
4248	1	2	depression	depression	0.3	3	3
4248	1	3	depression	depression	0.9	3	10
4248	1	4	depression	depression	0.9	3	10
4248	1	5	depression	mania	1.0	3	3
4248	2	3	depression	depression	0.3	3	10
4248	2	4	depression	depression	0.2	3	10
4248	2	5	depression	mania	0.3	3	3
4248	3	4	depression	depression	1.0	10	10
4248	3	5	depression	mania	0.7	10	3
4248	4	5	depression	mania	0.5	10	3
4953	2	3	mania	mixed	0.7	10	3
4953	2	4	mania	depression	0.9	10	10
4953	3	4	mixed	depression	0.8	3	10
5656	1	2	euthymia	euthymia	0.8	7	9
5656	1	3	euthymia	depression	0.9	7	7
5656	1	4	euthymia	depression	0.4	7	3
5656	2	3	euthymia	depression	0.8	9	7
5656	2	4	euthymia	depression	0.7	9	3
5656	3	4	depression	depression	1.0	7	3
5659	1	2	euthymia	euthymia	0.4	3	10
5736	2	3	depression	mixed	0.4	10	10
5768	2	3	euthymia	euthymia	1.0	10	10
5768	2	4	euthymia	euthymia	1.0	10	10
5768	3	4	euthymia	euthymia	1.0	10	10

(*continued*)

Table 2. (*continued*)

Patient ID	Visit A	Visit B	Assessment A	Assessment B	Grouping agreement	Valid days A	Valid days B
6139	3	4	mania	mixed	0.0	3	6
6139	3	5	mania	depression	0.0	3	2
6139	4	5	mixed	depression	0.0	6	2
6601	1	3	euthymia	euthymia	1.0	2	6
6601	1	4	euthymia	depression	1.0	2	6
6601	3	4	euthymia	depression	1.0	6	6
8866	1	2	depression	mixed	0.9	3	9
8866	1	3	depression	depression	0.7	3	8
8866	2	3	mixed	depression	0.7	9	8
9341	3	4	mania	mixed	0.8	5	3
9341	3	5	mania	euthymia	0.2	5	5
9341	4	5	mixed	euthymia	0.0	3	5
9829	1	2	depression	depression	0.6	2	10
9829	1	3	depression	depression	1.0	2	10
9829	1	4	depression	depression	1.0	2	10
9829	1	5	depression	depression	1.0	2	10
9829	2	3	depression	depression	0.6	10	10
9829	2	4	depression	depression	0.6	10	10
9829	2	5	depression	depression	0.6	10	10
9829	3	4	depression	depression	1.0	10	10
9829	3	5	depression	depression	1.0	10	10
9829	4	5	depression	depression	1.0	10	10

3.3   Limitations

There is some uncertainty related to the exact starting or ending date of affective episode that was diagnosed during the psychiatric assessment.

Moreover, one of the main challenges related to learning algorithms lies in the appropriate handling of large amount of missing data. These could be partly explained by patients' non-adherence to study conditions, in particular among patients in hypomanic/manic state. We observed that manic patients tended to delete the BDmon application or switch off their phones. Consequently, future approaches could assume that some missing data is informative.

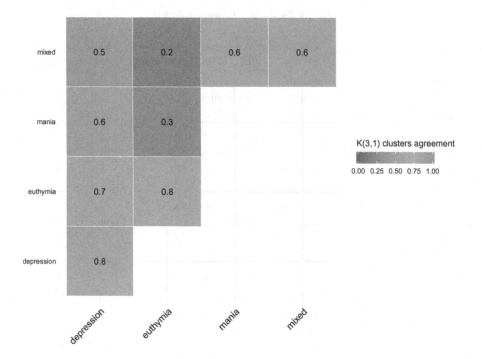

Fig. 2. Degree of agreement between clusters averaged over all possible pairs of visit within the testing scenarios

4   Conclusion and Future Work

The use of smartphone apps allows for convenient collection of large amounts of data about BD patients, including not only their social activity but also acoustic features of their voices. To develop a useful system for detection (or even prediction) of the phase change these data need coupling with psychiatric assessments, which is a bottleneck of this approach. In this paper, we address it with the use of an unsupervised learning (clustering) algorithm applied individually for every patient.

Verification of the proposed approach for pairs of visits, shows that the states obtained with unsupervised learning and the affective states of BD patients obtained from the psychiatric evaluations are interrelated. In particular, for concordant psychiatric assessments during both visits we notice higher similarity of the distributions of clusters than for discordant assessments (e.g. mixed state – euthymia). Furthermore, for the following concordant psychiatric assessments during both visits: euthymia – euthymia and depression – depression, the average compliance is very high and amounts to approximately 0.8.

In our application, psychiatric assessments were obtained bimonthly – much more rarely than patient monitoring data collected on daily basis. Unsupervised learning is based on the latter set only, however it is possible to enhance the possible clustering method by adding constraints following from the diagnostic data. This leads to the field of semi-supervised learning, which is a promising area of further study and applications in monitoring of BD patients.

Another direction for future research is the investigation of the temporal stability of the clustering results. It can be done with the use of control charts that enable generation of notifications of possible phase change for the patient or their doctor. Recently, control charts have been applied to support bipolar disorder phase detection [11,18], which suggests their adequacy for monitoring the clustering results in the BD context, and remains a promising direction for future research.

Future research will also concern automatic feature selection, trying to account for confounding factors such as medication intake effects, monitoring the stability of clusters and benchmarking the proposed approach with the state-of-the-art clustering and predictive algorithms.

Acknowledgments. The study was submitted to the Office for Registration of Medicinal Products, Medical Devices and Biocidal Products in accordance with Polish law. This work was partially financed from EU funds (Regional Operational Program for Mazovia) – a project entitled "Smartphone-based diagnostics of phase changes in the course of bipolar disorder" (RPMA.01.02.00-14-5706/16-00). The authors thank psychiatrists that participated in the observational trial for their commitment and advice. The authors thank the researchers Weronika Radziszewska and Anna Olwert from Systems Research Institute, Polish Academy of Sciences for their support in data preparation and analysis, as well as Małgorzata Igras-Cybulska and Bartosz Ziółko from Techmo sp. z o.o. for their support in the extraction of acoustic features.

Ethical Issues. The study obtained the consent of the Bioethical Commission at the District Medical Chamber in Warsaw (agreement no. KB/1094/17).

References

1. Ayadi, M.E., Kamel, M.S., Karray, F.: Survey on speech emotion recognition: features, classification schemes, and databases. Pattern Recogn. **44**(3), 572–587 (2011). https://doi.org/10.1016/j.patcog.2010.09.020. http://www.sciencedirect.com/science/article/pii/S0031320310004619
2. Catala-Lopez, F., Genova-Maleras, R., Vieta, E., Tabares-Seisdedos, R.: The increasing burden of mental and neurological disorders. Eur. Neuropsychopharmacol. J. Eur. College Neuropsychopharmacol. **23**(11), 1337 (2013)
3. Cummins, N., Scherer, S., Krajewski, J., Schnieder, S., Epps, J., Quatieri, T.F.: A review of depression and suicide risk assessment using speech analysis. Speech Commun. **71**, 10–49 (2015). https://doi.org/10.1016/j.specom.2015.03.004. http://www.sciencedirect.com/science/article/pii/S0167639315000369
4. Eyben, F., Weninger, F., Gross, F., Schuller, B.: Recent developments in openSMILE, the Munich open-source multimedia feature extractor. In: Proceedings of the 21st ACM International Conference on Multimedia, pp. 835–838. ACM (2013)
5. Faurholt-Jepsen, M., Busk, J., Frost, M., Bardram, J.E., Vinberg, M., Kessing, L.V.: Objective smartphone data as a potential diagnostic marker of bipolar disorder. Aust. N. Z. J. Psychiatry **53**(2), 119–128 (2019). https://doi.org/10.1177/0004867418808900. PMID: 30387368

6. Gideon, J., Provost, E.M., McInnis, M.: Mood state prediction from speech of varying acoustic quality for individuals with bipolar disorder. In: 2016 IEEE International Conference on Acoustics, Speech and Signal Processing (ICASSP), pp. 2359–2363. IEEE (2016)
7. Gliddon, E., Barnes, S., Murray, G., Michalak, E.: Online and mobile technologies for self-management in bipolar disorder: a systematic review. Psychiatr. Rehabil. J. **40**(3), 309–319 (2017). https://doi.org/10.1037/prj0000270
8. Grande, I., Berk, M., Birmaher, B., Vieta, E.: Bipolar disorder. The Lancet **387**(10027), 1561–1572 (2016). https://doi.org/10.1016/S0140-6736(15)00241-X. http://www.sciencedirect.com/science/article/pii/S014067361500241X
9. Gravenhorst, F., et al.: Mobile phones as medical devices in mental disorder treatment: an overview. Pers. Ubiquit. Comput. **19**(2), 335–353 (2015)
10. Grünerbl, A., Muaremi, A., Osmani, V.: Smartphone-based recognition of states and state changes in bipolar disorder patients. IEEE J. Biomed. Health Inform. **19**(1), 140–148 (2015)
11. Kaczmarek-Majer, K., et al.: Control charts designed using model averaging approach for phase change detection in bipolar disorder. In: Destercke, S., Denoeux, T., Gil, M.Á., Grzegorzewski, P., Hryniewicz, O. (eds.) SMPS 2018. AISC, vol. 832, pp. 115–123. Springer, Cham (2019). https://doi.org/10.1007/978-3-319-97547-4_16
12. Kamińska, D., Sapiński, T., Anbarjafari, G.: Efficiency of chosen speech descriptors in relation to emotion recognition. EURASIP J. Audio. Speech. Music Process. **2017**(1), 3 (2017). https://doi.org/10.1186/s13636-017-0100-x
13. Karam, Z.N., et al.: Ecologically valid long-term mood monitoring of individuals with bipolar disorder using speech. In: 2014 IEEE International Conference on Acoustics, Speech and Signal Processing (ICASSP), pp. 4858–4862. IEEE (2014). https://doi.org/10.1109/ICASSP.2014.6854525
14. Kohonen, T.: Self-Organizing Maps. Springer, Heidelberg (1995). https://doi.org/10.1007/978-3-642-97610-0
15. Kuhn, M.: Building predictive models in R using the caret package. J. Stat. Softw. Articles **28**(5), 1–26 (2008). https://doi.org/10.18637/jss.v028.i05. https://www.jstatsoft.org/v028/i05
16. Muaremi, A., Gravenhorst, F., Grünerbl, A., Arnrich, B., Tröster, G.: Assessing bipolar episodes using speech cues derived from phone calls. In: Cipresso, P., Matic, A., Lopez, G. (eds.) MindCare 2014. LNICST, vol. 100, pp. 103–114. Springer, Cham (2014). https://doi.org/10.1007/978-3-319-11564-1_11
17. Or, F., Torous, J., Onnela, J.P.: High potential but limited evidence: using voice data from smartphones to monitor and diagnose mood disorders. Psychiatr. Rehabil. J. **40**(3), 320 (2017)
18. Vazquez-Montes, M., Stevens, R., Perera, R., Saunders, K., Geddes, J.R.: Control charts for monitoring mood stability as a predictor of severe episodes in patients with bipolar disorder. Int. J. Bipolar Disord. **6**(1), 7 (2018). https://doi.org/10.1186/s40345-017-0116-2
19. Wehrens, R., Kruisselbrink, J.: Flexible self-organizing maps in kohonen 3.0. J. Stat. Softw. Articles **87**(7), 1–18 (2018). https://doi.org/10.18637/jss.v087.i07, https://www.jstatsoft.org/v087/i07

Explainable Machine Learning for Modeling of Early Postoperative Mortality in Lung Cancer

Katarzyna Kobylińska[1]([✉])(iD), Tomasz Mikołajczyk[4]([✉]),
Mariusz Adamek[2]([✉])(iD), Tadeusz Orłowski[3]([✉]), and Przemysław Biecek[1,4]([✉])(iD)

[1] Faculty of Mathematics, Informatics and Mechanics, University of Warsaw,
Warsaw, Poland
zwierzcho@gmail.com, przemyslaw.biecek@gmail.com
[2] Faculty of Medicine and Dentistry, Medical University of Silesia, Katowice, Poland
m.adamek@e.pl
[3] National Institute of Tuberculosis and Lung Diseases, Warsaw, Poland
tm.orlowski@gmail.com
[4] Faculty of Mathematics and Information Science,
Warsaw University of Technology, Warsaw, Poland
t.mikolajczyk@gmail.com

Abstract. In recent years we see an increasing interest in applications of complex machine learning methods to medical problems. Black box models based on deep neural networks or ensembles are more and more popular in diagnostic, personalized medicine (Hamet and Tremblay 2017) or screening studies (Scheeder et al. 2018). Partially because they are accurate and easy to train. Nevertheless such models may be hard to understand and interpret. In high stake decisions, especially in medicine, the understanding of factors that drive model decisions is crucial. Lack of model understanding creates a serious risk in applications.

In our study we propose and validate new approaches to exploration and explanation of predictive models for early postoperative mortality in lung cancer patients. Models are created on the Domestic Lung Cancer Database run by the National Institute of Tuberculosis and Lung Diseases. We show how explainable machine learning techniques can be used to combine data driven signals with domain knowledge. Additionally we explore whether the insight provided by model explainers give valuable information for physicians.

Keywords: Interpretable machine learning · Explainable artificial intelligence · Lung cancer · Personalized medicine · Computational medicine · Early postoperative mortality

---

P. Biecek was financially supported by NCN Opus grant 2016/21/B/ST6/02176. K. Kobylińska and T. Mikołajczyk were financially supported by Polish Centre for Research and Development (Grant POIR.01.01.01-00-0328/17).

M. Marcos et al. (Eds.): KR4HC-ProHealth 2019/TEAAM 2019, LNAI 11979, pp. 161–174, 2019.
https://doi.org/10.1007/978-3-030-37446-4_13

1   Introduction

Surgical excision of lung cancer is radical and therefore the most effective way of treatment. On the other hand surgical thoracic procedures entail high risk of postoperative morbidity or even death. The decision whether the patient is qualified for a surgery depends on the clinical features and performance status. One of the well known factors that are related to higher postoperative risk of death is age. The multiple comorbidities in the elderly constitute another risk factors (Glotzer et al. 2013). Even though old age is not a contraindication for a surgery, the patient's other features need to be carefully examined to assess the chances of positive surgery outcome (Zuin et al. 2010).

The process of such decision could be supported and improved by machine learning (ML) algorithms. In the current common model the decision depends on knowledge, intuition and experience of the specific doctors.

In this paper we introduce five machine learning models that predicts the probability of 3-month survival after lung cancer surgery based on the patient features available prior to surgery. Simultaneously the goal is to explain such model in order to understand the specific prognosis for a patient. Such a model not only supports the surgeon's decision but also indicates the risk factors. Moreover, it presents the factors that should be modified before the surgery to increase the probability of individual's survival.

The more understandable a model is, the more likely will an user trust in its predictions. That is why it is important not only to prepare accurate ML model but also explain its predictions. According to (Gilpin et al. 2018), eXplainable Artificial Intelligence (XAI) allows models to be more understandable and transparent. The approaches like Shapley values (Lundberg and Lee 2017), Locally Interpretable Model-agnostic Explanations (Ribeiro et al. 2016), Break-Down (Staniak and Biecek 2018) or auditor (Gosiewska and Biecek 2018) could ensure the models perform correctly or identify hidden problems, for example data inaccuracy. The XAI methods help to detect the most important features and conduct the what-if analysis (Biecek 2018). To our knowledge this is first large scale study that shows how model explainers work on real world data.

2   Methodology

2.1   Data Set

This study is based on data retrieved from Domestic Lung Cancer Database which provides medical history of 32 698 patients with operable lung cancer collected during 12 years (2002–2016). The data in the study comprise the smoking history (Table 1), examination results, cancer risk factors, symptoms and comorbidities (Table 2), radiological and pathological features of lung nodules (Table 3).

Some of the variables had to be transformed. For example levels of stage is transformed into numeric variable ranging from 1 to 4, where 1 corresponds to lung cancer staging 1a, 1.5 corresponds to 1b, 2 corresponds to 2 and so on.

Variable packyears measures patients' exposure to tobacco. For each patient, it is calculated as the number of years a patient has smoked multiplied by the number of packs of cigarettes per day.

The aim of this study is to analyse the short-term results of the lung cancer surgery. The early, 3-month postoperative mortality is equal to 7%. Those patients have higher median of years of smoking, packyears and age than survivors. However, the majority of analyzed variables are similar for patients who died and survived.

Table 1. Descriptive statistics of variables linked with the smoking status.

	Dead	Alive	Overall
Patients smoking	2 241	30 457	32 698
No	695 (31%)	10091 (33.1%)	10786 (33%)
Yes	1546 (69%)	20366 (66.9%)	21912 (67%)
Years of smoking			
Mean (SD)	24.2 (19.3)	21.4 (19)	21.6 (19)
Median [Min, Max]	30 [0, 80]	25 [0, 80]	25 [0, 80.0]
Cigarettes count			
Mean (SD)	14 (11.4)	12.9 (11.9)	12.9 (11.9)
Median [Min, Max]	20 [0.00, 60]	20 [0, 61]	20 [0, 61]
Quitted smoking (months ago)			
Mean (SD)	19.2 (60.9)	19.4 (60.6)	19.4 (60.7)
Median [Min, Max]	0 [0, 480]	0 [0,480]	0 [0, 480]
Packyears			
Mean (SD)	25.5 (23.4)	22.4 (23)	22.6 (23.1)
Median [Min, Max]	30 [0, 165]	20 [0, 189]	20 [0, 189]

2.2 Modeling

In order to prepare the most accurate predictive models, few types of machine learning models were examined: random forest (Breiman 2001), logistic regression model, lasso, XGBoost and svm. The logistic regression and lasso model are frequent choice for binary classification problems and are widely used in medical applications. The logistic regression model is easy to interpret, sometimes at the cost of precision. On the other hand, lasso model is chosen as an example of regression analysis with regularization in order to improve the performance. Random Forest, XGBoost and svm are a black box models that are difficult to interpret, but the results are very often better than results of traditional models.

Table 2. Descriptive statistics of cancer risk factors, symptoms, examination results and commorbidities.

	Dead	Alive	Overall
Sex			
Man	1577 (70.4%)	19398 (63.7%)	20975 (64.1%)
Woman	664 (29.6%)	11059 (36.3%)	11723 (35.9%)
Age			
Mean (SD)	65.4 (8.23)	63 (8.59)	63.2 (8.59)
Median [Min, Max]	66 [18, 88.0]	63 [15, 90]	63 [15, 90]
Cancer burden			
No	2020 (90.1%)	27202 (89.3%)	29222 (89.4%)
Yes	221 (9.9%)	3255 (10.7%)	3476 (10.6%)
External risk factors			
No	1847 (82.4%)	25132 (82.5%)	26979 (82.5%)
Yes	394 (17.6%)	5325 (17.5%)	5719 (17.5%)
Respiratory system diseases			
No	1981 (88.4%)	27809 (91.3%)	29790 (91.1%)
Yes	260 (11.6%)	2648 (8.7%)	2908 (8.9%)
Sputum			
No	2204 (98.3%)	29890 (98.1%)	32094 (98.2%)
Yes	37 (1.7%)	567 (1.9%)	604 (1.8%)
Bronchial lavage			
No	2149 (95.9%)	29135 (95.7%)	31284 (95.7%)
Yes	92 (4.1%)	1322 (4.3%)	1414 (4.3%)
Weight loss			
Mean (SD)	0.55 (2.36)	0.44 (2.07)	0.44 (2.09)
Median [Min, Max]	0 [0, 30]	0 [0, 80]	0 [0, 80.0]
Zubrod performance			
0	1168 (52.1%)	16705 (54.8%)	17873 (54.7%))
1	866 (38.6%)	11562 (38%)	12428 (38%)
2	193 (8.6%)	2139 (7%)	2332 (7.1%)
3	14 (0.6%)	51 (0.2%)	65 (0.2%)
Metastasis			
No	2133 (95.2%)	29416 (96.6%)	31549 (96.5%)
Yes	108 (4.8%)	1041 (3.4%)	1149 (3.5%)
Enlarged nodes			
No	1663 (74.2%)	24150 (79.3%)	25813 (78.9%)
Yes	578 (25.8%)	6307 (20.7%)	6885 (21.1%)
Symptoms			
No	929 (41.5%)	13689 (44.9%)	14618 (44.7%)
Yes	1312 (58.5%)	16768 (55.1%)	18080 (55.3%)
PCO2			
Mean (SD)	38.7 (7.06)	38.6 (10.9)	38.6 (10.6)
Median [Min, Max]	38 [2.5, 111]	38 [2.42, 639]	38 [2.42, 639]
Missing	1462 (65.2%)	20720 (68%)	22182 (67.8%)
APTT			
Mean (SD)	32.2 (14.7)	30.3 (7.56)	30.4 (7.96)
Median [Min, Max]	30.1 [3.02, 200]	29.7 [0.027, 200]	29.7 [0.027, 200]
Missing	1714 (76.5%)	17396 (57.1%)	19110 (58.4%)

Table 3. Descriptive statistics of radiological and pathological features.

	Dead	Alive	Overall
Lung			
Left	930 (41.5%)	13342 (43.8%)	14272 (43.6%)
Right	1311 (58.5%)	17115 (56.2%)	18426 (56.4%)
Stage			
Mean (SD)	1.85 (0.828)	1.74 (0.781)	1.75 (0.785)
Median [Min, Max]	1.5 [1, 4]	1.5 [1, 4]	1.50 [1.00, 4]
Tumor dimension			
below 1	36 (1.6%)	541 (1.8%)	577 (1.8%)
[1-2)	307 (13.7%)	4934 (16.2%)	5241 (16.0%)
[2-3)	572 (25.5%)	8270 (27.2%)	8842 (27%)
[3-5)	1104 (49.3%)	14891 (48.9%)	15995 (48.9%)
[5-7)	146 (6.5%)	1220 (4%)	1366 (4.2%)
[7-10)	62 (2.8%)	512 (1.7%)	574 (1.8%)
above 10	14 (0.6%)	89 (0.3%)	103 (0.3%)
Initial histopathological diagnosis			
Adenocarcinoma	189 (8.4%)	2682 (8.8%)	2871 (8.8%)
Adenosquamous carcinoma	3 (0.1%)	43 (0.1%)	546 (0.1%)
Atypical carcinoma	3 (0.1%)	83 (0.3%)	86 (0.3%)
Bronchoalveolar carcinoma	3 (0.1%)	45 (0.1%)	48 (0.1%)
Non-small cell carcinoma	568 (25.3%)	7369 (24.2%)	7937 (24.3%)
Large cell lung carcinoma	11 (0.5%)	131 (0.4%)	142 (0.4%)
Neuroendocrine carcinoma	4 (0.2%)	81 (0.3%)	85 (0.%)
Pleomorphic carcinoma	2 (0.1%)	18 (0.1%)	20 (0.1%)
Small cell lung carcinoma	6 (0.3%)	105 (0.3%)	111 (0.3%)
Squamous carcinoma	428 (19.1%)	5384 (17.7%)	5812 (17.8%)
Typical carcinoma	16 (0.7%)	397 (1.3%)	413 (1.3%)
Other	10 (0.4%)	174 (0.6%)	184 (0.6%)
Not defined	998 (44.5%)	13945 (45.8%)	14943 (45.7%)

2.3   Model Explanations

In this study the explaining methodology is used in order to interpret and understand machine learning models' predictions. All of those approaches are model agnostic so can be applied to every model, regardless of the model structure.

Two presented explainers focus on methods for level of a single observation. The sequential variable attribution decomposes model prediction into each variable contribution $v(f, x^*, i)$ for a particular observation x^* and scoring function f. Such contribution follows local accuracy and it will sum up to the model prediction in point x^*:

$$f(x^*) = baseline + \sum_{i=1}^{p} v(f, x^*, i) \tag{1}$$

The full algorithm is presented in (Staniak and Biecek 2018).

The what-if analysis (Gosiewska and Biecek 2019) presents the model responses if a change of one analysed feature would have occurred. It allows to understand how the changes in variables influence the model response. To formally define what-if analysis, let $X = (X_1, ... X_n)$ be a vector of variables and $f : X \rightarrow R$ be a scoring function for the predictive model.

Then for a single point x and j-th variable the what-if profile is equal to:

$$CP^{f,j,x}(z) = f(x|^j = z) \tag{2}$$

where $f(x|^j = z)$ means the value of the model for data point x with j-th feature changed to z value keeping all others unchanged.

The partial dependence plot (Hastie et al. 2009) is a global solution that considers all instances and presents the dependencies between continuous feature and the machine learning model response. This methodology calculates the marginal effect of a feature on the predicted values (Molnar 2018).

Variable Importance helps to understand which features are significant on the response. The method to calculate the influence of the variables on the outcome uses model agnostic algorithm, so it is possible to compare variable importance across different models. The main idea of the variable importance calculation is to compute the chosen loss function for full model and then apply for the randomized values of the variable ML model and then compute the loss function. The loss function for each variable calculated in that way corresponds to its importance.

3   Results

The data set was divided into two subsets, the training one that contains 85% of the initial instances and testing one (the rest of the data). The response variable 'Survived 3 months' was highly unbalanced because the postoperative mortality is equal to 7%. Even though during modeling process the threshold was set to 0.93, there were some shortages in examined data set. The missing values were imputed using random values with probabilities from the variables distribution. The set of logistic regression predictors was limited by collinearity of some of the variables.

3.1   Performance of Fitted Models

Based on clinical, smoking and lung scan variables, models predicting 3 month survival after surgery were calculated. The performances of the models were computed by the area under the precision recall curve (AUPRC). This measure is a useful metric to differentiate between few models in a case of a problem of imbalanced classes. The plot Fig. 1 presents the AUPRC measure for each model computed on training and testing data sets. Since xgboost model has similar AUPRC value on both testing and training data sets, the model seems not to be over-fitted. Random forest has much better performance on training data set. Logistic regression and lasso model have very similar performance on both data sets. Although, the svm model has really high performance on the training data set, this model has the lowest performance on the testing data set. So the model seems to be over-fitted.

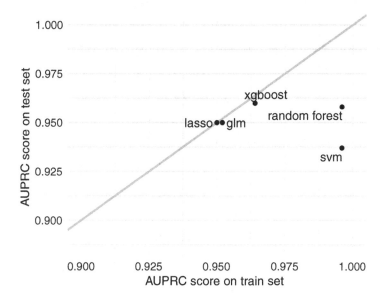

Fig. 1. The comparison of AUPRC measure for 5 different models validated on two data sets: testing and training. It is interesting to see that SVM overfits while xgboost behaves pretty well.

3.2 Methodology for Global Explainations

Three different models are compared using global explaining methods: logistic regression (as an example of simple and additive model), xgboost (an example of a model that can catch deep interactions) and random forest (a model that could catch only shallow interactions but is quite stable).

The results of the variable importance plots indicate that xgboost and random forest have very similar value of the root mean square error (RMSE), whereas logistic regression has a little bit higher value of that error. The Fig. 2 shows importance of a specific variable for each model. The longer the variable's bar is, the more significant is this feature. According to the plot, "APTT" (Activated Partial Thromboplastin Time) and "Age" are the most important variables for random forest and xgboost models. Random forest indicates also "Cigarettes Count", "Smoking years" and "Packyears" whereas xgboost shows "Stage", "Cigaretes Count" and "Quit smoking" as an informative ones. Logistic regression points "Age", "Tumor Dimension", "Sex", "Packyears" and "Respiratory System Diseases" as important variables.

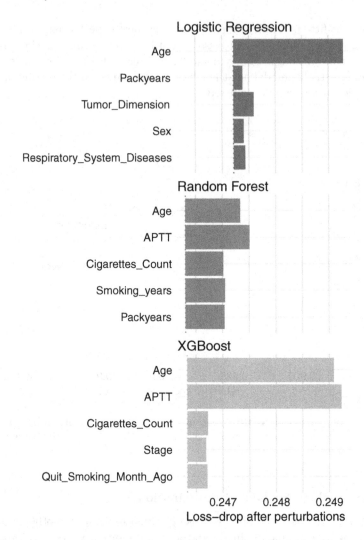

Fig. 2. Variable Importance plot shows the most significant variables for each model. All models agree that age is the most important variable. RF and Xgboost make use also from APTT.

For the most important variables it is worth to present the partial dependence plots. This methodology helps to understand how the relationship between those influential variables are formed and how the response differs between the models. As "APTT", "Age", "Packyears" are significant for at least two models, those variables will be illustrated on the partial dependence plots (Fig. 3).

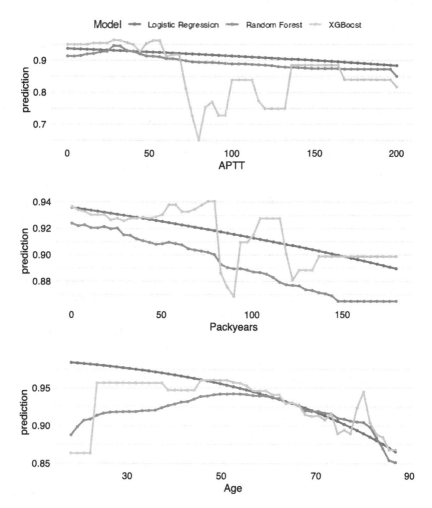

Fig. 3. Partial Dependence Plots for three significant variables. Each color corresponds to different model. Interestingly, those models differ most when it comes to age variable.

Partial dependence plots present the relationships the model has learnt. On x-axis the plot shows the range of the analyzed variable. On the y-axis is the mean prediction from the model. Random forest and logistic regression have quite similar dependency between the "Packyears" variable and the response. The dependency seems to be intuitive: the bigger value of packyears the worse the prediction is. For example, a person who has 100 packyears has the random forest response equal to 0.89, whereas person with 0 packyears has higher model prediction, equal to 0.93. PDP indicate that "APPT" and "Age" have a non-linear relationships with the random forest model's response. The biggest

differences in models' responses can be observed for the "Age" variable. Furthermore, the xgboost model response dependencies seems to be not stable.

Logistic regression, as a traditional model, has a simpler interpretation, but
this model may use variables in a misleading way. The logistic regression could
catch only linear dependencies. So the partial dependence plots of black box
models could be used to re-code some of the important variables in order to
improve regression model. According to random forest partial dependence plot,
two variables: "Age" and "APTT" should be transformed. If the level of "APTT"
is higher than 40, then the value of new transformed variable is assigned to 1,
otherwise it is 0. Similarly, the "Age" variable is transformed. If the value of this
feature is in the interval $(40, 64)$ then the value of the new variable is assigned to
0, otherwise to 1. Those transformed variables are used to prepare new logistic
regression model.

3.3   Methodology for Local Explanations

What-if and sequential variable attribution can give very interesting insights
into the probability of 3 month survival for specific patient. It could be useful
especially before the decision for specific patient is done. Those explainers can
support the surgeon's decision, because they give the opportunity to see each
feature's contribution to final prognosis. Moreover, the what-if profiles could
show which feature should be improved in order to increase the patient chances.
The plots could be used as a kind of personalized medicine.

Table 4. Features of a selected patient.

Feature	Value	Feature	Value
Sex	Woman	Respiratory system diseases	No
Age	69	External risk factors	Yes
Smoking	Yes	Initial histopathological diagnosis	Not defined
Years of smoking	44	Lung	Right
Cigarettes count	16	Sputum	No
Quitted smoking (months ago)	0	Bronchial lavage	No
Packyears	35	Tumor dimension	3-5
Cancer burden	No	PCO2	35.6
Enlarged nodes	Yes	Stage	3
Weight loss_kg	0	Metastasis	No
Symptoms	Yes	APTT	0
Zubrod performance	0		
Survived 3 months:		No	

The Fig. 4 presents the sequential variable attributions of random forest,
xgboost and logistic regression for a specific patient. Detailed information on
the chosen patient features are presented in the Table 4. The dotted, vertical line

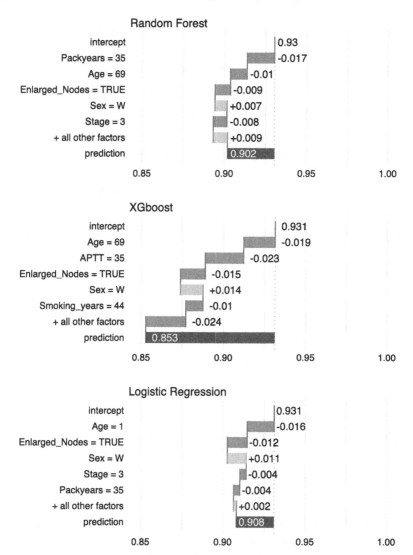

Fig. 4. Sequential variable attribution plots show the impact of variables to the prediction for the chosen patients. Green bars correspond to positive whereas red bars correspond to negative influence. Those bars sum up to the final model prediction (purple bar). The vertical line indicates the average model response. All models predict lower risk than an average, but they differ woth possible explanations. (Color figure online)

on each plot corresponds to the average models' responses (for each model it is equal 0.93). The red bars identify features that have negative contribution and worsen the prediction from the model's mean, whereas the green bars indicate

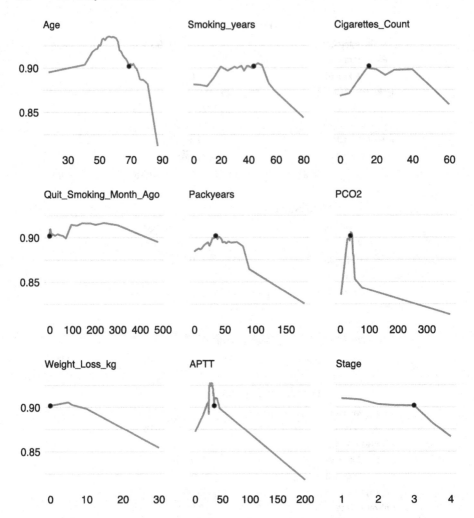

Fig. 5. The what-if analysis for a single patient (see Table 4). Blue dots stand for models predictions for a patient while red curves stand for hypothetical model responses after modifications for selected variables. (Color figure online)

the features that improve the prediction. The features that have close to zero contribution are presented as 'all other factors' bar.

The models final predictions are presented on the purple bar. The models classified the chosen patient as not surviving (the predictions are lower than the set threshold). However, the decisions were made in a slightly different way. The models indicate that age equal to 69 and enlarged nodes have negative impact, whereas being a woman has positive influence. Random forest indicates also negative contribution of packyears equal to 35 and stage equal to 3A. Xgboost points that APTT and number of years the person has smoked has negative contributions to final prognosis.

The what-if analysis for random forest model is presented on the Fig. 5. All numeric variables are presented on that plot. On each plot it is shown what the random forest model response would be if the selected variable would have changed while other input variables stay the same. Such analysis is especially useful if the variable level (for example the way of treatment) could be changed.

4 Discussion

Modeling of the early postoperative mortality is a very hard task. Lots of factors may contribute to the patient survival. We have used five machine learning models for this task, namely the Random Forest model, Support Vactor Machine model, Xgboost model, Lasso model and Logistic Regression model. Accuracy of each models on validation data set was moderate. But contrary to the classical black-box, modeling the accuracy was not the most important outcome.

Three models with the higher performance measures were equipped with methods for explainable machine learning, though they could be used to support surgeons' decision on classification patient for a lung cancer surgery. Moreover, the explainer methodology gives an insight into which patients' features should be taken under consideration. We presented global solutions that help to understand relationships of predictor and the machine learning model response, figure out the most important variables and present the models' residuals.

Global model explainers are important to better understand models. But we conclude with the observation that in the field of medicine local explanations are even more important. It is because they help to understand how particular features attribute to the final model decision, which variables are used to predict the outcome for a given patient and what can be done to change model prediction.

Acknowledgements. Przmysław Biecek was financially supported by NCN Opus grant 2016/21/B/ST6/02176. Katarzyna Kobylińska and Tomasz Mikołajczyk were financially supported by Polish Centre for Research and Development (Grant POIR.01.01.01-00-0328/17).

References

Biecek, P.: DALEX: explainers for complex predictive models in R. J. Mach. Learn. Res. **19**(84), 1–5 (2018)

Breiman, L.: Random forests. Mach. Learn. **45**(1), 5–32 (2001)

Gilpin, L.H., Bau, D., Yuan, B.Z., Bajwa, A., Specter, M., Kagal, L.: Explaining explanations: an overview of interpretability of machine learning (2018)

Glotzer, O., Fabian, T., Chandra, A., Bakhos, C.: Non-small cell lung cancer therapy: safety and efficacy in the elderly. Drug Healthc. Patient Saf. **22**, 113–121 (2013)

Gosiewska, A., Biecek, P.: Auditor: an R Package for Model-Agnostic Visual Validation and Diagnostic. arXiv e-prints, page arXiv:1809.07763 (2018)

Gosiewska, A., Biecek, P.: iBreakDown: Uncertainty of Model Explanations for Non-additive Predictive Models (2019)

Hamet, P., Tremblay, J.: Artificial intelligence in medicine. Metabolism **69**, S36–S40 (2017). Insights Into the Future of Medicine: Technologies, Concepts, and Integration

Hastie, T., Tibshirani, R., Friedman, J.: The Elements of Statistical Learning: Data Mining, Inference, and Prediction. SSS, 2nd edn. Springer, New York (2009). https://doi.org/10.1007/978-0-387-84858-7

Lundberg, S., Lee., S.-I.: A unified approach to interpreting model predictions. arXiv e-prints (2017)

Molnar, C.: Interpretable machine learning. A guide for making black box models explainable (2018)

Ribeiro, M.T., Singh, S., Guestrin, C.: Model-agnostic interpretability of machine learning. arXiv e-prints (2016)

Scheeder, C., Heigwer, F., Boutros, M.: Machine learning and image-based profiling in drug discovery. Curr. Opin. Syst. Biol. **10**, 43–52 (2018). Pharmacology and drug discovery

Staniak, M., Biecek, P.: Explanations of model predictions with live and breakdown packages. R J. **10**(2), 395–409 (2018)

Zuin, A., et al.: Pneumonectomy for lung cancer over the age of 75 years: is it worthwhile? Interact. CardioVasc. Thorac. Surg. **2010**(10), 931–935 (2010)

Author Index

Printed in the United States
By Bookmasters